S0-AVO-110

PRAISE FOR
THE PRACTICALLY MEATLESS GOURMET

"*The Practically Meatless Gourmet* is a gift to cooks who love the taste of meat. Carlson's recipes are right at the cutting edge of today's dietary advice: They emphasize flavor, texture, and enjoyment, but are low in fat, saturated fat, and cholesterol. The book explains how to use meat, stocks, and concentrates as flavoring agents, and should be a great boon to cooks concerned about health as well as cost. *The Practically Meatless Gourmet* reveals exactly why Asian and Mediterranean dietary patterns are so delicious and so healthy."

—Dr. Marion Nestle,
    Department of Nutrition and Food Studies, N.Y.U.

"*The Practically Meatless Gourmet's* exciting approach—using meat, fish, and poultry as seasonings instead of major foods—will help shift your focus toward a healthy and flavorful diet based on plant foods."

—Gene Spiller, D.Sc., Ph.D.,
    Director of The Health and Research Studies Center,
    Author of *The Super Pyramid Eating Program*

Most Berkley Books are available at special quantity discounts for bulk purchases for sales and promotions, premiums, fund-raising or educational use. Special books, or book excerpts, can also be created to fit specific needs.

For details, write or telephone Special Markets, The Berkley Publishing Group, 200 Madison Avenue, New York, New York 10016; (212) 951-8891

The Practically Meatless Gourmet

CORNELIA CARLSON

BERKLEY BOOKS, NEW YORK

THE PRACTICALLY MEATLESS GOURMET

A Berkley Book / published by arrangement with the author

PRINTING HISTORY
Berkley trade paperback edition / February 1996

All rights reserved.
Copyright ©1996 by Cornelia Carlson.
Book design by Irving Perkins Associates.
This book may not be reproduced in whole or in part, by mimeograph or any other means, without permission. For information address: The Berkley Publishing Group, 200 Madison Avenue, New York, New York 10016.

ISBN: 0-425-15131-X

BERKLEY®
Berkley Books are published by The Berkley Publishing Group, 200 Madison Avenue, New York, New York 10016. BERKLEY and the "B" design are trademarks belonging to Berkley Publishing Corporation.

PRINTED IN THE UNITED STATES OF AMERICA

10 9 8 7 6 5 4 3 2 1

*To Mel, who ate every bite
and patiently read every word*

Contents

INTRODUCTION   1

1. MEATS AS FLAVORINGS   6

2. INGREDIENTS: BASIC GRAINS AND EXOTIC FLAVORS   25

3. SOUPS, CASSEROLES, AND OTHER THICK DISHES   34

4. SAUCED PASTAS   72

5. STEAMED GRAINS: RICE AND COUSCOUS   101

6. PILAFS AND SIMILAR PRETOASTED GRAIN DISHES   141

7. FRIED GRAINS AND NOODLES   164

8. PIZZAS AND SIMILAR GRAIN-WRAPPED FOODS   177

9. GRAIN SALADS   197

    MAIL ORDER SOURCES   228

    SELECTED BIBLIOGRAPHY   231

    INDEX   233

Introduction

Though there was a lot of meat on the table, he would not take it out of proportion with his rice.

—Confucius, 500 B.C.

This is a cookbook for health-conscious Americans who love the succulence and seductive flavors of meat but fear its burden of fat. The recipes reflect an ancient culinary pattern that still prevails outside the industrialized world. There, rice, wheat, corn, and other high-carbohydrate grains are the heart of every day's meals, and minor amounts of high-fat meats are merely one of many seasonings. There, too, fat-stimulated diseases are rarely seen.

In the same way, all of these recipes are focused on grains and are seasoned with meats. Thus all are low in fat and high in complex carbohydrates.

As you flip through the recipes, you'll recognize many familiar ethnic dishes such as pastas and pizzas, pilafs and couscous, stir-fries and chilies, winter soups and summer pasta salads. All this sounds like customary fare, but it comes with a twist. Each recipe was created or adapted to fit a super-lean, meat-seasoned profile that resembles the dish's ancient and healthy heritage more than the meat- and fat-laden versions seen in American cookbooks. Here all recipes conform to stringent nutritional standards:

- *Total fats* provide no more than 20 percent of the dish's calories
- *Saturated fats* provide no more than 5 percent of the dish's calories
- *Carbohydrates* provide at least 60 percent of the dish's calories
- *Proteins* provide 8–20 percent of the dish's calories

These values reflect a new understanding of an optimal diet. They emphasize the positive aspects of complex carbohydrates and the need to watch protein intake, as well as the need to reduce fat even more than the current USDA/American Heart Association guidelines suggest. In addition, most recipes contain an abundance of vegetables and/or fruits, foods that are our main source of antioxidants, anticancer phytochemicals, and of several vitamins and minerals. This may sound like recipes designed by formula rather than taste. Not at all. The world is full of flavorful dishes that fill this bill.

Expanding Your Recipe Repertoire

To get the most from this book, use its recipes as a nucleus of meat-seasoned dishes, and begin collecting more recipes that reflect your own taste and experience. You'll find a wealth of complex carbohydrate-rich, low-fat dishes in most ethnic cookbooks or in those devoted to soups, salads, casseroles, pasta, or other hearty foods. If you're uncertain about a dish's nutritional makeup and think it contains unwanted fat, review the asapao recipes that appear on pages 36 to 37 and similar recipes that introduce each section of this book. They show some simple ways of cutting out fat and increasing carbohydrates without sacrificing flavor.

Don't hesitate to tinker with these recipes, either. As long as you substitute similar ingredients (e.g., pasta for rice or lamb for beef) you'll have little impact on the recipe's nutritional values. Certainly you should vary spices and noncaloric flavorings in any way you like.

Don't be discouraged if a favorite recipe won't yield to your fat-squeezing methods. Some meaty recipes are best left as they stand, to be enjoyed occasionally in their fatter glory.

If you find an abrupt adjustment to small meat servings uncomfortable, try adding a little extra meat in your initial ventures. Just make sure you trim the fat from it scrupulously. Compare the figures in the introductory dual recipes such as the asapao recipes on pages 36 and 37 to see how extra meats (even very lean meats) decrease the meal's complex carbohydrates.

With time, after your palate has adjusted to meat's seasoning potential, you'll find that instead of craving more meat, you'll want less, or perhaps even none. Act on your taste and reduce the meat accordingly.

Shifting from Meat-Focused to Meat-Seasoned Meals

This book's recipes represent a worldwide-tested, lifelong approach to maintaining health as well as a way to cut cholesterol, lower blood pressure, or lose some weight. Most of us understand the health benefits of a meat-seasoned diet intellectually, long before this style of cooking becomes second nature. Move toward this style at your own pace. Some of these suggestions may help you get there sooner.

Choose your initial meat-seasoned ventures from familiar cuisines so that you don't suffer culinary culture shock along with relinquishing large servings of meat. If you like pasta, start with the pasta-based recipes found in chapters 3, 4, and 9. If pizzas are a favorite food, prepare those in chapter 8. If Chinese food piques your palate, start in chapters 5 and 7. Move into recipes of more exotic cuisines as you become accustomed to eating less meat.

Become more discriminating about meat. When you eat a large serving, look at it carefully. Taste it carefully. Is it really delectable or is it dense, dry, tough, and meagerly flavored? If the latter is true, ask yourself whether you're eating it from hunger, desire, or habit. When you've become more conscious of meat quality, you'll miss it less and be willing to restrict your meaty indiscretions to an occasional first-class steak or roast.

Select meat cuts that furnish optimum flavor with minimum fat. Chapter 1 details the best choices, ways to trim their fat, and methods to enhance their flavor.

Use nonfat meat flavorings instead of meats. An especially good device is to cook grains in meat stocks. You won't yearn for pieces of meat when your mouth is full of other meaty-flavored food. For simple stock recipes and comments on meaty-tasting products, see chapter 1.

Reduce the quantities of oil used to sauté meats or other ingredients. On pages 19–20 you'll find hints on how to do the job with a minuscule amount.

Choose chewy or highly textured grains or toasted grain dishes such as pilafs and paellas or fried rice and noodles. You'll miss two of meat's pleasurable attributes (chewiness and toasted taste) less, if you emphasize these factors in other foods.

Incorporate abundant vegetables into the dish. Select seasonal and preferably aromatic or pungent varieties. They can add dramatic flavor and textural interest (along with a bundle of vitamins, minerals, and other protective molecules) if you cook them briefly.

Shake the salt habit. Stimulate your palate with fresh herbs and aromatic spices instead. Their volatile oils act on the nose's receptors (what we think of as taste) like many of the compounds in roasted meats. Whenever appropriate, include a little acidic flavoring like vinegar, lemon juice, or wine balanced with a pinch of sugar or freshly ground pepper. These elements will stimulate your mouth's taste buds much as salt does.

Keep your refrigerator and pantry stocked with flavorful ethnic sauces and pastes. Around the world, cooks rely on these whenever meat is scarce. Chapter 2 lists many.

Get in touch with the flavors of other foods. Taste and smell individual ingredients as you use them. Register the smell of grated orange peel or freshly roasted and brewed coffee. Taste a vine-ripened tomato or sugary sweet corn plucked from the plant. Each is as complex and seductively flavored as any meat.

Eat lots of pasta, rice, or similar grain salads for lunch. Most people find they feel less sluggish and have fewer late-afternoon hunger pangs than they do after eating the standard burger and fries.

Become more aware of how you feel after you've eaten other meals. If you feel dull and crabby after eating a very meaty or high-fat meal, and more energetic after eating lots of complex carbohydrates, make note of it. That should be as much inducement to change your diet as any cardiologist's threat.

Reverse your shopping priorities. Stop at the produce aisles first and plan your meals around the most appealing selections. Next, make sure you have all the staple items you'll need, and only then visit the meat department.

Keep your eye out for new *lite* products. Some will be as bogus as that word's spelling, but others may cut fat radically without sacrificing flavor.

Keep track of your grocery receipts. Even if you spend more on the recipe's fresh produce or the most expensive grains (e.g., wild rice), you'll still save money. Although health and gastronomic pleasure should be of greater concern than economy, it's great when the two correspond.

Take a fresh look at your dinner plate. Most Americans segregate their foods into three piles: the predominant meat entrée and two trivial side dishes. In less affluent countries, the all-important grain fills the plate, topped with vegetables, and embellished with meat. There, meals are literal examples of the USDA's figurative Food Pyramid, and no one bothers with counting servings or their size.

CHAPTER 1

Meats as Flavorings

Meat is a sensual food: juicy, chewy, and fragrantly flavored. No wonder people relish it. Probably early man gnawed as happily on his sinewy grilled mastodon as we do on our grain-fed steaks. Unfortunately, these pleasurable flavors come packaged with a superabundance of fat. Yet with a little care, you can enjoy the flavor of meat with little of the fat.

Meaty Pleasures and Ways to Augment Them

When you use meats as a flavoring, focus on these thoughts:

Get the most out of every morsel of meat. Select meat, poultry, and fish with the greatest inherent flavor (as long as the choices are reasonably lean). For example, if you like chicken, use stronger-flavored thighs (skinless and well-trimmed) instead of breast. With fish, select sweet-flavored shellfish and sea bass or strong-tasting tuna, salmon, or even shark. For some suggestions on red meats, see Selecting Meat Cuts page 8.

Heighten the flavor of meats. Their most intense, roasted flavors develop on the surface, so anything you can do to increase the surface area will enhance these. Whenever appropriate, dice meats or slice them into slivers before you cook them. This common Asian cooking practice not only intensifies flavor but makes the serving seem more generous. Don't restrict this technique to stir-fried dishes; it applies to almost any dish in this book.

Rely on meat, poultry, and fish stocks. They furnish the full flavor and none of the fat of their parent meats. Whenever you have the time, make your own. You'll hardly miss the actual meat when you use these dense, complexly flavored broths to season other foods. Detailed recipes appear at the end of this chapter. Resort to salty, canned bouillon and chicken stock only when you have no other choice.

Fat has flavor. Trim off as much fat as possible, but don't worry about leaving a very *small* amount of marbled fat. It carries some of the species-specific flavors or those related to the animal's diet (e.g., corn-fed beef), and the strongly flavored heat-catalyzed oxidation products of fatty acids. Their culinary payback will offset their cardiovascular threat.

Mimic meat's pleasures—both texture and taste—with other foods. Around the world, cooks compensate for meager meat servings with many devices. Here are a few.

Onions and garlic possess sulfurous molecules similar to those in meats, especially poultry. Whether cooks recognize the similarity consciously or subliminally, virtually every cuisine relies on these assertive vegetables to give a round, full, almost meaty nuance to any savory dish.

Toast or sauté other ingredients besides the meat. The taste of toasted grain in pilafs is as appealing as that of the meat.

Include flavor-enhancing foods (what the Japanese call *umami*) like dried mushrooms, fish and meat extracts, and seaweed. Embellish your recipes with any of these whenever the cuisine or other ingredients warrant their use. Many of the dried mushrooms are particularly valuable because their texture is chewy and meatlike.

Use other assertive, taste bud teasers in place of meats. Aromatic herbs and spices act on our sense of smell, much as does meat's fragrance. Chilies stimulate pleasurable sensations. Pungent black pepper irritates the taste buds, making them more receptive to other foods.

Use thick, well-seasoned sauces whenever appropriate. They coat your mouth in the same appealing way that the fat in meat does.

Rely on chewy grains and crisp vegetables to replace meat's dense texture. Whole grains, briefly cooked pasta, and any crunchy vegetable will give you much the same sense of having something to sink your teeth into.

Quantity

Because meat's flavors are so intense, a little of it goes a long way. Two ounces per person is usually enough to flavor any main-dish meal. Most of the recipes in this book suggest this amount. A few call for more fish. And some, using highly flavored smoked meats, require only one ounce per serving.

The table on the next page lists the approximate yields of various cuts of meat after you've trimmed away the fat and bone. The table is no more than a loose guide. If you're more skilled with a knife than I am, you may pry more meat free. If your butcher leaves more or less fat attached to his cuts, you'll get somewhat different values.

For some types of meat, the proportion of meat to fat and bone varies with the size of the original carcass. Generally, larger animals have a higher ratio of meat to bone than do smaller animals. This is especially true of poultry, hams, leg of lamb, whole fish, and prawns.

Selecting Meat Cuts

As you move from meat-focused to meat-seasoned meals, change the way you shop for meats. Stop looking at a meat cut and thinking, *How many of these should I cook for each person?* Instead, look at each piece and visualize how many little hunks of lean meat are nestled in it, each one of which can spike several people's individual meal.

Base your choices on the same criteria you would use if meat were the meal's major food: flavor, fat content, cost, and tenderness.

Most tender cuts come from little-used muscles, generally those farthest from the feet. Typical cuts in this class are T-bone steaks and lamb loin chops. Tender cuts should be cooked very briefly to retain their soft, moist texture. Over-

Meat	Cut	Trimmed oz. per lb. untrimmed
Beef		
	chuck, blade	8
	rump	13½
	round	13½
	London broil	14½
	flank	16
	heart	13½
Pork		
	loin, boneless	13½
	sirloin, boneless	13½
	shoulder, boneless	12
	picnic ham	8½
	butt ham	8
	shank ham	8
Lamb		
	shoulder blade	8
	loin chop	8½
	rib chop	6
	sirloin chop	9½
	leg, sirloin	9½
	leg, shank	10½
Chicken		
	thigh*	10½
	drumstick*	11
	breast*	9½
	whole (4 lb.)*	6½
Turkey		
	breast*	12
	thigh*	11
	drumstick*	11
Duck	whole*	6
Rabbit	whole*	10½
Average fish		
	steak	14½
	filet	16
Prawns		13

*Larger pieces may yield more trimmed meat than smaller pieces.

cooking dries and toughens them. They are costly and aren't used much in this book's recipes. Save them for a rare indulgence.

Tougher cuts of meat are as flavorful and are much cheaper. To tenderize these meats, you can either braise them for a lengthy period or break down their muscle fibers by bashing or cutting. These techniques make tough cuts amenable to quick-cooked, stir-fry recipes.

Select meat with easily trimmed fat. For the most part, this means fat that lies in discrete layers around individual muscles. If the fat's too well marbled within the muscle, you'll drive yourself crazy trying to pare it out, and you may end up with more fat than you want, despite your efforts.

Avoid ground meats. Even those that seem lean are usually very fatty. For example, ground beef labeled 15 percent fat actually derives 64 percent of its calories from fat. (Almost 75 percent of the meat is noncaloric water, so the 15 percent fat comprises a majority of the remaining weight.)

Buy larger cuts of meat than you need for one meal. They're often cheaper than smaller pieces, and you'll save time by trimming several meals' worth of meat at one time. Freeze the extra portions as described below.

There are some regional differences in butchers' terminology and ways of cutting up the carcass. If you're unfamiliar with a cut mentioned in this book, ask your butcher what it's called in your locality.

BEEF

Beef is America's favorite meat. Despite this, annual per capita beef consumption has decreased from its mid-1970s high of seventy pounds to a current fifty-five pounds. Appropriately, the decline parallels concerns with meat and fat's contributions to cardiovascular diseases.

There's no reason to quit eating beef entirely. Just choose it carefully, trim it well, and eat modest amounts most of the time. You'll find that chuck, rump, round, and flank are the best bets.

Chuck contains a varied group of muscles. Two of the smaller in this group are quite tender, but most are tougher and need some tenderizing. Its moderate fat content keeps the meat juicy, despite these procedures.

You can use chuck in virtually all the beef recipes in this book. It is the preferred cut for braised dishes, where leaner cuts would become leathery. You can also use chuck cuts in stir-fried dishes if they're cut wafer-thin and briefly cooked.

Buy chuck bone-in as long as it is cheaper than its boneless derivative, and save the bones for stock. To cut it up, trim off the fat that encircles the piece. Then cut the meat off the bone(s). Cut or pull the meat apart at the fat margins separating the muscle groups. Trim off and discard as much of this fat as possible.

The *rump* is intermediate in fat content, tender enough to be used in stir-fried dishes, and still fat enough to braise. It is almost always sold as a piece large enough to roast, with a pad of fat on one surface. Trim this off carefully by running a sharp knife just below the fat while pulling it away with your free hand.

Beef *round* also contains several muscles, some more tender than others. Top round is the most tender and best for stir-fried dishes. Bottom round and eye of round tend to be tougher and need some tenderizing. You can include them in braised dishes, though their low fat content gives them a dry taste.

Round is easy to trim since the fat is obvious and restricted to edges and muscle margins. Cut as for chuck. Bones, if any are left in, are trivial.

Flank steak is a small, grainy cut that requires attentive cooking. This is the true London broil, though you'll see that name given to other cuts. It is delicious in stir-fried dishes if briefly cooked.

Avoid most other beef cuts. The very tender rib and loin sections are fat, expensive, and best saved for an occasional feast. The remaining cuts are either too difficult to trim, e.g., oxtails and short ribs, or contain very high cholesterol levels. These include most organ meats such as liver, brains, or thymus (sweetbreads).

Beef *heart* is one delicious and overlooked exception. It has a very low fat content. Its cholesterol concentration, though about twice that of other beef muscles, is a third that of liver. Virtually all the fat is external to the heart and is easy to trim off, and the muscle itself is easy to cut. It is tasty, well-textured, and extremely cheap. Try it initially in a highly seasoned stir-fry dish. Slivers of it will remain tender and chewy and no one will guess the meat's origin.

VEAL

Although veal is generally leaner than beef, its mild taste provides little seasoning punch. Save veal for elegant feasts.

LAMB

Lamb was domesticated in the Middle East at least 7,000 years ago. It remains a favorite meat in that area and is relished in much of the rest of the world, yet Americans eat less of it than any other meat, perhaps because they view its flavor as high. This decisive flavor is precisely what makes lamb the best seasoning meat. A small amount lends a dense and alluring, earthy, sweet, meaty-musky perfume to a large amount of blander foods.

By definition, all lamb is young and therefore tender. Appropriate cuts for this book's recipes include the shoulder and the leaner leg.

Lamb *shoulder* resembles beef chuck. It corresponds to the same part of the animal's carcass, its fat content is intermediate between other lamb cuts, and it's generally cheap.

Select shoulder chops with a minimum of marbled fat. It's difficult, though not impossible, to trim. Don't worry about the fat around the edges. It's simple to hack off. Some butchers sell boneless shoulder roasts. They're not worth the extra cost.

After trimming as much fat as possible, the remaining meat is likely to be in small pieces. Measure the quantities needed for individual recipes and freeze the portions.

A *leg* of lamb refers to the hind legs. A full cut includes the upper *sirloin* and the lower *shank* sections. The sirloin adjoins the loin and is almost as tender as that cut. It is sometimes sold sliced into chops. When they're available, buy them. They're generally leaner than shoulder chops, are as easy to trim, and have the same bonus bones. The lower *shank* portion of the hind leg is always sold as a roast. Its meat is also lean and tender.

To prepare either of these cuts for seasoners, first pare off the surface fat. Run a sharp knife down the length of the fatter side of the leg, cutting through the fat until you feel the muscle. Repeat down the fat on the leaner side. Then, beginning at the wider end of the roast, insert the knife into the margin between the muscle and fat layer. Carefully slice along this margin, feeling your way so that you don't take a lot of meat off with the fat. Use your hands to strip back the loosened fat. Use the knife and your hands to release the fat farther down the leg. At the base, the layer is thinner and more difficult to pull off. Cut the meat off the leg bone in large sections. Trim off any obvious fat within the muscle. Cut the meat into requisite portions, wrap carefully, and freeze. Save the bone for a large kettle of soup. If you have a heavy cleaver capable of cutting the bone, whack it into sections and save them with the meat.

Lamb *ribs* and *loin* are delicious meats and are fairly lean if you trim them well. They're expensive and best left for an occasional treat.

Lamb shanks (from the front legs) and breasts are much fattier and more difficult to trim. Avoid these cuts.

PORK

Pork has a mild, sweet flavor and delicate texture. You can use well-trimmed shoulder, loin, or fresh hams for any pork-containing recipe in this book.

Pork *loin* is sold in chops or roasts. It is easier to see how much fat is on a chop than a roast, and a chop is also easier to cut up. If you buy chops, trim away as much fat as possible and save the bones. *Center loin* chops are usually less marbled and thus on the dry side. Save them for a special occasion. *Sirloin* and *blade* chops from the outer loin sections are a little fattier and make more succulent seasonings.

If you choose a loin roast, trim the exterior fat off first. Then run a sharp knife along the bone to release the meat. Work from both ends of the roast until you've freed as much meat as possible, then cut through the meat to pull the hunk free. Alternatively, you can cut into the meat and slice hunks off the bone. In either case, trim as much interior fat off the meat as you can.

Pork *shoulder* is fattier than loin. It is often called Boston butt and is sold (like its beef and lamb counterparts), cut into steaks, chops, or a roast. Cut the shoulder pieces in the same way as loin.

Fresh hams are the pig's legs. *Picnics* are the forelegs, cut just below the shoulder. *Butt* and *shank* hams are respectively the upper and lower section of the pig's hind legs. All are usually smoked, but occasionally your butcher may have fresh hams as well. Food tables indicate all three have similar fat content, but in my experience, they vary considerably. To trim any of these, first slice off the exterior fat. Cut a circle around the bottom of the leg just above the area where the skin remains attached. Cut down to the bone. Next, slice down the length of the ham, again cutting to the bone. Use your hands to expose the bone. Cut the meat away from it, using the point of a sharp knife. Remove and save the bone. Trim out as much fat as you can, cut it into portions, wrap, and freeze.

Smoked hams make delicious seasonings but suffer from their high sodium and nitrite contents. Used as a condiment instead of a slab of meat, these problems are unimportant unless you're on a very restrictive diet. Still, it's best to avoid the saltiest and/or smokiest hams. Ask your butcher for those with the least or substitute smoked turkey sausage, if you prefer.

Buy hams bone-in. The bone will enrich a generous stockpot or kettle of beans. Trim carefully, as you would a fresh ham (see above). If it is precooked, you can cut it into hunks, wrap it carefully, and freeze for up to two months.

If uncooked, trim away as much exterior fat as possible, then bake or braise the whole piece. After it is cooked, let the ham cool until you can handle it comfortably, then rip it into appropriate portions, wrap it carefully, and store it in the refrigerator for three to four days, or in the freezer for up to two months.

If you buy a Smithfield ham or similar genuine article, cook it in a more elegant way, eat heartily, and save any leftover scraps (and the bone) to season soups, pilafs, and sundry dishes.

Ignore pig's feet, spareribs, and country ribs. Their fats are hard to remove.

CHICKEN AND TURKEY

These two fowl are great meat bargains, usually available at rock-bottom prices. Their fat is mostly in and around the skin and easy to trim. Buy whole, rather than cut-up, chickens. They're cheaper and supply more debris for stocks.

To prepare whole birds, rinse them, cut them into pieces, and then trim off their skin and fat.

Lay the bird on its back on a large, washable cutting board. Lift a drumstick and thigh with your left hand (if you're right handed). Cut between the thigh and body cavity starting on the breast side and moving around to the back side. After cutting through the flesh to the bone, snap the leg out of the socket, and cut it free with a knife. Cut the thigh away from the drumstick by slicing along the ridge of yellow fat on the inside surface. Continue cutting along the outside surface. Snap the two bones as above and cut them through with a knife. Repeat with the other leg. Cut the wings off the body in the same fashion. Stand the chicken up on the neck opening. Run a sharp, heavy knife along the breast bone starting at the bottom (which is upended). Cut through the meat and bone at one side of the ridge. Pry the bird open. Release the breast halves from the back by slicing through the ribs at their thinnest point.

Use your hands to pull the skin off the thighs and breast. Pull the drumstick skin off, starting at the top and cutting it off at the bottom. Pull off whatever loose fat you can with your hands and cut and scrape the remaining off with a knife. The fat and skin are not included in classic stock recipes, but they are useful. Read the chicken stock recipe on page 22 before you toss them out.

Save the wings and back for the stockpot. They're difficult to trim. Add the neck to this pile. It is not good for anything but flavoring. You can either add the gizzard, heart, and liver to the stock mixture (though they do make the broth cloudy) or save them for pasta sauces.

Add the leg and breast bones to the stockpot as well. To remove the thigh bone, run a knife through the muscle lengthwise along the ribbon of yellow fat. Cut down to the bone. Pull the muscle away from the bone, scraping with the knife as necessary to free it. To bone the drumstick, slice lengthwise through the muscle from top to the base. Pull the muscle off the bone, freeing it of tendons as you go, and scraping it, if necessary, with a knife. To dislodge the breast bones, run the knife along the bone, scraping the meat away from it. Move along the attached ribs, gently scraping with the knife, and pull the flesh away with your hands.

Segregate the breast meat from the leg meat, then divide each into portions, wrap carefully, and freeze. Be sure to freeze the liver and gizzard separately as well.

Unless it's Thanksgiving, buy turkey already cut up. Breast meat is very lean once you have removed the skin. It tends to be dry if you don't cook it carefully. Skinned drumsticks are also lean but have the disadvantage of numerous stringy tendons. Turkey thighs are the simplest to deal with. They're also lean and are easier to trim. All provide an abundance of meat for a minuscule price.

Trim each cut as though it were an oversized chicken. Cut the meat into portions and freeze as usual. Save the skin and bones for turkey-flavored soups. Don't mix them with chicken bits. Turkey's flavor is too distinct for all-purpose stocks.

CHICKEN AND TURKEY PRODUCTS

Most ground turkey products are very lean. They also tend to have meager flavor. For this reason I prefer to trade off the additional fat of many other meats for their much denser flavors. Low-fat smoked turkey sausage is one exception. It makes a good ham substitute, but like those latter fragrant meats, it is usually quite salty. Check package labels if you're watching your salt intake.

DUCK

Duck has the reputation of being one of the fattest meats. That's true for the whole carcass, but if you skin and trim this bird before you cook it, the flesh won't be much fatter than chicken. You'll throw away a lot of the duck, so the final meat yield is far more expensive than chicken or turkey. It is worth the price for an occasional treat of its earthy flavor and succulent texture.

Duck is usually purchased frozen. Thaw it quickly in cold water and cut it up as soon as it's barely thawed. Cut and trim the duck as though it were a chicken. Freeze the giblets for pasta seasoning. Freeze or cook the remaining meat immediately. Be sure to save all the duck debris for stock. It is heavenly.

RABBIT

Rabbit is a very lean animal that tastes much like chicken. If it's not cut up, treat it like a chicken, first cutting off the legs, then cutting up the breast and back. Because the pieces will be relatively small or have little meat, you may want to serve these as whole pieces on top of a pilaf or in a stew. Or you can dice the meat for stir-fried or sautéed dishes.

Fish and Shellfish

Fish is gaining a favored place on Americans' tables as we turn away from large servings of meats. Not only are most fish much leaner than red meat, the fat some contain may actually be beneficial.

Leaning toward fish makes equal culinary sense, since as a group they present an enormous variety of flavors and textures. Many, like sea bass and sole, have faintly sweet or buttery flavors and delicate textures. Others, like salmon, catfish, or shark, are decidedly flavored or like swordfish have a steaklike texture. Some cost more than an average meat, but the expense is made up by the fact that there is little or no wasted material.

If you remove skin and bones before cooking, be sure to save them for fish fumet (see page 23). The same is true for shellfish shells. In both cases, be sure to freeze or cook them immediately.

Storing Meats

The cardinal principles in storing all meats are to keep them briefly, and keep them cold. Stop by the meat counter just before you check out, not when you first enter the store, then take it directly home to your refrigerator.

If you're buying prepackaged meat from a supermarket, select a package whose pull date is several days in the future. Hold the package to your nose, and if it has the faintest high or putrid hint, reject it. Avoid meat with an opalescent sheen on its surface. If you are buying from a butcher, ask him how fresh it is and how long you can safely keep it.

Once home, rewrap it loosely with waxed paper and store in the coldest part of your refrigerator at 34 to 40 degrees F. Within this temperature range you can keep meat from one to three days, depending on how fresh it was when you bought it, and whether the temperature is at the higher or lower end of the suggested range.

Use the same criteria to select and store poultry, but remember that it doesn't keep as well as meat. Therefore, store it no longer than one or two days at the lowest temperature suggested.

Fish is even more fragile. Because most fish come from cold waters, their attendant bacteria (and endogenous enzymes that also degrade this food) are more active at low temperatures than the bacteria associated with meat and poultry. Therefore, cook fish the day you buy it, or if it's very fresh, store it for one day at close to 32 degrees F. When you purchase fish, make sure it has no fishy smell or surface opalescence, dents, or cracks. If it is whole, make sure the eyes are clear, not opaque. If possible, ask your butcher or fishmonger which fish is freshest, and act on his advice.

If, despite your efforts, the meat or fish smells off, throw it out and eat something else. Today's meat serving is never worth tomorrow's intestinal distress.

Don't dice, grind, or otherwise chop your meat until you're ready to cook or freeze it. Most of meat's bacteria inhabit its surface. As soon as the surface is punctured, the bacteria find fresh breeding grounds. Ground meat usually has many times more bacteria than the same weight of an intact piece.

Use cutting boards that you can wash in very hot water. Wash everything that comes in contact with raw meats, fish, or poultry—including your hands—immediately after use in hot, soapy water.

Freezing Meats

Be sure to freeze meat as soon as you've brought it home if you suspect you can't cook it within its safely refrigerated time. Cut it into single-meal portions and wrap tightly in waxed paper, plastic wrap, or aluminum foil, forcing as much air out of the packages as possible. Then wrap in a second airtight plastic bag or container. Label and store in your freezer for one to two months at 10 to 15 degrees F. If you have a chest freezer set below 0 degrees F, you can store these for as long as 3 to 6 months.

Avoid freezing fish. It readily becomes dry, tough, and fishy flavored. And it may have been frozen already for transfer from boat to market.

Thaw meats shortly before you cook them. Thirty minutes is sufficient to thaw most 2- to 16-ounce pieces of 3/4- to 1-inch thick meat before chopping or slicing.

Often thawed meats weep. Save the juice and add it to any sauce or stock that accompanies the meat, but be sure to cook these juices for at least a few minutes to kill any bacteria.

Label meat packages legibly and try to maintain order in your freezer. It will save time later when you search for what you need.

Cooking Tips

When you cook meats, be sure they reach safe temperatures. Beef and lamb are usually cooked to at least 135 to 140 degrees F (rare) and pork usually to 150 degrees F to kill any trichinae, the round worms that produce trichinosis. Some people believe that cooking to 140 degrees F kills any salmonella present in poultry, but others suggest it should be cooked to 165 degrees. I opt for the more cautious, high temperature. Fish should be cooked until it's opaque, flaky, and steaming, but not to the dry stage.

You won't need to measure meat temperatures for many recipes in this book since the meat is usually diced into small bits or thin slices, which cook rapidly to requisite temperatures. If you're in doubt, be sure to cut into the meat or fish and make sure it's cooked throughout.

Most meats should be cooked briefly over a moderate heat. Ideally, the surface should acquire a lightly browned patina and the interior should be cooked just long enough to gelatinize the protein, but not dry and toughen it. If the meat's surface is wet, and that's especially true of thawed meats, it won't brown as well as a dry surface. If you want more intensely browned meats, pat the surface moisture off with paper towels before you sauté it.

Very tough meat cuts require much longer cooking to tenderize. Braise these at a low temperature for several hours.

Brown meats at a moderate temperature. Charring them produces nasty flavors and potentially carcinogenic compounds.

Sauté with a Minimum of Oil

You can lubricate most skillets adequately with one teaspoon of oil, and you never need more than two teaspoons.

Measure the oil into the skillet and set it over low to medium heat. Tilt the pan occasionally so that little oil streaks run out from the center. As the oil warms, it will become more fluid and appear slightly rippled and lively. At this point, you can tilt the pan and the oil will run freely across it.

Add the food when the oil has this lively look. Don't let it heat to the smoking point. At that high temperature, oil begins to degrade and oxidize. Be sure to move small bits of food around so that all sides are browned and none stick to the pan.

Basic Stocks

The recipes that follow are fundamental to the book's dishes. Each provides robust flavor, just a few calories and virtually no fat, cholesterol or sodium. They can be as elaborate as the French saucier's or as simple as a few bones or meat scraps tossed in a pot with some herbs and water. You'll find that the next few recipes require intermediate effort and produce excellent, all-purpose stocks. For the densest flavor, cook the concentrated beef flavoring (page 22). It looks murky but tastes wonderful.

Most of these stocks require several hours of cooking, but none require more than a few minutes of active work. All keep well in the freezer for at least two months, so make large batches and freeze the extra stock in one- or two-cup-sized, airtight containers.

Whenever possible, buy meat bone-in and freeze the bones until you have enough to make two or three quarts of stock. Or buy meaty soup bones from your butcher.

If you have a small bone or two in the freezer but no stock, you can enrich whatever you're cooking by simmering the bones directly in a soup, sauce, or even in a grain-based dish like a pilaf. This instant stock won't be as robust or complex as long-cooked stocks, but it will at least be free of the fake flavors and saltiness of dried or canned bouillon. Be sure to sauté the bones as well as the meat to intensify their flavor.

Beef Stock

BUY THE MEATIEST SHIN AND MARROW BONES AVAILABLE. IF YOU MAKE STOCK FROM BONES SAVED FROM CHUCK OR SIMILAR MEATS, LEAVE A LITTLE MEAT ON THEM. THE MEATIER THE BONES, THE LESS YOU'LL NEED. IF YOU DON'T HAVE A LARGE STOCKPOT, YOU CAN DIVIDE THE INGREDIENTS INTO TWO POTS AFTER ROASTING THE BONES.

3–6 pounds beef bones
1 large onion
1 carrot
1–2 ribs celery
1 medium turnip (optional)
1 medium tomato (optional)
2–3 sprigs of thyme or
   1 teaspoon chopped thyme

6–8 large parsley sprigs
5–10 peppercorns or 1/4 teaspoon
   freshly ground pepper
5 allspice berries or 1/8 teaspoon
   ground allspice
2–3 bay leaves, preferably fresh
3½–4 quarts water

Preheat the oven to 400 degrees. Put the bones in a roasting pan and roast them until they become fragrant and browned on the surface. This takes about 15 minutes.

While they roast, chop the vegetables into large chunks and toss them into a 6-quart or larger stockpot along with the herbs and spices. Add the bones and any juices from the roasting pan. Add a little water to the roasting pan and deglaze any coagulated juices. Add them to the stockpot. Add the remaining water, cover, and bring the liquid just to a boil. Reduce the heat to low.

If you want a clear stock, skim and discard the scum rising to the top. Simmer the stock for 3 to 4 hours.

Cool it in a sink full of icy water, then refrigerate until very cold. Lift the congealed fat off the top. Strain the stock into a large mixing bowl and discard the vegetables and bones. Measure relevant quantities of stock into labeled plastic (not glass, which breaks) containers. These will keep in the freezer for 3 to 4 months.

YIELD: about 10 cups

Concentrated Beef Flavoring

Add 1 pound of beef chuck meat (cut into ½-inch cubes) and half as many bones to the previous recipe. For simplicity, brown both in a little oil in the stockpot instead of a separate pan in the oven. Add the remaining ingredients (plus ½ cup red wine if you like), and cook as above. When straining the stock, mash some of the solids through the strainer. That will lend a denser flavor, though it won't be a true, clear stock.

Chicken Stock

USE THE SKINS YOU'VE PEELED OFF CHICKEN PARTS TO ENRICH THIS STOCK. IT'S NOT CLASSIC TECHNIQUE, BUT THIS STOCK IS MEANT FOR ROBUST FOODS, NOT CLASSIC DAINTIES. YOU CAN USE MORE OF SOME BONES OR CHICKEN PARTS AND LESS OF OTHERS THAN IS SUGGESTED BELOW. JUST AIM FOR THE SAME GENERAL QUANTITY.

2 chicken backs, wings, gizzards, hearts, and livers
A few chicken bones or skins from 1 or 2 chickens (optional)
2–3 stalks celery
1 carrot
1 onion
1 turnip (optional)
6–8 parsley sprigs

2–3 bay leaves, preferably fresh
2–3 sprigs of fresh thyme or 1–2 teaspoons dried
8–10 peppercorns or ¼ teaspoon freshly ground pepper
3–4 allspice berries or ¹⁄₁₆ teaspoon ground
3½–4 quarts water

Put all the ingredients in a gallon or larger stockpot. Cover and bring the liquid to a boil. Reduce the heat and simmer slowly 3 to 4 hours. Skim off the scum occasionally.

Cool the pot in a sink full of ice water, then chill in the refrigerator. Remove the congealed fat and the debris. Pour the liquid in 1- or 2-cup plastic containers and freeze for up to 3 months.

YIELD: about 10 cups

Fish Fumet

Fish acquire unpleasant flavors when frozen for any length of time, so be sure to use fresh material for this stock. Once prepared, you can store it in the freezer where it will retain good flavor for up to 2 months.

If possible, use a mixture of different fish. The resulting stock will be more complexly flavored than one that relies on a single type. Avoid oily fish like salmon, whose pungent flavors will overwhelm this delicate juice. You can also substitute some prawn shells or other shells for the fish, though they also tend to dominate the flavor.

1½ pounds fish heads, bones, and/or skin
6 cups water
1 cup dry white wine
1 leek, chopped, or 1 small onion, sliced
2 peppercorns

¼ lemon, peel and juice (optional)
1 sprig fresh parsley or 1 celery top (optional)
1 teaspoon chopped fresh lemon thyme or 1 bay leaf (optional)

Put all the ingredients in a large stockpot, cover, and bring slowly to a boil. Simmer for 30 to 45 minutes, let it cool slightly, then strain through a fine-mesh sieve. Measure out portions into freezer containers if you aren't using it within two days.

YIELD: **about 6 cups**

Braised Ham and Its Pot Liquor

THIS RECIPE WAS INSPIRED BY JULIA CHILD'S DELICIOUS ENTRÉE, JAMBON BRAISÉ AU MADÈRE (MASTERING THE ART OF FRENCH COOKING, VOLUME I). HERE, IT PRODUCES TWO SEASONERS INSTEAD: COOKED HAM AND A CONCENTRATED STOCK. AN OUNCE OR TWO OF HAM PER SERVING IS ALL YOU'LL NEED TO FLAVOR SAUCES, AND ONE TO THREE ICE CUBES OF THE FROZEN STOCK WILL BEEF UP THE FLAVOR OF A SUBSTANTIAL KETTLE OF SOUP OR SAUCE. BOTH STORE WELL FOR TWO TO THREE MONTHS IN THE FREEZER.

6–10 pound smoked ham shank
  or butt
1 cup dry Madeira or sherry
2 sliced carrots
1½ cups sliced mushrooms

1 cup chopped onion
2–4 bay leaves, preferably fresh
1–2 teaspoons chopped fresh or
  dried thyme
¼–½ teaspoon peppercorns

Trim as much fat off the exterior of the ham as possible. Put it in a large stockpot, add the Madeira, sprinkle the vegetables and herbs around the meat, and add enough water to cover the ham. Cover the pot and bring the liquid to a boil. Reduce the heat and simmer gently for at least two hours *and* until the meat's interior temperature reaches 130 degrees if it is a precooked ham, or 160 degrees if it was an uncooked ham.

When the meat is cooked, lift it out of the stock, set it on a platter to cool, and save any juices that run out of it. At the same time, set the stockpot in a basin of very cold water to cool it. Set it in the refrigerator to chill further.

As soon as the meat is cool enough to handle, cut it into the small portions needed to flavor a recipe, trimming and discarding any fat you encounter. Wrap each piece separately with plastic, then store the batch in a second airtight container. Freeze.

When the stock has chilled and its fat has solidified, skim it off. Pour the liquid into ice cube trays or other freezer containers, and freeze. If you use ice trays, remove the stock cubes as soon as possible. Run warm water over the bottom of the tray, pop the cubes out, and store them in a doubled set of plastic bags.

CHAPTER 2

Ingredients: Basic Grains and Exotic Flavors

Wherever meat is scarce, cooks replace its savor with aromatic spices, pungent sauces, and other complex and assertive flavorings. Most of these you'll find in supermarkets or natural food stores. Check your local ethnic stores for the few remaining items. If you can't find foods locally, contact the purveyors listed in Mail Order Sources on page 228–230.

Sauces, Pastes, and Extracts

Ketjap manis is a sweet Indonesian soy sauce, and *ketjap asem* is a similar, but saltier, version. Both are available in Oriental and Dutch food stores.

Hoisin sauce is a Chinese paste based on fermented soybeans and rice blended with sugar, vinegar, and spices. Most supermarkets carry it; Oriental stores should carry several brands.

Chili paste with garlic and similar hot bean pastes are available in Oriental markets. When added with a light touch, they're delicious. Otherwise, they'll take your head off. Canned sauces tend to bulge. Buy brands that are packed in jars.

Orange flower water adds a wonderful fragrance to mild couscous. You'll find it in Middle Eastern markets and many gourmet stores.

Rose water, used with a light touch, gives an intriguing edge to rice or bulgur pilafs, as well as to Middle Eastern pastries. It's available in Middle Eastern and gourmet stores.

Oyster sauce is made from oyster extracts mixed with sugar. Though delicious, many brands contain monosodium glutamate (MSG). Read the label if you have reactions to that compound. Supermarkets carry oyster sauce and better Oriental markets carry several brands.

Fish sauces are fundamental to Vietnamese and Thai cooking. In their native regions, they are called *nuoc mam* and *nam pla* respectively. Made from fermented fish, they're very stinky, but delectable when used discreetly. Buy these in Oriental markets.

Tamarind concentrate is used in Indian cuisines, and it is sold here in Middle Eastern and Indian grocery stores. It's very tart. You can substitute lemon juice.

Tahini is a paste made from raw sesame seeds. It's a necessary ingredient in many Middle Eastern recipes and is found in stores catering to clientele from that region. Oriental sesame paste is made from toasted seeds, is more strongly flavored, and is available in Oriental markets.

Harissa is a searingly hot paste used in Moroccan cooking. You can heat up your couscous with other hot peppers if you can't find this in gourmet or Middle Eastern markets. Store tubes of harissa in the refrigerator. If you buy it in a can, transfer the contents to a plastic jar and store it in the freezer.

Miso pastes, made from fermented soybeans and grain, are extremely salty, but a mere spoonful will give a meaty taste to any soup. These Japanese products are available in many supermarkets and any Oriental grocery store.

Dry Flavorings

Dried mushrooms, such as shiitake and porcini mushrooms, lend unparalleled earthy, meaty flavors to dishes containing little or no meat. You can buy packages of a few shiitakes in many supermarkets, but they're much cheaper in Oriental markets. The even more expensive porcinis are available in Italian delicatessens and gourmet stores. Insects love both. If you suspect they contain larvae, freeze these for a week or two before storing. If your kitchen is infested, be sure to transfer them to impervious containers. Store both in a cool, dry place.

Wood ear fungus is virtually tasteless, but adds crunchy texture to Chinese soups. Buy these in Oriental markets and soak before using.

Lily buds, also known as *golden needles*, provide an elusive sweet-smoky note to Chinese soups and stir-fried dishes. Their vibrant orange color darkens rapidly, but they're edible for up to a year after purchase. You'll find these in Oriental markets.

Dashi is a Japanese dried soup stock made from dried bonito flakes and dried kômbu (seaweed). Avoid commercial mixes, which contain MSG. You'll find the individual components as well as the mix in Oriental grocery stores and some supermarkets. Both can be stored in a cool kitchen for a year as long as you keep insects out of their packages.

Sun-dried tomatoes add a smoky note to sauces. Store those packed in oil in the refrigerator, and the less-expensive, dry variety in your cupboard.

Oils

Store all oils in the refrigerator unless you use them up very rapidly. Once they smell or taste rancid, throw them out. Substantial evidence indicates rancid oils are as unhealthy as they are unpalatable.

Canola oil is high in monounsaturated fats. It has little flavor and is the best choice for sautéing foods when you don't want to taste the oil.

Extra-virgin olive oil is also high in monounsaturated fatty acids. Its rich flavor compensates for that of meats.

Sesame oil is even more densely flavored. Often 1/4 to 1/2 teaspoon is sufficient to perfume a dish for several people. Oriental markets usually carry more highly flavored oil from toasted seeds. Buy this type in preference to natural food brands.

Spices and Herbs

Spices are the backbone of many ethnic cuisines. To keep them as fresh and flavorful as possible, buy whole spices and grind them as needed. Most whole spices remain pungent for three to twelve months when stored in a cool, dark place. Ground spices tend to deteriorate within one to four months. Whenever possible, purchase just enough to last for these durations. Supermarkets carry most of the common spices. Natural food stores do as well, often in bulk at cheaper prices. Ethnic food stores carry those their clientele favors. Check the listings in Mail Order Sources on page 228–230 if you can't find a spice locally.

BASIC SPICES

Allspice, whole or ground
Anise seed
Bay leaves
Capers
Caraway seed
Cardamom, whole seed or ground
  Cayenne
Celery seed
Cinnamon, stick or ground
Cloves, whole or ground
Coriander, whole seed or ground
Cumin, whole seed or ground

Dillseed
Fennel seed
Ginger
Horseradish
Mace
Mustard, seed, powder, and/or
  prepared
Nutmeg, preferably whole
Paprika
Peppercorns
Poppy seeds
Sesame seeds
Turmeric

FRESH HERBS

With few exceptions, herbs are always at their best when freshly cut. Most supermarkets carry a few. However, you'll have a much wider selection if you grow your own. A small corner of your garden can produce a bounty of herbs. Even a few pots on your balcony will supply you with fresh, aromatic herbs. These are some of the most useful.

Basil	Parsley
Chives	Rosemary
Cilantro	Sage
Dillweed	Savory
Marjoram	Tarragon
Mint	Thyme
Oregano	

EXOTIC SPICES

Ajwain is harsh and medicinally flavored. A pinch of ajwain gives an interesting sharp tingle to soups, stews, and breads. Substitute a mixture of thyme and celery seed, if necessary. Ajwain is used in Indian, Middle Eastern, and Ethiopian cuisines, so you'll find it in stores and by mail from sources specializing in those foods.

Asafetida is a spice that is unbelievably stinky, but the smallest pinch adds a delightful, meaty, garlicky zest to stews and even salad dressings. It is sold as a powder (compounded with flour and other gums) or in hard chunks of resin that are impossible to grind. Buy the powder. Used in Indian cuisines, you'll find this in Indian or Middle Eastern stores or mail order sources.

Chili peppers are fundamental to the world's spicy cuisines. At a minimum, you'll want these most versatile varieties or similar peppers in your cupboard: the ground mild California, warmer New Mexico, a medium to very hot cayenne, and whole hot hantaka.

Curry leaves, the product of a tall Indian shrub (*Murraya koenigii*), is a spice used to flavor that country's fish, dal, grain, and similar savory dishes. It is rarely included in commercial curry powder blends. You can buy the dried leaves, which have a pleasant, oily aroma, in Indian and Middle Eastern markets or from mail order suppliers. Fresh leaves from home-grown trees are rather acrid.

Epasote is used by cooks in many regions of Mexico in soups, stews, and especially the bean pot. This rank-flavored herb is reputed to be carminative (antiflatulent), and this property and its medicinal flavor loses nothing in drying. You will find the dried herb in well-stocked Hispanic markets and mail order sources.

Fenugreek is a maple/celery-flavored spice that lacks the pungency of most spices, but its persistent fragrance will perfume your kitchen for days. Cooks in parts of North Africa, the Middle East, and the Indian subcontinent use it primarily to flavor breads, vegetables, and bean or meat stews. Both whole and ground fenugreek are available in natural foods stores, Middle Eastern, and Indian markets.

Galangal, also called *laos* (Indonesian) or *kha* (Thai), is hot, pungent, and decidedly camphorous in its fresh state. When dried, its taste becomes subtle and woody. This ginger-family spice is used mostly in Southeast Asian cookery. You will find dried slices and/or powder in Oriental stores serving this clientele. Some carry the fresh or equally pungent frozen rhizomes as well.

Juniper berries, which you can buy in gourmet, natural food, and specialty spice stores, add an earthy dimension to vegetables, meat, or game. Add no more than one or two per serving. Crush them first, or remove them after the dish is cooked. Avoid adding too many. They can make a dish taste like pine. Caution: Very large quantities of juniper berries can cause uterine contractions. Pregnant women should avoid them entirely.

Nigella, also called *kalonji*, are black seeds that give a buttery but slightly bitter edge to Indian and Middle Eastern breads. They are also a favorite fish flavoring in India's Bengal region. Buy them from stores or mail order suppliers of those regions' foods.

Sansho pepper is lemon-flavored with a peppery hint. This Japanese spice adds a clean, refreshing note to any grain, poultry, or fish. Sold as a powder, it deteriorates rapidly. Buy small quantities and toss out any that is more than six months old. You'll find it in some Oriental and all Japanese markets and mail order houses.

Star anise is a licorice-flavored spice that is present in five-spice powder, a blend that adds a rich, spicy note to Chinese red-cooked stews. Once ground, its flavor deteriorates rapidly. Buy whole stars in Oriental markets or gourmet stores and grind them in an electric coffee mill right before you need them. You can also toss a whole one directly into the stew as though it were a bouquet garni. Star anise is available in Oriental and natural food stores.

Sumac is related to poisonous sumac, but this spice isn't toxic. In the Middle

East it's used to flavor breads, poultry, and fish. You can buy whole or ground sumac in Middle Eastern markets.

Szechuan peppercorn is no relation to black pepper, although this spice possesses a similar pungent, peppery flavor, but with slightly sweet, fruity overtones. It is a common element in the hotter Chinese cuisines, used to flavor vegetables, fish, fowl, and meats. Most Oriental markets carry this spice, as do many gourmet stores.

Wasabi, a pungent relative of horseradish, is used by Japanese cooks to give a mouth-singeing kick to sushi and sashimi. None of the fresh, Japanese-grown root currently reaches the United States. A few Japanese grocery stores carry frozen roots. Most Oriental stores carry the less pungent wasabi paste in tubes or the dried powder. Most supermarkets also carry the latter.

Garam masala is a blend of spices that's a staple in virtually every Indian kitchen. Each region, and even each family, favors its own recipe. You can buy one or more of these blends in Indian or Middle Eastern grocery stores, or you can make up your own using this basic mixture: 1 tablespoon each coriander seed, black pepper, cinnamon, and cumin, 1 teaspoon cardamom, and ½ teaspoon cloves. If possible, use whole spices and toast them briefly in a heavy skillet before grinding. If not, use recently ground spices.

Grains

In the world's peasant kitchens, grains remain the staff of life. Plentiful, cheap, and tasty, they are the central focus of many ethnic cuisines. Grains so dominate many cultures that their languages use the same word for *grain* and *food*. In these cuisines, a meal isn't considered a true meal if it doesn't contain some grain, and all other foods are nutritious or flavorful adjuncts to all-important grain.

Most of this book's recipes call for the familiar rice, pasta, and other grain products you can buy in your supermarket. These are a few more.

Amaranth is a nutritious pseudograin (a seed that resembles the true grass family grains like rice and wheat). It's as tiny as a poppy seed, with a curious flavor of beets and corn and a pleasant crunchy texture. Amaranth is available in natural food stores.

Arborio rice is a large, chubby Italian rice that absorbs an enormous amount of water. It is ideal for making paellas and salads, and it is required for making risotto. Spanish-grown Granza rice is similar. One or both should be available in better supermarkets, gourmet shops, and Italian food stores.

Basmati rice is a deeply flavored, beautifully textured long grain white rice variant grown in India and Pakistan. A luxury rice even in the countries producing it, basmati costs about three times the amount of an average long grain rice. It's worth the price. Basmati is an unrivaled accompaniment to Indian or Middle Eastern dishes. It's excellent in cold salads and unparalleled for spiced rice puddings or other desserts.

This product often contains stones, metal bits, and other debris. Be sure to check it carefully, then rinse thoroughly with water.

Black rice from Indonesia resembles wild rice with its striated purple brown hue, but it has a less nutty taste. It is sold in Asian markets.

Buckwheat is a pseudograin, like amaranth and quinoa. You'll find the earthy flavored kasha in supermarkets, and buckwheat noodles (blended with wheat flour) in natural food stores and Oriental markets. They'll be labeled *soba* in the latter stores.

Bulgur is steamed and parched wheat that is cracked and graded by particle size from zero or one (very fine) to four (the coarsest). The finest grades need no cooking and are best in salads like tabouli. When cooked, they tend to become mushy. Medium and coarse grades are the best selections for pilafs. For soups, use only number four grade and add it shortly before the soup is done. All retain most of the whole kernel's nutrients.

Couscous forms the base for many North African dishes. It is made by compressing durum wheat particles (semolina—see below) into coarser morsels. Since it is already cooked, you can simply rehydrate it for salads or steam it for hot dishes. You can buy it in many supermarkets, gourmet stores, and Middle Eastern grocery stores. The latter stores may carry *Magrebi couscous*, a giant form resembling tapioca pearls. Many natural food stores also stock whole wheat couscous.

Millet has a dry, chewy texture and buttery flavor that's pleasant in soups, salads, and casseroles. Most natural food stores carry the whole seed as well as millet flour. Don't buy more than you can use in a short time. It rapidly becomes rancid, especially if your kitchen is warm.

Oshi mugi is pressed barley. Packages are available in Japanese food stores.

Polenta is coarsely ground yellow cornmeal.

Quinoa (pronounced *keen-wah*) is a delicate pseudograin native to the Andes. Because it's more nutritious than most grains, agronomists are eager to grow it in expanded settings. Quinoa seeds are coated with soapy, bitter molecules called saponins, so it must be rinsed well before it is cooked. To clean it, put the seeds in a large sieve and rinse for about fifteen seconds. Use a fine-meshed sieve; the seeds will run through a coarse mesh. Alternatively, you can put the seeds in a large bowl filled with water. Stir, then pour off the water. Repeat this process two or three times. The amount of saponin varies from batch to batch. It tends to be almost absent from the best quality, labeled *altiplano*. This high-grown grade is white and sweet flavored. It needs minimal rinsing. Quinoa labeled *valley* is slightly yellow, more roughly flavored, and may have more saponin. Gray to tan colored quinoa is probably domestically grown or *sea-level* Peruvian grown. It tends to be more bitter. Some batches, particularly of this latter type, contain unpleasant gritty material. Be sure to remove any dark seeds and pebbles.

Rye and *triticale* share an assertively earthy and faintly sour flavor, which isn't surprising since triticale is a hybrid of rye and wheat plants. The whole berries have a chewy texture that is especially appealing in soups, salads, casseroles, and pilafs. Natural food stores carry both.

Semolina flour is the gritty textured hard wheat used to make the best pastas and some renditions of Italian gnocchi.

Texmati rice is a long grain hybrid of Indian basmati and domestic brown rice strains. It is the premier whole grain rice for pilafs, possessing both the nutty flavor of brown rice and some of basmati's perfume.

Wild rice is the acme of grains, with an alluring, nutty, smoky flavor. Though not a true rice, it resembles its plainer sister in appearance, preparation, and the aquatic conditions it requires for growth. However, there is considerable variation in the liquid and time needed to cook different batches of this rice, so watch carefully when you prepare this luxury grain. You can buy it in better supermarkets, gourmet shops, and natural food stores.

CHAPTER 3

Soups, Casseroles, and Other Thick Dishes

A steaming cauldron of soup conjures visions of the hearth, security, and bone-warming pleasure. During winter weather, much of the world thrives on heat-retentive soups and casseroles. Many are based on the staples of the winter kitchen: grains, dried beans, root vegetables, and preserved meats. These starchy stews seem the thickest and most warming. Simple peasant fare, these satisfying dishes are inexpensive and easy to make.

You can expand your repertoire of these hearty, low-fat dishes by adapting the recipes you'll find in most ethnic, casserole, and soup cookbooks. Be sure to check Italian cookbooks for risotto, polenta, and gnocchi recipes, Mexican and Spanish cookbooks for dry soups, Chinese and other Oriental books for rice and noodle soups, and British cookbooks for barley soups. Select those that contain a substantial proportion of grain and/or beans. Review the other ingredients and adjust them as necessary to pare out fat. Watch out particularly for the amount and kind of meat. Choose the leanest meat consistent with the recipe and trim it well. Include no more than two ounces of meat per serving. Rely on meat stocks for flavor and pungent vegetables and/or beans for extra texture and taste. Also note the amount of oil or fat used to sauté meats and other foods. One to two teaspoons per serving is ample. Look for other high-fat ingredients like cheese or sour cream, especially in casseroles. Try to restrict these to one tablespoon per serving.

The two versions of asapao that appear on the following pages show how easily you can adapt recipes. The original recipe derives virtually all of its 40 percent fat calories (and its 14 percent saturated fat) from lard and chicken. The adapted version also relies on traditional ingredients, but it emphasizes the leanest ones. In it, rice becomes the basic element, a small amount of fish and olive oil replace the original version's chicken and lard, and extra vegetables and herbs make up for the cheese. The taste remains; the fat doesn't.

Traditional Asapao

2 tablespoons lard
8 small chicken thighs with skin
1 cup rice
3 cups chicken stock
1 cup tomatoes
4 ounces ham

1 cup sweet red pepper
2/3 cup peas
1/4 cup olives
1/4 cup parsley*
1/4 cup Parmesan cheese
Tabasco sauce to taste*

SERVES 4

NUTRITIONAL CONTENTS (PER SERVING)

Food*	Calories	Protein	Total fat	Saturated fat	Carbohydrate
		gram (% cal.)	gram (% cal.)	gram (% cal.)	gram (% cal.)
Lard	58	—	6 (8%)	2.5 (3%)	—
Chicken	275	30 (18%)	16 (21%)	4.5 (6%)	—
Rice	173	3 (2%)	trace	—	39 (23%)
Stock	15	3 (2%)	trace	—	—
Tomato	12	trace	trace	—	2 (1%)
Ham	47	6 (4%)	2 (3%)	1.0 (1%)	—
Pepper	10	trace	—	—	2 (1%)
Peas	18	1 (1%)	—	—	3 (2%)
Olive	26	trace	3 (4%)	0.3 (trace)	trace
Cheese	46	4 (2%)	3 (4%)	2.0 (3%)	trace
Total	680	47	30	10.3	46
% of calories		29%	40%	14%	27%

*Ingredients with trivial calories aren't shown.

Adapted Asapao

2 teaspoons olive oil	2 cups lima beans
8 ounces catfish	1/4 cup olives
1 1/2 cups rice	1/4 cup parsley*
2 cups onion	6–8 cloves garlic*
1/2 cup clam broth*	1 tablespoon thyme*
2 cups tomatoes	2 teaspoons coriander*
2 ounces ham	2 teaspoons paprika*
2 cups bell pepper	Tabasco to taste*

SERVES 4

NUTRITIONAL CONTENTS (PER SERVING)

Food*	Calories	Protein		Total fat	Saturated fat	Carbohydrate
		gram (% cal.)		gram (% cal.)	gram (% cal.)	gram (% cal.)
Oil	21	—		2 (3%)	0.3 (trace)	—
Fish	58	10	(7%)	2 (3%)	(trace)	—
Rice	259	5	(4%)	trace	—	58 (42%)
Onion	31	1	(1%)	trace	—	7 (5%)
Tomato	24	1	(1%)	trace	—	5 (4%)
Ham	24	3	(2%)	2 (3%)	0.5 (1%)	—
Pepper	20	1	(1%)	trace	—	3 (2%)
Lima beans	95	6	(4%)	trace	—	17 (12%)
Olive	26	trace		3 (5%)	0.3 (1%)	trace
Total	558	27		9	±1.1	90
% of calories		20%		15%	3%	65%

*Ingredients with trivial calories aren't shown.

Asapao

THIS IS THE COMPLETE RECIPE THAT APPEARS ON PAGE 37.

2 teaspoons olive oil
½ pound boneless catfish fillet, chopped
1½ cups long grain white rice
2 cups chopped onions
½ cup bottled clam broth
4 cups water
2 cups chopped tomatoes
2 ounces ham, diced
2 cups chopped pimiento or red bell pepper

2 cups lima beans
¼ cup chopped olives
¼ cup chopped fresh parsley
6–8 cloves garlic, mashed
1 tablespoon chopped fresh or dried thyme
2 teaspoons ground coriander seed
2 teaspoons sweet Hungarian paprika
Tabasco or similar hot sauce to taste

Heat the oil in a large pot over medium heat. Sauté the fish until it's slightly golden.

Add the rice and onion and cook until the latter is soft.

Add the remaining ingredients and simmer for at least 30 minutes. Taste for seasoning and add more hot sauce if needed.

SERVES 4—558 cal.; 9g (15% of cal.) total fat; ±1.1 g (3%) saturated fat; 90 g (65%) carbohydrate; 40 mg cholesterol; and ±600 mg sodium per serving

Fish Soup

SAFFRON'S VIBRANT COLOR AND ALLURING ASTRINGENT TASTE MAKE THIS AN ELEGANT SOUP.
FOR A SIMPLE (AND CHEAPER) DISH, YOU CAN LEAVE THIS INGREDIENT OUT.

2 teaspoons olive oil
4–8 cloves garlic, mashed or minced
6 cups homemade fish fumet
   (see page 23)
1 cup dry white wine
4 cups chopped fresh tomatoes
1 green pepper, diced

1 sweet red pepper, diced
3–4 bay leaves
Large pinch saffron (optional)
2 oranges
1 pound orzo, riso, or
   similar small pasta
½ pound diced sea bass

Cook the oil and garlic in a large stockpot over a low flame until it becomes fragrant, then add the liquids, vegetables, and spices.

Squeeze the orange juice and set aside. Add a large piece of the peel to the soup.

Simmer the soup over medium heat for 20 to 30 minutes.

Cook the pasta in another pot until it is barely tender (about 7 to 10 minutes). Drain and add to the soup along with the orange juice and sea bass. Simmer just until the soup is very hot and the fish is cooked through. Remove the orange peel and bay leaves, then serve.

SERVES 4—639 cal.; 6 g (8% of cal.) total fat; 1.2g (2%) saturated fat; 106g (66%) carbohydrate; 23mg cholesterol; and 147mg sodium per serving

Pozole

PORK DOMINATES MANY RECIPES FOR THIS MEXICAN SOUP. THIS VERSION RELIES MORE ON RICH STOCK FOR TASTE AND LARGER QUANTITIES OF VEGETABLES FOR TEXTURE. CANNED HOMINY IS VERY SALTY. BE SURE TO RINSE IT THOROUGHLY.

¼ pound lean, fat-trimmed, boneless pork

2 medium-sized skinned, boned, fat-trimmed chicken thighs

2 32-ounce cans hominy

2 cups chopped onion

2 cups chopped fresh tomatoes

2 tablespoons chopped fresh oregano or 2 teaspoons dried oregano

½–3 teaspoons mild to medium hot ground red chili

¼–1 teaspoon chopped epasote (optional)

2 teaspoons sugar

8 cups homemade chicken stock (see page 22)

3 cups sliced zucchini

4 10- to 12-inch flour tortillas

3 cups loosely packed shredded lettuce

2 cups sliced radishes

Dice the pork and chicken. Drain and rinse the hominy.

Put the first 10 ingredients in a stockpot. Cover and bring to a boil. Reduce the heat to low and simmer for at least 1½ hours.

Add the zucchini and simmer another 10 minutes.

Warm the tortillas on a dry griddle or in a low oven or microwave and keep them warm in a napkin-lined basket or bowl.

Put the lettuce and radishes in serving bowls.

Serve the soup in large soup bowls, allowing diners to sprinkle the lettuce and radishes into their own soup. The tortillas can be eaten as a bread or ripped into strips and tossed into the soup.

SERVES 4—599 cal.; 13g (20% of cal.) total fat; 3.2g (5%) saturated fat; 96g (64%) carbohydrate; 42mg cholesterol; and ±980mg sodium per serving

Harira

This nourishing soup is traditionally served after a sunrise-to-sunset fast during the Moslem holy days of Ramadan. Although this version contains less meat and oil than most, the stock and spices give it an equally rich flavor. You can cook the chicken thighs whole or diced.

2 teaspoons olive oil
4 small skinned, fat-trimmed
  chicken thighs
3 cups chopped onion
2 teaspoons ground cumin
2 teaspoons ground coriander
2 teaspoons turmeric
1 teaspoon cinnamon
1 teaspoon freshly ground black pepper
3/8 cup uncooked lentils

5–6 cups homemade chicken stock
  (see page 22)
2 cups chopped tomatoes
Juice of 2 lemons
2/3 pound winter squash
  (e.g., Hubbard)
1/2 pound capellini or
  other thin pasta
1–2 tablespoons sugar
2 tablespoons chopped fresh parsley

Heat the oil in a stockpot over medium heat. Sauté the chicken for a minute, then add the onion and spices. Cook an additional minute.

Rinse the lentils and check them for debris. Add them, along with the stock, tomatoes, and lemon juice, to the chicken. Cover the pot, raise the heat to bring the soup just to a boil, then reduce the heat and simmer it for 20 minutes.

Peel the squash, cut it into 1/2-inch cubes, and break the capellini into about 1-inch lengths. Add the squash and pasta to the soup and simmer for 15 minutes longer. Taste the soup for seasoning and add sufficient sugar to balance the lemon juice. Sprinkle with the fresh parsley and serve immediately.

SERVES 4—629 cal.; 8 g (11% of cal.) total fat; 2.1 g (3%) saturated fat; 108 g (69%) carbohydrate; 38 mg cholesterol; and 362 mg sodium per serving

Variation. You can use lamb cubes (trim all fat) instead of chicken, and/or cooked chickpeas in place of the lentils. Substitute vegetables freely.

Borscht

IN THE UKRAINE, BORSCHT IS OFTEN FLAVORED MORE WITH BEETS, RYE KVASS (A LIGHTLY FERMENTED BREW), AND MUSHROOMS, THAN WITH MEAT. THIS VERSION FOLLOWS SUIT.

½ pound lean, fat-trimmed,
  boneless beef chuck
2 teaspoons canola oil
Beef bones (optional)
2 cups chopped onions
6 cups homemade beef stock
  (see page 21)
1 cup beer
4 cups sliced fresh mushrooms
2 cups chopped, peeled beets
2 cups chopped, peeled turnips
2 cups chopped carrots

1 cup chopped celery
⅔ cup whole rye berries
¼ cup cider vinegar or lemon juice
2 tablespoons dillseed or
  chopped dillweed
3–4 bay leaves
2 tablespoons sugar
1 teaspoon freshly ground black
  pepper
2 cups chopped, peeled potatoes
2 bunches well-washed beet greens
  or 2 cups shredded cabbage

Cut the beef into ¼- to ½-inch cubes.

Heat the oil in a large stockpot over a moderate flame. Sauté the meat and any bones until lightly browned. Add the onions and sauté until they are limp, then add the remaining ingredients except the beet greens or cabbage. Cover, raise the heat, bring the liquid just to a boil, then reduce the heat, and simmer the soup gently for at least 40 minutes.

Add the beet greens or cabbage and simmer about 5 to 10 minutes longer. Serve very hot.

SERVES 4—523 cal.; 8g (14% of cal.) total fat; 3g (5%) saturated fat; 84g (64%) carbohydrate; 40mg cholesterol; 328mg sodium per serving

West African Rice and Fish Stew

BANANAS, WHICH COMPLEMENT THIS DISH'S SWEET, SPICY FLAVORS, REPLACE THE MORE AUTHENTIC PLANTAINS IN THIS SENEGALESE STEW. YOU CAN USE EITHER FRESH OR CANNED TOMATOES. THE SODIUM VALUE BELOW REFLECTS THE FRESH VARIETY. CANNED TOMATOES WILL DOUBLE EACH SERVING'S SODIUM CONTENT.

1 tablespoon plus 1 teaspoon olive oil
½ pound catfish fillet,
    cut in thin strips
1⅓ cups long or medium grain
    white rice
2 cups chopped onion
4 cups water
1½ cups (12 ounces) bottled clam
    juice
2 cups chopped fresh or
    canned tomatoes
3 tablespoons sugar

1–3 teaspoons mild cayenne or
    California chili powder
1 teaspoon ginger powder
1 teaspoon ground cinnamon
¼ teaspoon ground cloves
¼ teaspoon freshly grated nutmeg
Juice of 1 or 2 lemons
1 or more drops Tabasco or
    other hot sauce
1 cup chopped fresh cauliflower
2 large, firm bananas, sliced

Heat the oil in a large, covered skillet over medium heat. Sauté the fish strips until they are golden. Remove with a slotted spoon and set aside.

Add the rice and onions to the oil and sauté for 1 minute, then add the remaining ingredients (except the cauliflower, bananas, and fish strips), using the smallest amount of Tabasco and lemon juice indicated.

Cover the pan, bring to a boil, then reduce the heat to low and simmer the stew for about 10 minutes.

Add the cauliflower and bananas and simmer for 5 minutes. Add the fish and simmer 5 minutes longer. Taste and adjust the seasoning as desired and serve in large soup bowls.

SERVES 4—571 cal.; 8g (13% of cal.) total fat; 1.6g (3%) saturated fat; 104g (73%) carbohydrate; 32mg cholesterol; and 420mg sodium per serving

Drunken Beans and Hominy

FIGS AND BEER MAY SEEM ODD IN A CHILI, BUT BOTH IMPART SWEET, ROASTED FLAVORS THAT REPLACE SOME OF THE NUANCES OF MEAT.

½ pound lean, fat-trimmed pork shoulder, cubed
2 teaspoons olive oil
2 cups chopped onions
3 cups cooked pinto beans or 2 16-ounce cans pinto beans, drained
2 15-ounce cans hominy, drained and rinsed
3 cups dark beer
2 cups homemade chicken stock (see page 22)

¼ cup chopped dried figs
2–3 teaspoons mild or medium chili powder
2 teaspoons ground cumin
2 teaspoons chopped epasote (optional)
2 teaspoons chopped fresh or dried oregano
2–3 bay leaves
8 6-inch corn tortillas

Brown the meat cubes with the oil in a large, heavy, covered pot over medium heat. Add the onions and sauté until they're limp. Add the remaining ingredients except the tortillas. Cover and bring to a boil. Reduce the heat to low and simmer for about 45 minutes. Remove the bay leaves.

Warm the tortillas in a 300-degree oven for a few minutes. Serve with the chili.

SERVES 4—664 cal.; 11g (15% of cal.) total fat; 3.2g (4%) saturated fat; 100g (60%) carbohydrate; 40mg cholesterol; and ±735mg sodium per serving

Hopping John

THIS RECIPE IS CHARACTERISTIC OF THE MANY THICK RICE AND BEAN COMBINATIONS COOKED THROUGHOUT THE CARIBBEAN AND AMERICAN SOUTH. BLACK-EYED PEAS ARE TYPICAL OF AMERICAN RECIPES, PIGEON PEAS OF CARIBBEAN. MANY CALL FOR MUCH MORE MEAT THAN SUGGESTED IN THIS RECIPE. YOU DON'T NEED THE EXTRA.

2 cups long grain white rice
1/3 pound trimmed raw or
   cooked ham
1 tablespoon plus 1 teaspoon olive oil
2 1/2 cups water
2 1/2 cups homemade chicken stock
   (see page 22)
2 cups coarsely chopped onions

1 1/2 cup cooked pigeon peas or
   1 15-ounce can pigeon peas, drained
2 large green bell peppers, chopped
2 teaspoons sugar
2 tablespoons chopped fresh thyme
   or 2 teaspoons dried thyme
1/2 teaspoon ground mild red pepper
Hot sauce to taste

Briefly sauté the rice and ham in the oil, then add the remaining ingredients. Cover and bring to a boil. Reduce the heat to low and simmer until the rice is tender (about 20 minutes).

Serve, letting individual diners add more hot sauce to taste.

SERVES 4—644 cal.; 12g (17% of cal.) total fat; 3.4g (5%) saturated fat; 108g (67%) carbohydrate; 46mg cholesterol; and ±900mg sodium per serving

Gumbo

Typical Louisiana gumbos call for larger quantities of shellfish and/or rich sausages, and a roux made with lots of butter. A small amount of olive oil replaces it here. If you wish a smoked sausage flavor, substitute an equal quantity of trimmed ham for the shrimp. Use fresh (rather than canned) crab, if possible.

3 tablespoons olive oil

¼ cup flour

2 teaspoons Spanish or
   sweet Hungarian paprika

¼–2 teaspoons mild to hot cayenne

2 teaspoons ground allspice

2 teaspoons chopped fresh or
   dried thyme

4–6 cloves garlic, mashed

1 cup chopped onions

4 cups chopped tomatoes

4 cups homemade fish fumet
   (see page 23) or chicken stock
   (see page 22)

2 cups thinly sliced okra, fresh or
   frozen

1½ cups chopped green bell pepper

1⅓ cups chopped celery

1½ cups long grain white rice

3 cups water

½ pound fresh crab meat or
   2 5-ounce cans crab, rinsed

¼ pound cooked shrimp or
   chopped, cleaned prawns

½ cup chopped radish leaves
   (optional)

2 teaspoons filé powder

Tabasco or other Louisiana hot sauce
   to taste

Mix the olive oil and flour with a wooden spoon in a large, heavy stockpot. Warm the roux over the lowest heat possible, stirring frequently, until the mixture becomes a golden brown. This will take at least 20 to 30 minutes.

Stir in the paprika, cayenne, allspice, thyme, garlic, and onions and continue cooking for one minute more. Stir in the tomatoes, stock, okra, bell pepper, and celery.

Raise the heat and bring the liquid barely to a boil, then cover the pot, reduce the flame, and simmer over very low heat for 45 to 60 minutes, stirring several times.

About 20 minutes before the soup is cooked, steam the rice in the water.

About 5 to 7 minutes before serving, add the crab, prawns, radish leaves, and filé powder to the soup and continue simmering it until the fish is cooked.

Put the rice in large soup bowls and ladle the gumbo over it. Let each person add hot sauce to taste.

SERVES 4—599 cal.; 13g (20% of cal.) total fat; 2.6g (4%) saturated fat; 93g (62%) carbohydrate; 82mg cholesterol; and 611mg sodium per serving

Pasta e Fagioli

RECIPES FOR THIS SIMPLE ITALIAN DISH OFTEN CALL FOR MORE (AND/OR FATTER) PORK. IN THIS VERSION, A RICH CHICKEN STOCK AND THE DIVERSE MEDLEY OF INGREDIENTS MORE THAN MAKE UP FOR THE EXTRA PORK.

IF YOU COOK THE PASTA DIRECTLY IN THE SOUP, IT WILL BE THICKER THAN IF YOU COOK IT IN A SEPARATE POT. EITHER IS FINE.

1 tablespoon plus 1 teaspoon olive oil
½ pound lean, boneless,
    fat-trimmed pork, cubed
2 cups chopped onion
2 cups diced carrots
2 cups chopped celery
4 cups homemade chicken stock
    (see page 22)
3 cups chopped fresh tomatoes
1½ cups precooked or canned
    cranberry, fava, or kidney beans

1 cup red wine
¼ cup chopped fresh parsley
2 tablespoons chopped fresh or
    dried basil
2 teaspoons chopped fresh thyme
2 teaspoons chopped fresh rosemary
    or 1 teaspoon dried rosemary
1 teaspoon chopped fresh sage or
    ½ teaspoon dried sage
¾ pound macaroni or
    other small pasta

Heat the oil in a large stockpot over a medium flame. Sauté the meat in it until lightly browned, then add the onion, carrots, and celery. Cook until fragrant.

Add the remaining ingredients except the pasta, bring to a boil, then reduce the heat to low and simmer for at least 30 minutes.

Cook the pasta, either directly in the soup or in a different kettle of water. If you cook it in the soup, simmer long enough to soften the pasta (at least 10 to 15 minutes). If you cook it separately, drain it, then add to the soup and simmer together at least 5 minutes.

SERVES 4—707 cal.; 14g (18% of cal.) total fat; 3.1g saturated fat; 109g (62%) carbohydrate; 37mg cholesterol; and 115mg sodium per serving

Chili Colorado

YOU MAY BE PERPLEXED BY THE COCOA IN THIS CHILI, BUT IT PROVIDES AN ELUSIVE FLAVOR THAT NO ONE WILL IDENTIFY WITH CHOCOLATE. DON'T SUBSTITUTE HOT CHOCOLATE MIX FOR COCOA.

2 teaspoons olive oil
½ pound lean, fat-trimmed,
    boneless lamb, diced
2 cups chopped onions
8–10 cloves garlic, mashed
4 cups chopped fresh tomatoes
3½ cups cooked pinto beans or
    2 16-ounce cans pinto beans, drained
2 cups homemade lamb or beef stock
1 32-ounce can hominy, drained
    and rinsed

1–2 tablespoons ancho or other
    mellow chili powder
2 tablespoons chopped fresh oregano
    or 2 teaspoons dried oregano
1–2 tablespoons ground cumin
1 teaspoon chopped fresh sage or
    ½ teaspoon dried rubbed sage
1 teaspoon ground allspice
1 tablespoon cocoa

Brown the lamb with the oil in a large, covered pot over medium heat. Add the onions and garlic and cook until fragrant.

Add the remaining ingredients, except the cocoa, cover, and simmer at least 30 minutes.

Mix the cocoa with a tablespoon of water and stir it into the chili. Simmer 10 minutes longer before serving.

SERVES 4—519 cal.; 9g (16% of cal.) total fat; 2.7g (5%) saturated fat; 79g (61%) carbohydrate; 48mg cholesterol; and 825mg sodium per serving

Scotch Broth

½ pound lean, fat-trimmed,
   boneless lamb, diced
2 teaspoons olive oil
1 cup pearled barley
2 cups chopped onions
4 cups homemade beef or
   chicken stock (see page 21 and 22)
2 cups chopped carrots
2 cups chopped potatoes

1½ cups chopped turnips
1 cup chopped celery
2–3 cloves garlic, mashed
2 teaspoons chopped fresh thyme or
   1 teaspoon dried thyme
2-3 bay leaves
¼–1 teaspoon freshly ground black
   pepper
Pinch freshly grated nutmeg

Brown the lamb with the oil in a large, covered pot over medium heat. Add the barley and onion and sauté them until the barley is lightly toasted.

Add the remaining ingredients, cover, and simmer for about 45 to 60 minutes. Add a little water if the soup becomes too thick or begins to stick to the pot.

Serve in soup bowls, sprinkling extra pepper over the top.

SERVES 4—490 cal.; 9g (16% of cal.) total fat; 2.4g (4%) saturated fat; 78g (64%) carbohydrate; 48mg cholesterol; and 264mg sodium per serving

Mulligatawny

INDIAN VERSIONS OF MULLIGATAWNY (LITERALLY *PEPPER WATER*) ARE THICK, BEAN AND RICE BASED SOUPS. ENGLISH VERSIONS FEATURE FISH OR MEAT COOKED IN A THINNER BROTH. THIS RECIPE COMBINES THE ANGLICIZED CHICKEN AND THE INDIAN VEGETABLES AND LENTILS. SPICES MAKE UP MOST OF THE LENGTHY INGREDIENTS LIST. YOU CAN SUBSTITUTE A FLAVORFUL CURRY POWDER IF YOU PREFER. ADD IT TO TASTE.

2 large, skinned, fat-trimmed, boned chicken thighs
⅓ cup urid dal or brown lentils
8 cups homemade chicken stock (see page 22)
2 cups chopped turnips
2 cups chopped onions
2 cups chopped carrots
2 cups chopped celery
1 tablespoon ground cumin
2 teaspoons minced fresh gingerroot
2 teaspoons turmeric

2 teaspoons freshly ground black pepper
1 teaspoon cinnamon
½ teaspoon ground cardamom
¼ teaspoon ground cloves
Pinch asafetida (optional)
1½ cups long grain white rice
Juice of 1 lemon
2 tablespoons sugar
¼ cup chopped fresh cilantro (optional)

Cut the meat into ½-inch cubes. Rinse and drain the dal.

Heat the stock over a high heat in a very large stockpot. Add the chicken, dal, vegetables, and spices. Reduce the heat to low and simmer for at least 20 minutes.

Add the rice and simmer 20 to 40 minutes longer, depending on how thick a soup you want.

Stir in the lemon juice and sugar, cook 1 minute, then taste for seasoning. Add more of either or both to correct the tart/sweet balance and simmer an additional minute.

Sprinkle the cilantro over the soup, then serve.

SERVES 4—564 cal.; 5g (8% of cal.) total fat; 1.5g (2%) saturated fat; 99g (70%) carbohydrate; 36mg cholesterol; and 216mg sodium per serving

Mancha Manteles

MANCHA MANTELES LITERALLY MEANS *TABLECLOTH STAINER* IN SPANISH. THIS TRADITIONAL MEXICAN DISH CONTAINS A SEEMINGLY CURIOUS ASSORTMENT OF FRUITS AND VEGETABLES, BUT THE ULTIMATE MARRIAGE IS A DELICIOUS SWEET/SOUR STEW.

½ pound lean, fat-trimmed, boneless pork
2 teaspoons olive oil
2 cups chopped onion
6 cups homemade chicken stock (see page 22)
2 cups chopped tomatoes
2 cups chopped apple
1 dried ancho chili or 2–3 teaspoons mild or medium hot ground chili
¼–⅓ cup cider or wine vinegar
¼ cup sugar

2 tablespoons chopped fresh oregano or 2 teaspoons dried oregano
4–5 bay leaves
2 teaspoons cinnamon
½ teaspoon ground cloves
1 large yam, peeled and chopped
1 32-ounce can hominy
2 medium-sized bell peppers, chopped
2 cups chopped fresh pineapple
2 tablespoons ground, unsalted pumpkin seeds (optional)

Brown the pork with the oil in a very large covered pot over medium heat. Add the onions and cook until they're soft.

Add the stock, tomatoes, apple, chili, the smaller quantity of vinegar, sugar, and the spices and herbs. Cover, bring to a boil, then reduce the heat and simmer for about 20 minutes.

Add the yam and cook for 20 minutes.

Drain and rinse the hominy, add it to the stew, and cook 10 minutes longer. Then add the remaining ingredients. Cook for about 5 minutes, or until the yam is soft. Taste for seasoning and add additional vinegar or sugar to taste.

Serve in large soup bowls, or if you wish to serve on plates, scoop out the solids, reduce the liquid rapidly, and pour over the meat and vegetables.

SERVES 4—675 cal.; 14 g (19% of cal.) total fat; 3.9 g (5%) saturated fat; 111 g (65%) carbohydrate; 37mg cholesterol; and 762mg sodium per serving

Variations. You can substitute squash or green beans for the yam and/or replace the apple with other tart fruits. For a vegetarian version, replace the pork and bones with 1 cup chickpeas or another bean and add some extra herbs to beef up the juice.

Chicken Stew with a Chinese Taste

BABY CORN ADDS GREAT TEXTURE (AND FIBER) TO THIS MODIFIED CANTONESE DISH. YOU CAN EITHER DICE THE CHICKEN MEAT, OR COOK THE THIGHS INTACT.

4 small skinned, fat-trimmed, boned chicken thighs
2 tablespoons canola oil
4 cups diced potatoes (about 2 pounds)
2 cups coarsely chopped onions
2 tablespoons minced fresh gingerroot
1½ tablespoons sugar

2 tablespoons soy sauce
⅓ cup dry sherry
4½ cups water
2 8-ounce cans water chestnuts
1 15-ounce can baby corn, drained and rinsed or 2 cups frozen corn kernels
1½ tablespoons cornstarch

Brown the chicken with the oil in a large wok set over medium heat. Add the potato, onion, ginger, and sugar and cook until the potatoes are slightly golden.

Add the soy sauce, sherry, and water. Cover the wok, bring to a boil, then reduce the heat to maintain a simmer. Cook until the potatoes are soft, or for about 15 minutes.

Add the water chestnuts and corn and cook for 3 to 5 minutes longer. Mix the cornstarch with 2 tablespoons of water and add it to the wok. Stir and heat until the liquid thickens.

SERVES 4—598 cal.; 13g (20% of cal.) total fat; 2.8g (4%) saturated fat; 94g (63%) carbohydrate; 48mg cholesterol; and 794mg sodium per serving

Dry Soup with Mushrooms

THE NEXT FOUR SOUPS ARE EXAMPLES OF *SOPA SECAS* (DRY SOUPS), PREPARED THROUGHOUT THE HISPANIC WORLD. MOST OF THESE ALMOST CASSEROLELIKE SOUPS ARE BASED ON RICE, PASTA, TORTILLAS, OR OTHER GRAIN PRODUCTS. LIKE ITALIAN PASTAS, YOU CAN SERVE SMALL PORTIONS AS A FIRST COURSE OR LARGER HELPINGS AS THE MAIN DISH.

1 tablespoon olive oil
1/3 pound lean, fat-trimmed
  smoked ham, minced
2 cups chopped onions
2 cups thinly sliced mushrooms
2 cups long grain white or brown rice
6 cups homemade chicken stock
  (see page 22) or beef stock
  (see page 21)
2 cups chopped fresh tomatoes

1/4 cup chopped fresh cilantro or
  parsley (optional)
1 tablespoon ground coriander
1 tablespoon chopped fresh oregano
  or 2 teaspoons dried oregano
2 teaspoons ground cumin
1 tablespoon Spanish or
  sweet Hungarian paprika
1/4 cup Parmesan cheese

Preheat the oven to 350 degrees. Rub the interior of a 2-quart casserole with a bit of the oil.

Lightly sauté the ham in the remaining oil, then add the onions and mushrooms. Cook until they are fragrant and soft. Add the remaining ingredients, except the cheese. Cover, bring to a boil, reduce the heat, and simmer for 15 minutes (35 minutes for brown rice).

Pour the mixture into the casserole, sprinkle with the cheese, and bake for 20 minutes, then serve.

SERVES 4—605 cal.; 11g (16% of cal.) total fat; 3.1g (5%) saturated fat; 97g (64%) carbohydrate; 30mg cholesterol; 793mg sodium per serving

Cider Soup

APPLE CIDER GIVES A FAINTLY SWEET EDGE TO THIS SPANISH DRY SOUP.

½ pound lean, fat-trimmed
  boneless pork, cubed
1½ tablespoons olive oil
3½ cups apple cider
3–4 cups homemade chicken stock
  (see page 22)
2 cups chopped onion
4–5 cloves garlic, mashed
3 cups chopped turnips
2 tablespoons Spanish or
  sweet Hungarian paprika

1 tablespoon chopped fresh thyme or
  1 teaspoon dried thyme
2 teaspoons ground cumin
¼ teaspoon freshly grated nutmeg
3—4 bay leaves
1½ cups long grain white rice
1½ cup cooked kidney beans or
  1 15-ounce can kidney beans,
  drained
¼ cup chopped fresh parsley
Tabasco or other hot sauce to taste

Brown the pork with the oil in a large pot over medium heat.

Add the liquids, vegetables, spices, and herbs. Cover and bring the liquid to a boil. Reduce the heat and simmer for about 15 minutes.

Add the rice and beans and simmer 20 minutes. Stir in the parsley and add hot sauce to taste.

SERVES 4—614 cal.; 12g (18% of cal.) total fat; 3g (4%) saturated fat; 100g (65%) carbohydrate; 37mg cholesterol; and 246mg sodium per serving

Fidellini Soup

FISH AND TOMATOES ARE THE DOMINANT FLAVORS IN THIS SPANISH DRY SOUP. USE ANY FISH, BUT BE SURE TO REMOVE ANY BONES BEFORE COOKING.

1 pound fidellini, cappellini, or other fine spaghetti-type pasta
1½ tablespoons olive oil
½ pound boneless catfish fillet, diced
5–6 cloves garlic, mashed
6 cups chopped tomatoes
⅔ cup bottled clam juice
½ cup dry white or red wine

2 tablespoons Spanish or sweet Hungarian paprika
2 teaspoons finely chopped fresh or dried basil
4–5 bay leaves
¼ teaspoon freshly grated nutmeg
1 10-ounce package frozen chopped spinach or 6–8 cups coarsely chopped fresh spinach

Cook the pasta until tender in a large pot of water. Drain, rinse, and set aside.

Heat the oil over medium heat in a large, heavy pot and sauté the fish pieces until they become opaque. Add the garlic and sauté for a minute longer, but don't let the garlic burn.

Add the remaining ingredients except the pasta and spinach. Simmer the sauce for about 10 minutes, then add these two. Cook until very hot, then serve.

SERVES 4—653 cal.; 9g (13% of cal.) total fat; 1.7g (2%) saturated fat; 107g (67%) carbohydrate; 33mg cholesterol; and ±375mg sodium per serving

Mexican Lime Soup

THINNER VERSIONS OF THIS SOUP ARE SERVED THROUGHOUT THE YUCATAN PENINSULA. THIS RECIPE, ENRICHED WITH HOMINY AND MORE TORTILLAS, IS ALMOST A TRADITIONAL DRY SOUP.

4 small skinned, fat-trimmed chicken thighs

7 cups homemade chicken stock (see page 22)

1 16-ounce can hominy, drained and rinsed

2 cups chopped fresh tomatoes

2 cups chopped onions

Juice of two limes

10–12 cloves garlic, mashed

2 tablespoons chopped fresh oregano or 1 tablespoon dried oregano

2 tablespoons chopped fresh cilantro

2–3 bay leaves

1/4-2 teaspoons New Mexican chili powder

1 teaspoon chopped fresh or dried epasote (optional)

8 10-inch wheat tortillas (about 18 ounces total)

1 1/2 tablespoons olive oil

Put all the ingredients except the tortillas and oil in a large, covered pot. Bring the soup to a boil, then reduce the heat and simmer at least 30 minutes.

Cut the tortillas into 1/2-inch-wide strips.

Heat the oil in a large, heavy skillet and fry the tortilla strips in the oil. Turn the strips constantly so that all sides are lightly coated with oil and fried. Remove from the skillet when crisp and golden. Put them in a napkin-lined basket and let each diner add them to the soup.

SERVES 4—632 cal.; 12 g (18% of cal.) total fat; 2.9 g (4%) saturated fat; 98 g (63%) carbohydrate; 50mg cholesterol; and 515mg sodium per serving

Spinach Gnocchi

GNOCCHI DEFIES DESCRIPTION, THOUGH STIFF PORRIDGE PERHAPS COMES CLOSEST. WHEN CHILLED, CUT INTO SQUARES, THEN FRIED OR BAKED (AS IN THIS RECIPE), IT MAKES A MOST SATISFYING WINTER DISH. ITALIANS MAKE IT WITH POTATOES, FLOUR-THICKENED RICOTTA CHEESE, OR SEMOLINA. THE NEXT TWO RECIPES USE THE LAST OF THESE.

YOU CAN PREPARE BOTH THE GNOCCHI AND SAUCE UP TO A DAY IN ADVANCE. STORE IN THE REFRIGERATOR AND ASSEMBLE JUST BEFORE BAKING.

3 cups homemade beef or chicken stock (see pages 21 and 22)
2½ cups water
2 10-ounce packages frozen chopped spinach
¼ cup dry sherry (optional)
Pinch of freshly grated nutmeg

2 cups semolina
2 medium sized whole eggs
2 tablespoons Parmesan cheese
4 cups basic tomato sauce (page 78)
¼ pound diced cooked or raw ham
2 medium sized green or sweet red peppers, diced

Put the stock, water, spinach, sherry, and nutmeg in a large, heavy saucepan. Bring to a simmer over moderate heat. Sprinkle the semolina into the bubbling liquid, stirring constantly with a wooden spoon or wire whisk. Continue beating until it thickens, turning the heat lower if it sticks to the pan.

Beat the eggs in a large bowl and slowly beat the hot gnocchi mixture into it. Pour into two 9- x 13-inch baking dishes. Cover with plastic wrap and set in the refrigerator. Chill until stiff (about 4 hours). Prepare the sauce

About 30 minutes before serving, preheat the oven to 400 degrees.

Slice the gnocchi into 1-inch pieces, lifting them with a spatula so that the edges overlap a little. Sprinkle with the Parmesan cheese and bake until very hot and top is golden (about 15 to 25 minutes).

While gnocchi bakes, add the ham and peppers to the tomato sauce and simmer at least 5 minutes.

Serve the baked gnocchi with the sauce poured over it.

SERVES 4—699 cal.; 12g (15% of cal.) total fat; 3.3g (4%) saturated fat; 110g (63%) carbohydrate; 160mg cholesterol; and 642mg sodium per serving

Basil-Flavored Gnocchi

FRESH BASIL GIVES THIS DISH A DELICIOUS, SWEET, AROMATIC TONE.

2 cups nonfat milk
4 cups homemade chicken stock
(see page 22) or fish fumet
(see page 23)
½ cup chopped fresh basil
2 tablespoons dry sherry
2 cups semolina

2 medium sized whole eggs
2 tablespoons Parmesan cheese
⅓ pound shelled shrimp
2 cups thinly sliced fresh fennel
¼ cup chopped imported
black olives
4 cups basic tomato sauce (page 78)

Put the milk, stock, basil, and sherry in a large, heavy saucepan. Bring to a simmer over moderate heat. Sprinkle the semolina into the bubbling liquid, stirring constantly with a wooden spoon or wire whisk. Continue beating until it thickens, turning the heat lower if it sticks to the pan.

Beat the eggs in a large bowl and slowly beat the hot gnocchi mixture into it. Pour into two 9- x 13-inch baking dishes. Cover with plastic wrap and set in the refrigerator. Chill until stiff (about 4 hours).

About 30 minutes before serving, preheat the oven to 400 degrees.

Slice the gnocchi into 1-inch pieces, lifting them with a spatula so that the edges overlap a little. Sprinkle with the Parmesan cheese and bake until very hot and top is golden (about 15 to 25 minutes). Warm the sauce.

About 5 minutes before serving, add the shrimp, fennel, and olives to the simmering tomato sauce. Serve over the baked gnocchi.

SERVES 4—654 cal.; 12g (17% of cal.) total fat; ±3.2g (4%) saturated fat; 101mg (62%) carbohydrate; 179mg cholesterol; and 327mg sodium per serving

Peppered Polenta

THE MICROWAVE OVEN REPLACES THE LABORIOUS POLENTA PREPARATIONS OUR ITALIAN GRANDMOTHERS ENDURED. THE PRODUCT, IF NOT TO PURISTS' STANDARDS, IS QUICK TO MAKE AND DELICIOUS TO EAT.

3 cups chopped tomatoes
1½ cups chopped onions
⅓ pound cooked or raw ham, minced
3 tablespoons dry red wine
3 tablespoons chopped fresh basil or 2 tablespoons dried basil

2 cups polenta (coarse cornmeal)
2 medium green or red bell peppers, cored, seeded, and chopped
3½ cups homemade chicken stock (see page 22)
3½ cups water

Put the tomatoes, onions, ham, wine, and basil in a covered saucepan and simmer for at least 20 minutes. Add some water if sauce becomes too dry.

Put the polenta, peppers, and liquids in a 3-quart, microwave-safe casserole. Stir once and microwave it on high for about 10 minutes. Remove, stir, and microwave until all liquid is absorbed, stirring it every 3 or 4 minutes. The total cooking time should be about 20 to 30 minutes.

Serve the polenta with the sauce poured over it.

SERVES 4—474 cal.; 7g (13% of cal.) total fat; 2.1g (4%) saturated fat; 78g (66%) carbohydrate; 32mg cholesterol; and 800mg sodium per serving

Tamale Pie

COARSE POLENTA ADDS A CRUNCHY QUALITY TO THE CRUST OF THIS SOUTHWESTERN DISH.
YOU CAN USE NOTHING BUT REGULAR CORNMEAL, IF YOU PREFER.

1⅓ cups cornmeal
⅔ cup polenta or an additional
  ⅔ cup cornmeal
4½ cups water
Juice and peel of 1 lemon
2 teaspoons chopped fresh sage or
  rubbed dry sage
½ pound lean, fat-trimmed,
  boneless beef rump, minced
1 tablespoon plus 1 teaspoon
  olive oil
2 cups chopped onion

3–4 cloves garlic, mashed
3 cups chopped fresh tomatoes
1 32-ounce can hominy, drained
  and rinsed
2 cups chopped mild fresh pasilla or
  green bell pepper
2 teaspoons chopped fresh oregano
  or 1 teaspoon dried oregano
2 teaspoons ground cumin
½ teaspoon mashed juniper berries
  (optional)

Preheat the oven to 350 degrees.

Put the cornmeal and polenta in a saucepan with the water and bring it to a boil over medium heat. Reduce the heat and simmer, stirring constantly, until it becomes very thick (about 5 to 8 minutes). Stir in the lemon juice, grated peel, and sage. Set it aside to cool.

Brown the beef with the oil in a large, covered skillet over medium heat. Add the onion and garlic and cook until soft. Add the tomatoes, hominy, pepper, herbs, and spices. Cover, reduce the heat to low, and simmer for 20 minutes.

Grease two 9-inch square (or one 4-quart) casseroles with a little oil.

Cover the bottom and as much of the sides as possible with the cornmeal to form a crust. Scoop the meat/vegetable mixture into the crust and bake in the preheated oven for about 25 minutes, or until very hot.

Let the casserole set for a minute or two before serving.

SERVES 4—616 cal.; 13g (19% of cal.) total fat; 3.4g (5%) saturated fat; 100g (65%) carbohydrate; 35mg cholesterol; and ±600mg sodium per serving

Lasagna with Two Fillings

IF YOU USE FRESH BASIL, THIS LEAN LASAGNA WILL BE AS FLAVORFUL AS ANY LOADED WITH MEATIER SAUCES AND MOZZARELLA CHEESE. YOU CAN PREPARE IT IN ADVANCE, UP TO THE BAKING STEP, BUT BE SURE TO CHILL IT AS SOON AS IT IS ASSEMBLED, AND KEEP IT COLD UNTIL IT IS TIME TO BAKE IT.

3/4 pound lasagna noodles
2 teaspoons olive oil
2 cups chopped onion
4 cups chopped juicy fresh tomatoes
1½ cups chopped green bell pepper
¼ pound cooked ham, chopped
¼ cup chopped fresh (or dried) basil
2 10-ounce packages frozen chopped spinach

¼ cup dry sherry (optional)
Pinch of freshly grated nutmeg
¼ cup flour
1⅓ cups water
1 cup low-fat, low-sodium ricotta cheese

Preheat the oven to 350 degrees.

Cook the noodles in boiling water until they are barely tender or for about 10 to 13 minutes. Drain, rinse, and set aside.

Heat the oil over moderate heat in a large skillet and sauté the onion until it is limp. Add the tomatoes, bell pepper, ham, and basil. Cover and simmer until the sauce is thickened, or for about 15 to 20 minutes.

Break up the blocks of frozen spinach and put the pieces in a saucepan with the sherry and nutmeg.

Make a paste of the flour and a little of the water. Stir it into the spinach. Add the remaining water as well. Cook over a medium flame until the spinach is thawed and the sauce is thick. Stir in the cheese and set aside.

Grease a 10-x-14-inch or two 8-inch square baking pans with a little olive oil.

Line the bottom(s) with one-third of the noodles. Smear half the tomato sauce over them. Add a second layer of noodles and spoon all the spinach-cheese filling over it. Lay the remaining noodles on top and then spoon the rest of the tomato sauce over them.

Bake in the preheated oven until it is very hot (about 20 to 30 minutes). It will take longer if the casserole has been chilled.

Let the lasagna rest for a minute before cutting.

SERVES 4—650 cal.; 11 g (16% of cal.) total fat; 3.6 g (5%) saturated fat; 102 g (63%) carbohydrate; 35mg cholesterol; and 574mg sodium per serving

Wild Rice Casserole

SWEET SHELLFISH ARE PERFECT MATES FOR NUTTY-TASTING WILD RICE.

1½ cups wild rice
2½ cups water
4 cups sliced fresh mushrooms
2 tablespoons olive oil
¼ cup flour
3 cups milk
2 cups chopped onions
½ pound cleaned mussels or
scallops or shrimp

½ cup dry sherry
2 tablespoons sugar
1 teaspoon minced sage or
½ teaspoon dried rubbed sage
¼–1 teaspoon mild to medium hot
cayenne pepper
Pinch of freshly grated nutmeg

Simmer wild rice and water until the grains are tender and partially split (about 25 to 40 minutes), adding extra water as needed.

Preheat the oven to 350 degrees.

Cook the mushrooms in the oil in a large skillet until they are soft. Stir in the flour and cook another minute. Slowly stir in the milk, mashing out any lumps before adding more milk. Cook until thickened, then stir in the remaining ingredients, including the wild rice. Spoon into an oiled casserole and bake until the fish is cooked (about 20 minutes).

SERVES 4—573 cal.; 9g (14% of cal.) total fat; ±1.4g (2%) saturated fat; 86g (67%) carbohydrate; 20mg cholesterol; 265mg sodium per serving

Scalloped Casserole

2 cups long grain brown rice
2³/₄ cups water
²/₃ cup clam broth
2 10-ounce packages frozen spinach
Pinch of freshly grated nutmeg
4 cups sliced mushrooms

½ pound scallops or
 boneless sea bass, diced
2 tablespoons olive oil
2 tablespoons sherry
¼ cup grated Parmesan cheese

Steam the rice in the water and clam broth until tender (about 40 to 50 minutes).

Chop up the frozen spinach to speed thawing. Preheat the oven to 425 degrees. Grease a 10- x 14-inch casserole with a little olive oil.

Spread the cooked rice over the bottom of the casserole, distribute the spinach over the rice, dust with nutmeg, then layer the mushroom slices on top of the spinach. Top with the fish and drizzle the olive oil and sherry over the top. Dust with the Parmesan cheese and bake until the fish and mushrooms are cooked, or about 15 to 20 minutes.

Serves 4—552 cal.; 11g (18% of cal.) total fat; 3g (4%) saturated fat; 88g (64%) carbohydrate; 27mg cholesterol; and 450mg sodium per serving

Basic Risotto

SMALL PORTIONS OF RISOTTO CAN BE SERVED AS A FIRST COURSE, BUT IT MAKES AN EQUALLY GOOD WINTER MAIN-DISH MEAL. MANY VERSIONS OF THIS TRADITIONAL ITALIAN DISH ARE VEGETARIAN; THOSE WITH MEAT RELY MORE ON THEIR STOCKS FOR FLAVOR THAN ON ACTUAL PIECES OF MEAT. ITS VARIATIONS, USING DIFFERENT VEGETABLES AND SEASONINGS, ARE ALMOST LIMITLESS AS THE LIST BELOW SUGGESTS.

USE ITALIAN ARBORIO OR SPANISH GRANZA RICE. NO OTHER TYPE PRODUCES THE SAME DENSE, CREAMY TEXTURE. IF POSSIBLE, FOLLOW THE TRADITIONAL METHOD. IF YOU'RE PRESSED FOR TIME, YOU CAN USE THE MICROWAVE METHOD GIVEN IN THE NEXT RECIPE INSTEAD.

1½ tablespoons olive oil
2 cups Arborio rice
4 cups water
2 cups clam broth
1 cup white wine
2–3 cloves garlic, mashed

Grated peel of 2 oranges (optional)
3 cups thinly sliced fennel
2 cups chopped fresh tomatoes
½ pound boned sea bass,
  cut into ½-inch cubes

Heat the oil over low to moderate heat in a heavy, heat-proof casserole or enameled skillet, preferably one that is wide and shallow. Add the rice and stir with a wooden spoon to coat the grains. Sauté until they become translucent around the edges, but don't let them brown. This takes about 3 to 6 minutes.

While it cooks, mix the water, clam broth, and wine in a saucepan and heat almost to a simmer. Keep it at this temperature.

Add the garlic and orange peel to the rice and sauté it for a few seconds. Pour about ½ cup of the hot broth into the rice and stir almost continuously. Regulate the heat so that the rice and liquid barely simmer. As soon as the rice has absorbed the liquid, add an additional ½ cup of the hot broth, stirring as before. Repeat the process until you've added 4 cups.

Add the fennel and tomato and continue adding the remaining broth a little at a time. When all the broth is absorbed, the grains should be tender. Bite into one. If it is chalky and hard in the center, it isn't cooked. Add a little more water and cook the rice until it is soft throughout, and the mass is a little gummy. The total cooking time (after the sauté step) can vary from 25 to 40 minutes.

When the rice is very creamy, stir in the sea bass pieces and a little water or broth and continue cooking until the fish is cooked. Serve very hot.

SERVES 4—575 cal.; 9g (14% of cal.) total fat; 1.3g (2%) saturated fat; 90g (63%) carbohydrate; 23mg cholesterol; and ±500mg sodium per serving

Variations. Use bits of ham, sausage, or other smoked meats, fresh meats or poultry, fresh fish or shellfish, and almost any fresh vegetable, especially early spring asparagus, green beans, peas, shredded greens, or artichoke hearts. Mushrooms, particularly with some porcini added, are superlative. Use any meat, fish, or poultry stock, or diluted wine spiced with saffron or herbs. Several recipes, using some of these ingredients, follow.

Microwave Risotto

This risotto, cooked in the microwave, is based on foods you can keep on hand: dried mushrooms and spinach and cooked ham or sausage from the freezer. It may not rival a great chef's rendition, but it's tasty and takes no more than 10 minutes of active work.

2 10-ounce packages frozen spinach
1½ tablespoons olive oil
2 medium onions, coarsely chopped
2 cups Arborio or Spanish rice
¼ pound minced, fat-trimmed ham or hot Italian sausage
½–1 ounce dried mushrooms (porcini or shiitake)
2 tablespoons minced fresh or dried thyme

Pinch of freshly grated nutmeg
½ teaspoon freshly ground black or white peppercorns
6 cups homemade chicken stock (see page 22)
½ cup dry white wine
¼ cup grated Parmesan cheese

Chop the spinach into small chunks.

Put the oil and onion in a 3-quart microwave-proof container. Cook on high until onions are limp. Stir in the rice and cook on high for 2 minutes.

Stir in the spinach and all other ingredients and microwave on high for 10 minutes. Remove, stir, and return to microwave for 10 minutes longer. Repeat as needed until the rice is soft and the liquid absorbed.

Serves 4—573 cal.; 10g (16% of cal.) total fat; 2.6g (4%) saturated fat; 93g (65%) carbohydrate; 20mg cholesterol; and 463mg sodium per serving

Risotto with Grapes

Marsala wine ties the sweet taste of grapes to the earthy flavors of mushrooms and chicken gizzards and hearts. You can use breast or thigh meat if you prefer.

1½ tablespoons olive oil
2 cups Arborio rice
4–8 cloves garlic, mashed or minced
6 cups homemade chicken stock (see page 22)
½ cup marsala or dry sherry
2 tablespoons white wine or rice vinegar

2 teaspoons sugar
1 tablespoon chopped fresh or dried thyme
6 ounces chicken gizzards and/or hearts, diced, or 2 medium skinned, boned chicken thighs, diced
2 cups mushroom slices
2 cups seedless grapes, cut in half

Heat the oil over low to moderate heat in a heavy, heat-proof casserole or enameled skillet, preferably one that is wide and shallow. Add the rice and garlic. Stir with a wooden spoon to coat the grains. Sauté until they become translucent around the edges, but don't let them brown. This takes about 3 to 6 minutes.

Mix the liquids, sugar, and thyme in a small saucepan and simmer over low heat.

Add the chicken bits and mushrooms to the rice and sauté until the former are golden. Toss in the grapes and add about ½ cup of the hot liquid into the rice and stir almost continuously.

Regulate the heat so that the rice and liquid barely simmer. As soon as the rice has absorbed the liquid, add an additional ½ cup of the hot broth, stirring as before. Repeat the process until you have added 4 cups. Add the remaining broth a little at a time. When all the broth is absorbed, the grains should be tender. Bite into one. If it isn't cooked, add a little more hot water and cook the rice until it is soft throughout, and the mass is a little gummy. The total cooking time (after the sauté step) can vary from 25 to 40 minutes.

Serve as soon as the rice is creamy.

Serves 4—581 cal.; 7g (11% of cal.) total fat; 1.1g (2%) saturated fat; 100g (69%) carbohydrate; 70mg cholesterol; and 437mg sodium per serving

Risotto with Peas

⅓ pound hot Italian sausage
2 tablespoons olive oil
2 cups Arborio rice
2 cups chopped onion
Juice and grated peel of 2 lemons

6 cups homemade chicken stock (see page 22)
3 cups fresh or frozen peas
½ cup chopped fresh basil

Crumble the sausage.

Heat the oil over low to moderate heat in a heavy, heat-proof casserole or enameled skillet, preferably one that is wide and shallow. Add the rice and stir with a wooden spoon to coat the grains. Sauté until they become translucent around the edges, but don't let them brown. This takes about 3 to 6 minutes. Add the sausage and onion and cook until the onion is limp.

Warm the stock and the lemon juice in a saucepan and keep it almost simmering. Pour about ½ cup of the hot broth into the rice and stir almost continuously. Regulate the heat so that the rice and liquid barely simmer. As soon as the rice has absorbed the liquid, add an additional ½ cup of the hot broth, stirring as before. Repeat the process until you've added 4 cups.

Add the peas, basil, and lemon peel. Continue adding the stock a little at a time. When all the broth is absorbed, the grains should be tender. Bite into one. If it isn't cooked, add a little more hot water and cook the rice until it is soft throughout, and the mass is a little gummy. The total cooking time (after the sauté step) can vary from 25 to 40 minutes. Serve immediately.

SERVES 4—616 cal.; 12g (18% of cal.) total fat; 2.4g (4%) saturated fat; 100g (65%) carbohydrate; 25mg cholesterol; and 640mg sodium per serving

Risotto with Asparagus

THIS RECIPE DEMONSTRATES HOW DEBRIS—PRAWN SHELLS AND THE WOODY ENDS OF AS-
PARAGUS—CAN PRODUCE A FLAVORFUL BROTH.

10 ounces prawns with shells
1 pound thin asparagus spears
5½ cups water
1¼ cups dry white wine
2–3 bay leaves
2 teaspoons chopped fresh or
   dried thyme
½ teaspoon freshly ground white or
   black pepper

2 tablespoons olive oil
2 tablespoons chopped shallots or
   4 cloves of garlic, mashed
2 cups Arborio rice
Pinch saffron threads
Juice of 1 lemon
2 tablespoons chopped fresh parsley

Remove the prawn shells and trim off the tails. Put shells and tails in a
saucepan. Rinse and devein the prawns, cut into ½-inch pieces, and set aside.

Snap off the woody asparagus bottoms and add them to the shells in the
saucepan, along with the water, wine, bay leaves, thyme, and pepper.

Cut the tender asparagus tops into ¾-inch lengths and set aside.

Simmer the shell stock for about 15 minutes.

Heat the oil in a heavy enameled skillet or similar pan over a moderate flame.
Sauté the prawn pieces until they turn pink (about 2 to 4 minutes).

Add the shallots and sauté briefly, then remove both with a slotted spoon.
Reduce the heat and add the rice to the hot oil. Sauté until rice becomes
translucent around the edges, but don't let it brown. This takes about 3 to 6
minutes.

Strain the shell stock, return the liquid to the saucepan, and keep it warm
over low heat. Pour about ½ cup of the hot broth into the rice and stir almost
continuously. Regulate the heat so that the rice and liquid barely simmer. As
soon as the rice has absorbed the liquid, add an additional ½ cup of the hot
broth, stirring as before. Repeat the process. When rice has absorbed about 5
cups, add the asparagus tips. Continue adding stock and cook at least 5 min-

utes longer, using more liquid if necessary. As soon as the rice is cooked, add the prawns and shallots and the lemon juice. Sprinkle with parsley and serve.

SERVES 4—585 cal.; 12g (19% of cal.) total fat; 1.8g (3%) saturated fat; 91g (62%) carbohydrate; 87mg cholesterol; and 193mg sodium per serving

CHAPTER 4

Sauced Pastas

Few foods are as popular as pasta in America, in Italy, in fact, in most of the world. Wheat, rice, and bean thread noodles play a major role in Chinese cuisine. The Japanese are fond of buckwheat noodles and many other varieties. Thailand's famous dish, mee krob, is a rice noodle product. Almost every country that grows appreciable wheat has a favorite pasta product. Ribbons of rishta noodles are popular in much of the Middle East. The Greeks are proud of their thin fides and rice-shaped orzo pastas. India's vermicelli-thin semiyan is typically reserved for desserts, while the similar Moroccan sheriya does double duty in both sweet dishes and soups. Jewish cooks prepare egg noodles and bowties, and barley-shaped farfel. All Northern and Eastern European cuisines relish some form of noodle, like nudeln (German), nouilles (French), and galuska (Hungarian). Spain's favorite, fideo, is now a staple food in much of Hispanic America. Italy's love affair with pasta is too obvious to mention.

Pasta's ubiquitous popularity suggests its saucing potential. You can eat pasta every night for decades without duplicating a dish.

While pastas are virtually fat-free, what you put on them often isn't. As you'll see in this chapter, it's easy to prune much of the fat out of most pasta recipes without losing any flavor.

Watch out particularly for the amount and kind of meat used in the sauce. Always choose the leanest cut possible, trim it well, and include the smallest amount needed for flavor. Two ounces of meat and a flavorful stock usually provide plenty of taste. Substitute vegetables for texture and flavor. Consider whether a small helping of fish could replace a larger serving of meat.

The amount of oil used to sauté meats or other foods can also be reduced. One to three teaspoons of oil per serving is ample.

Cheese, cream, and other high-fat ingredients can be cut to no more than one tablespoon per serving.

Cook large helpings of the pasta itself, and cook it al dente. If it has a chewy texture, you won't crave meat.

For an example of how easy it is to cut out fat, take a look at the two recipes for pasta with homemade ragu sauce which follow. The original recipe, which resembles several in popular Italian cookbooks, has 45 percent fat calories. The adapted version relies on pasta for its substance and additional vegetables and herbs for flavor. It's just as tasty, but has two-thirds less fat.

Techniques

Pastas are among the easiest foods to cook. Most forms cook within minutes, and some, like rice pastas, cook within seconds. Unfortunately, pastas should be served as soon as they're cooked or they become sticky, nor do they reheat well. Be sure to coordinate the timing of the sauce and pasta preparations.

If you always use the same pan to cook pasta, make a mental note of how long it takes to bring a potful of water to a boil. Factor that time into your preparations.

Cooking Dried Pastas

Bring a large kettle of water to a rolling boil. Dribble in the pasta and stir it briefly with a large fork or slotted spoon. Keep the water boiling and cook, stirring once or twice, until the pasta is barely tender and chewy. Taste the pasta often until it reaches this toothsome point, which the Italians refer to as al dente.

Drain the pasta immediately or it will become sticky or even mushy. Don't rinse; just make sure you toss it with the sauce as soon as possible.

If you've miscalculated and the sauce isn't ready, drizzle a little olive oil over the pasta, toss it to mix, and keep it warm until the sauce is cooked. The oil helps keep the pasta strands apart.

Cooking Fresh Pasta

The recipes in this book assume you're using dried pasta. If you do use fresh, cook an extra quarter pound for every pound of dried pasta in the recipe. Cut the cooking time as well. Fresh pastas cook twice as fast as dried, so start tasting them sooner, and make sure you have the sauce prepared in advance.

Nonwheat Pastas

Although the best pastas are made from hard wheat, you'll find pastas made from other grains in most natural food stores. Most carry amaranth, buckwheat, corn, rice, and/or quinoa pastas. Be sure to check the labels carefully. Some contain wheat in addition to the alternative grain.

Spaghetti with Homemade Ragu Sauce

8 ounces ground beef chuck
8 ounces pork shoulder
2 tablespoons olive oil
1 cup onion
½ cup celery
4 cloves garlic*

4 cups tomatoes
½ cup dry red wine
2 teaspoons thyme*
2–3 bay leaves*
2 teaspoons oregano*
1 teaspoon rosemary*
½ pound spaghetti

SERVES 4

NUTRITIONAL CONTENTS (PER SERVING)

Food*	Calories	Protein	Total fat	Saturated fat	Carbohydrate
		gram (% cal.)	gram (% cal.)	gram (% cal.)	gram (% cal.)
Beef	146	11 (7%)	11 (15%)	5.0 (7%)	—
Pork	163	9 (5%)	14 (19%)	5.0 (7%)	—
Oil	62	—	7 (9%)	0.8 (1%)	—
Onion	15	trace	trace	—	3 (2%)
Celery	2	trace	—	—	1 (1%)
Tomato	48	2 (1%)	1 (1%)	0.1 (trace)	10 (6%)
Wine	24	—	—	—	1 (1%)
Pasta	210	7 (4%)	1 (1%)	0.1 (trace)	44 (26%)
Total	670	29	34	11.0	59
% of calories		17%	45%	15%	36%

*Ingredients with trivial calories aren't included.

Adapted Spaghetti with Ragu Sauce

8 ounces trimmed beef chuck
2 teaspoons olive oil
1 cup onion
6–8 cloves garlic*
4 cups tomatoes
2 cups mushrooms
1 cup celery
1 cup carrots

1 cup dry red wine
1 cup water*
2 teaspoons thyme*
3–4 bay leaves*
2 teaspoons oregano*
1 teaspoon rosemary*
1 teaspoon fennel seeds*
1 pound spaghetti

SERVES 4

NUTRITIONAL CONTENTS (PER SERVING)

Food*	Calories	Protein	Total fat	Saturated fat	Carbohydrate
		gram (% cal.)	gram (% cal.)	gram (% cal.)	gram (% cal.)
Beef	103	12 (7%)	6 (8%)	2.9 (4%)	—
Oil	20	—	2 (3%)	0.3 (trace)	—
Onion	15	trace	trace	—	3 (2%)
Carrot	12	trace	trace	—	3 (2%)
Celery	5	trace	trace	—	1 (1%)
Mushroom	15	1 (1%)	trace	—	2 (1%)
Tomato	48	2 (1%)	1 (1%)	0.1 (trace)	10 (6%)
Wine	48	—	—	—	2 (1%)
Pasta	420	15 (9%)	1 (2%)	0.2 (trace)	87 (51%)
Total	686	30	10	3.5	108
% of calories		18%	14%	4%	64%

*Ingredients with trivial calories aren't included.

Spaghetti with Homemade Ragu Sauce

THIS IS THE COMPLETE RECIPE THAT APPEARS ON PAGE 75.

½ pound lean, fat-trimmed boneless
  beef chuck
2 teaspoons olive oil
1 cup chopped onions
6–8 cloves garlic, mashed
4 cups chopped tomatoes
2 cups sliced fresh mushrooms
1 cup diced celery
1 cup chopped carrots
1 cup dry red wine

1 cup water
2 teaspoons chopped fresh or
  dried thyme
3–4 bay leaves
2 teaspoons chopped fresh or
  dried oregano
1 teaspoon chopped fresh or
  dried rosemary
1 teaspoon crushed fennel seed
1 pound spaghetti

Dice the meat.

Heat the oil in a large, covered skillet over medium heat. Sauté the meat briefly, add the onions and garlic, and cook until fragrant. Add the remaining ingredients except the pasta, and simmer for at least 30 minutes. Longer is better.

Cook the pasta until it is al dente, drain, toss with the sauce, and serve.

SERVES 4—686 Cal.; 10g (14% of cal.) total fat; 3.5g (4%) saturated fat; 108g (63%) carbohydrate; 40mg cholesterol; and ±200mg sodium per serving

Basic Tomato Sauce

You can produce an almost limitless variety of sauces based on this simple recipe by adding bits of fresh vegetables, olives, fish, shellfish, ham, sausage, or other meats, and spices or herbs to suit your taste. A few of the latter are mentioned below. Use it to top any pasta shape or to bind pasta together in a casserole. Thickened, it makes a fine coating for pizzas. Make a double batch and freeze the extra. It will keep for two to three months.

Fresh tomatoes, especially when home grown, produce a more savory sauce. If they aren't available, you can substitute canned tomatoes. Their nutritional composition isn't too different from the fresh except for the salt added during canning. See the note below if you use the canned type.

2 teaspoons olive oil
2 cups chopped onions
4–6 cloves garlic, minced or mashed
4 cups chopped fresh or
  canned tomatoes
1/2 cup chopped fresh parsley or
  minced celery tops
2 teaspoons sugar

3–4 bay leaves
2 tablespoons chopped fresh basil or
  dried basil
2 teaspoons chopped fresh thyme or
  dried thyme
1/4 teaspoon freshly ground black
  pepper

Heat the oil in a large skillet or saucepan over medium heat. Sauté the onions and garlic until they are fragrant and limp.

Add the remaining ingredients, cover the pan, and simmer gently at least 30 minutes. Add a little water if the sauce becomes too thick.

To reduce the sauce for pizza topping, raise the heat and boil, stirring constantly, until the sauce is sufficiently thick.

Be sure to remove the bay leaves before serving.

SERVES 4 as pasta sauce for 1 pound dry pasta or to cover two 10-inch round pizzas—58 cal.; ±1.5 g (23% of cal.) total fat; 0.2g (3%) saturated fat; 9g (62%) carbohydrate; 0mg cholesterol; and ±35mg sodium per serving

Note: The sodium content will be about 675mg per serving if you use canned tomatoes.

Variations. Use your imagination to season this sauce, or try adding some of these flavorings (one at a time) to modify its taste, keeping in mind the other ingredients you'll add to the sauce.

2 teaspoons oregano and/or
  1 teaspoon rosemary
½ cup dry red wine
Peel of an orange and/or
  2 teaspoons fennel seed

1–2 teaspoons Thai fish sauce
2 teaspoons ground coriander plus
  a pinch of cumin and chili powder
Pinch of saffron threads and/or
  a pinch of freshly grated nutmeg

For an example, try the next recipe. It's based on this sauce with some chopped sweet peppers and flavorings of ham and lemon.

Pasta with Peppers and Ham

THIS IS A DISH YOU CAN THROW TOGETHER IN ABOUT 20 MINUTES IF YOU'VE MADE THE SAUCE IN ADVANCE. IF NOT, YOU CAN USE A COMMERCIAL PASTA SAUCE. SEEK OUT THE TASTIEST, LOW-FAT BRAND POSSIBLE.

4 cups basic tomato sauce
  (see page 78)
2 teaspoons olive oil
2 cups chopped onions
2 green or red bell peppers, cored,
  seeded, and diced

⅓ pound diced, lean, fat-trimmed,
  raw or cooked ham
2 teaspoons lemon peel (optional)
1 pound spaghetti or similar long
  pasta

Prepare the sauce ahead and keep warm.

Heat the oil in a covered skillet over medium heat. Add the onion and sauté until it is limp.

Add the sauce, peppers, ham, and lemon peel. Cover and simmer for 10 to 15 minutes.

While it simmers, cook the pasta until it is al dente (about 7 to 11 minutes). Drain, toss with the sauce, and serve.

SERVES 4—668 cal.; 10g (13% of cal.) total fat; 2.3g (3%) saturated fat; 116g (77%) carbohydrate; 22mg cholesterol; and 498mg sodium per serving

Pasta Puttanesca

THE TITLE OF THIS ROMAN DISH MEANS WHORE'S PASTA. NOTE ITS HIGH SODIUM CONTENT. IF YOU'RE ON A SALT-RESTRICTED DIET, REPLACE THE ANCHOVIES WITH TOMATO-PACKED SARDINES AND OLIVE OIL.

2 2-ounce cans anchovies
2 teaspoons oil from anchovies
6–8 cloves garlic, mashed
2 cups chopped tomatoes
1 cup dry white wine
2 teaspoons chopped fresh or
dried rosemary

1 pound spaghetti or linguini
½ cup chopped fresh parsley
½ cup chopped green olives
½ cup grated Parmesan cheese

Drain the anchovies in a strainer, saving 2 teaspoons of the oil as well as the fish. Mash the filets.

Heat the oil in a large skillet over moderate heat. Sauté the garlic briefly, then toss in the tomatoes, wine, rosemary, and anchovies. Simmer over low heat.

Cook the spaghetti until it's al dente (about 7 to 11 minutes). Drain immediately.

Stir the parsley and olives into the sauce, then toss with the pasta. Sprinkle with the cheese and serve.

SERVES 4—614 cal.; 13 g (19% of cal.) total fat; 3.6g (5%) saturated fat; 94g (61%) carbohydrate; ±20mg cholesterol; and 1,370mg sodium per serving

Buckwheat Noodles and Glazed Onions

THIS DISH IS A HYBRID OF VARIOUS CUISINES, USING A FRENCH-INSPIRED PEPPERY BEEF AND ONION CONCENTRATE TO SAUCE THE EARTHY ORIENTAL BUCKWHEAT NOODLES.

½ pound lean, fat-trimmed boneless
  beef, diced
2 teaspoons freshly ground black
  pepper
2 teaspoons olive oil
6 cups thinly sliced onions
1 tablespoon sugar

1 tablespoon flour
1 cup homemade beef stock
  (see page 21)
1 cup dry red wine
2 tablespoons cognac (optional)
14 ounces Oriental buckwheat
  noodles

Mix the beef and pepper, then sauté the mixture with the oil in a large stock-pot. Cook until the meat is browned, then add the onions. Reduce the heat to low, cover, and cook, stirring occasionally, for about 15 minutes, or until the onions are very soft.

Sprinkle the sugar and flour over the beef and onions. Cook for about 1 minute, then add the beef stock, wine, and cognac. Bring the sauce to a boil, then reduce the heat and simmer for about 15 minutes, covered.

Cook the pasta until it is al dente (about 3 to 7 minutes). Drain, toss with the beef and onion mixture, then serve.

SERVES 4—663 cal.; 11g (15% of cal.) total fat; 3.6g (5%) saturated fat; 102g (62%) carbohydrate; 35mg cholesterol; and ±150mg sodium per serving

Pasta Basilico

YOU CAN PREPARE THIS DISH IN A HURRY, USING EITHER TRUE SCALLOPS OR THE CHEAPER BITS OF SKATE THAT SOMETIMES PASS FOR THEM. BOTH ARE DELICIOUS. USE FRESH BASIL ONLY. ITS AROMATIC SWEETNESS IS THE PERFECT MATCH WITH THE SCALLOPS.

½ cup (packed) fresh basil leaves
½ pound scallops
1 pound dry linguini or
   similar long pasta
2 tablespoons olive oil

6–8 cloves garlic, mashed or minced
1 cup fish fumet (see page 23) or
   clam broth
½ cup dry white wine
¼ cup grated Parmesan cheese

Mince the basil leaves as fine as possible with a sharp knife and set them aside. If the scallops are large, cut them up and set them aside.

Cook the linguini until it is al dente (about 7 to 10 minutes).

While it cooks, heat the olive oil over moderate heat in a medium-sized skillet. Toss in the garlic and sauté for a few seconds before adding the scallops. Sauté just until they are opaque and cooked through. Add the basil, fish fumet, and wine. Heat just until the liquid is very hot.

Drain the pasta as soon as it is cooked, toss with the sauce and cheese, and serve very hot.

SERVES 4—598 cal.; 12g (18% of cal.) total fat; 2.8g (4%) saturated fat; 91g (61%) carbohydrate; 27mg cholesterol; and 382mg sodium per serving

Pasta and Prawns

ORANGE PERKS UP THE FLAVOR OF THE NEXT THREE PASTA RECIPES. THE FRUIT'S PEEL, AS WELL AS ITS JUICE, IS INTEGRAL TO THIS ONE.

2 medium-sized green bell peppers
2 medium-sized red bell peppers or pimientos
4–8 large cloves garlic, minced or mashed
Juice and peel of 2 large oranges
1 tablespoon plus 1 teaspoon olive oil
1 pound spaghetti
½ pound shelled prawns, cut in ½-inch pieces
1 cup dry white wine
¼ cup grated Parmesan cheese

Slice the peppers and pimientos into matchstick-sized pieces and put them in a bowl with the garlic. Grate the orange peel and mix it into the peppers. Add half the oil.

Squeeze the orange juice and set aside separately.

Set a large skillet over moderately high heat. When very hot, toss in the pepper mixture and stir vigorously.

As it sautés, cook the pasta until al dente (about 7 to 11 minutes).

Add the prawn pieces to the peppers, and as soon as they are pink, add the wine. Scrape up any coagulated juices stuck to the pan. Reduce the heat, add the orange juice, and simmer on low heat.

Drain the spaghetti, toss together with the sauce and cheese, then serve.

SERVES 4—649 cal.; 9g (13% of cal.) total fat; 2.3g (3%) saturated fat; 105g (65%) carbohydrate; 89mg cholesterol; and 166mg sodium per serving

Pasta and Monkfish

Orange adds a subtle note to this tomato/fish sauce. Use grated lemon peel if an orange isn't handy.

2 tablespoons olive oil
1 cup chopped onion
2–3 cloves garlic
3 cups chopped tomatoes
1 cup dry white wine
1 cup water
2 tablespoons chopped fresh parsley
1 tablespoon chopped fresh basil or
  2 teaspoons dried basil

2–3 bay leaves
Pinch of saffron threads (optional)
1 strip (about 1 x by inches) orange
  or lemon peel
2 teaspoons sugar
3/4 pound monkfish, membranes
  and/or bones removed
1 pound spaghetti

Heat the oil in a large skillet over medium heat. Sauté the onions and garlic in it until they are soft. Add the remaining ingredients except the fish and spaghetti. Cover the pan, raise the heat just enough to keep the sauce simmering, and cook for about 20 to 30 minutes.

While sauce cooks, trim the monkfish and chop it into 1/2-inch cubes.

Cook the spaghetti until it is al dente (about 7 to 11 minutes). Drain immediately.

About 2 minutes before the spaghetti is cooked, remove the bay leaves and orange peel and add the monkfish pieces to the sauce. Cook it over low heat until the fish is done (about 2 to 3 minutes). Toss with the pasta and serve.

Serves 4—644 cal.; 10g (14% of cal.) total fat; 2g (3%) saturated fat; 100g (62%) carbohydrate; ±21mg cholesterol; and 100mg sodium per serving

Spicy Pasta Wheels

ROTELLE (WHEEL-SHAPED PASTA) TRAP THE BITS OF HOT SAUSAGE THAT FLAVORS THIS SAUCE.
USE A CORKSCREW OR SHELL-SHAPED PASTA IF YOU PREFER.

1/3 pound hot Italian sausage
2 teaspoons olive oil
2 cups chopped onions
4 cups chopped tomatoes
2/3 cup dry red wine
1/4 cup chopped olives
1 piece (about 2 inches square) fresh orange peel (optional)

1 tablespoon chopped fresh oregano
2 teaspoons sugar
1 teaspoon crushed fennel seed
1/8–1/2 teaspoon mild to hot cayenne (optional)
1 pound rotelle or other pasta with crevices

Crumble the sausage and brown in a heavy, covered skillet. Remove with a slotted spoon and drain on paper towels. Discard any grease in the pan.

Heat the oil in the same pan and sauté the onions in it until they're soft. Add the meat and the remaining ingredients except the cayenne and the pasta. Use the smallest amount of cayenne, then add more to taste. Simmer for about 20 minutes.

Cook the pasta until it is al dente (about 7 to 12 minutes). Drain, toss with the sauce, and serve.

SERVES 4—662 cal.; 12g (16% of cal.) total fat; 3.7g (5%) saturated fat; 105g (63%) carbohydrate; ±40mg cholesterol; and ±550mg sodium per serving

Fettuccini Carbonara

THIS IS A LEAN VERSION OF A TRADITIONAL ITALIAN DISH. EVEN WITHOUT THE USUAL CREAM
IT IS TASTY AND VERY SIMPLE TO MAKE.

2 large whole eggs
½ cup nonfat milk
2 tablespoons chopped fresh basil or
   1 tablespoon dried basil
1 tablespoon chopped fresh oregano
   or 2 teaspoons dried oregano
¼ teaspoon freshly grated nutmeg

1 pound fettucini or other wide
   spaghetti-type noodle
1½ tablespoons olive oil
¼ pound lean, fat-trimmed
   smoked ham, minced
6–8 cloves garlic, mashed
2 tablespoons grated Parmesan cheese

Beat the eggs, milk, herbs, and nutmeg together and set it aside.

Cook the pasta until it is al dente (about 7 to 12 minutes). Drain immediately.

While it cooks, heat half the oil over medium heat in a large skillet. Sauté the
ham and garlic until fragrant.

Toss the pasta into the skillet, drizzle with the remaining oil, then stir the egg
mixture into the pasta with a fork, lifting it to mix as the eggs cook. Scrape it
out of the pan as soon as the eggs are congealed, sprinkle with the Parmesan
cheese, and serve.

SERVES 4—580 cal.; 12g (19% of cal.) total fat; 3.3g (5%) saturated fat;
89g (61%) carbohydrate; 185mg cholesterol; and 446mg sodium per
serving

Pasta with Black Olives

RED WINE, LAMB, AND PUNGENT, OIL-CURED BLACK OLIVES CONTRIBUTE MUCH TO THIS SAUCE'S FLAVOR.

½ pound lean, fat-trimmed lamb
  (leg or shoulder)
2 teaspoons olive oil
3 cups chopped onions
1 cup dry red wine
1½ cups homemade beef or
  chicken stock (see pages 21 and 22)
¼ cup chopped black olives,
  preferably oil-cured

4–5 bay leaves
2 teaspoons chopped fresh or
  dried thyme
2 teaspoons chopped fresh or
  dried rosemary
1 pound spaghetti, linguini, or
  similar pasta

Cut the lamb into small cubes.

Heat the oil in a covered skillet over a moderate flame and brown the meat pieces in it. Lower the heat, add the onions, and sauté until they are limp. Add the wine, stock, olives, and herbs. Bring to a boil, then reduce the heat and simmer the sauce for about 20 minutes. Remove the bay leaves.

Cook the pasta until it is al dente (about 7 to 11 minutes). Drain and toss with the sauce.

SERVES 4—658 cal.; 12g (16% of cal.) total fat; 2.8g (4%) saturated fat; 100g (61%) carbohydrate; 48mg cholesterol; and 345mg sodium per serving

Pasta with Agrodulce Sauce

Meat cooked in a sweet-sour (agrodulce) sauce is a Roman specialty that dates back to ancient times. Dried fruits, like the prunes in this recipe, were probably early components, but chocolate's inclusion occurred only after New World foods arrived in the sixteenth century. Though an unlikely sounding pair, these two foods add an elusive, smoky flavor that few could identify.

½ pound lean, boneless pork
1½ teaspoons olive oil
1½ cups thinly sliced mushrooms
3 tablespoons sugar
⅓ cup white or rice wine vinegar
¾ dry white wine
1½ teaspoons cinnamon
⅛ teaspoon nutmeg
3 medium-sized dry, pitted prunes
¾ cup chopped carrot

¾ cup chopped onion
¾ cup chopped celery
5–6 bay leaves
1½ teaspoons chopped fresh sage leaves or 1 teaspoon dried rubbed sage
2 cups chicken stock (see page 22)
¼ ounce (¼ of a square) unsweetened chocolate
¾ pound fettucini

Cut the pork into ½-inch cubes and set them aside.

Heat the oil in a heavy, covered skillet or large saucepan over medium heat. Sauté the pork until it is lightly browned. Add the mushrooms, sugar, vinegar, wine, and spices to the pork and bring to a simmer.

Put the prunes, carrot, onion, celery, bay leaves, sage, and stock in a small, covered saucepan. Cover, bring to a boil over high heat. Reduce the heat and simmer for about 10 minutes, then remove the bay leaves and put the rest of the mixture in a blender jar. Add the chocolate and puree, then add the mixture to the pork and mushroom sauce. Simmer together for about 20 minutes longer.

Cook the pasta until it is al dente (about 7 to 12 minutes). Drain and toss with the sauce.

Serves 4—524 cal.; 10g (17% of cal.) total fat; 3g (5%) saturated fat; 78g (60%) carbohydrate; 37mg cholesterol; and 108mg sodium per serving

Pasta from Two Worlds

EASTERN FLAVORS MEET THOSE OF THE WEST IN THIS SIMPLE RECIPE.

1 pound spaghetti or other long pasta

12 halves sun-dried tomatoes, packed in olive oil

1/2 pound thresher shark, diced

2 tablespoons minced fresh ginger

2 cloves garlic, minced

2 large bunches kale (about 1 pound total), shredded

8 medium-sized fresh tomatoes, chopped

1/3 cup clam broth or chicken stock

1–2 teaspoons soy sauce

2 tablespoons olive oil

Cook the pasta until it is al dente (about 7 to 11 minutes).

Put the sun-dried tomatoes in a very large skillet or wok along with about 1 tablespoon of the oil they're packed with. Warm over medium heat. Cut each piece in half as it heats.

Add the shark, ginger, and garlic and sauté until the fish is cooked.

Toss in the kale and stir-fry it until it's limp.

Add the fresh tomatoes, clam broth, and soy sauce and simmer for 2 to 3 minutes.

After draining the pasta, toss it with the olive oil first, then the sauce.

SERVES 4—685 cal.; 15g (20% of cal.) total fat; ±2.8g (4%) saturated fat; 106g (62%) carbohydrate; ±35mg cholesterol; and low but variable sodium per serving

Variations. You can substitute another salty fish (or half the quantity of diced ham) for shark. If you use dry tomatoes rather than those packed in oil, soak them briefly in a little water before chopping, and add an extra tablespoon of olive oil to sauté the fish.

Pasta with Pine Nuts

SAUTÉED BROCCOLI RABE, A LEAFY FORM OF BROCCOLI, IS SUPERLATIVE WITH PASTA. IF IT'S NOT IN SEASON, SUBSTITUTE REGULAR FRESH BROCCOLI.

1 pound linguini or other long pasta
3 tablespoons olive oil
1/4 pound ham, diced
1 1/2 pounds broccoli rabe, chopped
3 tablespoons pine nuts
5–6 cloves garlic, mashed
1/2 cup homemade beef stock
   (see page 21) or chicken stock
   (see page 22)

1/4 cup dry sherry
1 teaspoon wine vinegar
Pinch of freshly grated nutmeg
2 tablespoons Parmesan cheese

Cook the pasta until it is al dente (about 7 to 12 minutes).

Heat 1 tablespoon of the oil in a large skillet over medium heat. Brown the ham bits in it, then add the broccoli, pine nuts, and garlic. Sauté until the broccoli is barely tender.

Add the liquids and nutmeg and bring to a simmer.

Toss the drained pasta with the remaining oil, then with the sauce, and finally with the cheese.

SERVES 4—658 cal.; 14g (19% of cal.) total fat; 3.5g (5%) saturated fat; 99g (60%) carbohydrate; ±25mg cholesterol; and ±500mg sodium per serving

Juniper-Scented Pasta

THE EARTHY FLAVORS OF JUNIPER BERRIES, MUSHROOMS, AND WINE GIVE THIS PASTA SAUCE A FAINTLY GAMEY TASTE.

1/2 pound fat-trimmed, boneless pork shoulder, diced
2 teaspoons olive oil
2–4 cloves garlic, mashed
2 cups finely chopped carrots
3 cups finely sliced mushrooms
2 tablespoons chopped olives
2 teaspoons chopped fresh thyme or 1 teaspoon dried thyme

2 juniper berries, mashed in a mortar
2–3 bay leaves
1/2 cup dry red wine
2 cups rich, homemade beef stock (see page 21)
1 pound linguini or other long pasta
2 teaspoons cornstarch
1/4 cup grated Parmesan cheese

Sauté the meat in the oil in a covered skillet until lightly browned, then add the garlic, carrots, and mushrooms and sauté another minute. Add the olives, herbs, wine, and stock, cover, and simmer 20 to 30 minutes.

Cook the pasta until it is al dente (about 7 to 12 minutes). Drain immediately.

Mix the cornstarch with a tablespoon of water. Stir it into the sauce, cook until thickened, then toss with the pasta and cheese.

SERVES 4—632 cal.; 10g (14% of cal.) total fat; 3.1g (4%) saturated fat; 98g (62%) carbohydrate; 100mg cholesterol; and 352mg sodium per serving

Caraway Noodles

CARAWAY SEEDS ADD A PUNGENT NOTE TO THESE MEAT-SPIKED NOODLES. SERVE THEM WITH PUNGENT GREENS OR PICKLED CRAB APPLES.

1/2 pound lean, fat-trimmed boneless beef chuck, chopped

4 teaspoons olives oil

2 cups chopped onions

2 tablespoons sweet Hungarian paprika

4 cups sliced mushrooms

4 cups homemade beef stock (see page 21)

2–3 bay leaves

2 teaspoons chopped fresh or dried thyme

1 cup nonfat sour cream or nonfat, unflavored yogurt

2 tablespoons cornstarch

1 pound dry egg noodles

1–2 teaspoons caraway seeds

2 tablespoons chopped fresh parsley (optional)

Brown the meat in half the oil in a large, covered skillet. Add the onion. Sauté until soft, then add the paprika, mushrooms, stock, bay leaves, and thyme. Cover and simmer for about 30 to 40 minutes.

Mix the sour cream and cornstarch together and set aside.

Just before the sauce is ready, cook the noodles until they are soft (about 4 to 7 minutes). Drain noodles, put them back in the pot, dribble the remaining oil over them, and toss together with the caraway seeds.

Stir the sour cream mixture into the meat sauce and cook over very low heat until it is hot, but don't let it boil or it will curdle. Remove the bay leaves and stir in the parsley. Pour over the noodles and serve.

SERVES 4—670 cal.; 15g (19% of cal.) total fat; 3.8g (5%) saturated fat; 100g (60%) carbohydrate; 45mg cholesterol; and 194mg sodium per serving

Fusilli with Tuna

USE ANY CORKSCREW-SHAPED PASTA FOR THIS DISH. ITS GROOVES ARE A PERFECT TRAP FOR THIS SIMPLY MADE SAUCE. ALWAYS USE FRESH PARSLEY.

1 pound fusilli, rotelli, or other corkscrew-shaped pasta
1 9-ounce can water-packed albacore tuna, drained
1 cup dry white wine

$1/2$ cup chopped fresh parsley
Juice and peel of 2 lemons
2 tablespoons pickled capers
2 tablespoons olive oil
4–8 cloves garlic, mashed

Cook the pasta until it's al dente (about 8 to 12 minutes).

Puree the remaining ingredients in a blender.

Drain the pasta as soon as it's cooked, toss with the sauce, and serve.

SERVES 4—607 cal.; 10g (15% of cal.) total fat; 2.6g (4%) saturated fat; 92g (61%) carbohydrate; 38mg cholesterol; and ±400mg sodium per serving

Spaghetti with Red Clam Sauce

Canned clams make this pasta an inexpensive, simple dish, even if it lacks the finesse of sauces made with fresh clams. Note that canned tomatoes will triple the sodium content.

1½ tablespoons olive oil
2 cups chopped onions
2–4 cloves garlic, mashed
3 cups chopped fresh or canned tomatoes
2 6½-ounce cans clams with juice
½ cup dry red wine
2 tablespoons chopped fresh or dried basil

2 teaspoons chopped fresh oregano or 1 teaspoon dried oregano
1 teaspoon chopped fresh or dried rosemary
3–4 bay leaves
1 pound spaghetti

Heat the oil in a large skillet over medium heat. Sauté the onions and garlic in it until they are soft. Add the remaining ingredients, except the spaghetti, and simmer at least 15 minutes. Remove bay leaves.

Cook the spaghetti until it's al dente (about 7 to 11 minutes). Drain, toss with the sauce, and serve.

Serves 4—618 cal.; 8g (12% of cal.) total fat; 1g (1%) saturated fat; 104g (67%) carbohydrate; 35mg cholesterol; and ±300mg sodium per serving

Spaghetti with White Clam Sauce

LIKE ITS RED COMPANION, THIS SAUCE IS DESIGNED FOR CANNED CLAMS AND RAPID COOK-
ING. IF YOU HAVE TIME AND A SOURCE OF GOOD CLAMS, BE SURE TO USE THEM INSTEAD.
SCRUB THEM WELL, REJECT ANY WITH OPEN OR BROKEN SHELLS, AND STEAM IN THE SAUCE
JUST UNTIL THE SHELLS OPEN.

1½ tablespoons olive oil
2 cups minced onions
2 tablespoons chopped basil,
  preferably fresh
2 teaspoons chopped fresh or
  dried thyme

2 10-ounce cans clams with juice
½ cup dry white wine
¼ cup chopped green olives
1 pound spaghetti
2 tablespoons grated Parmesan cheese

Heat the oil in a large skillet over a moderate flame. Sauté the onions until they
are limp, then add the remaining ingredients except the pasta and cheese. Cover
and simmer for at least 10 minutes.

Cook the spaghetti until it is al dente (about 7 to 11 minutes). Drain, toss
with the sauce and cheese, then serve.

SERVES 4—656 cal.; 13g (18% of cal.) total fat; 2.5g (3%) saturated fat;
99g (60%) carbohydrate; 65mg cholesterol; and 466mg sodium per
serving

Stout Noodles

BEEF BRAISED IN DARK BEER IS A TYPICAL FLEMISH MAIN DISH, THAT IS OFTEN SERVED WITH A SIDE DISH OF NOODLES. HERE THE ROLES OF NOODLES AND MEAT ARE REVERSED.

$^1/_2$ pound lean, fat-trimmed boneless beef chuck, minced
2 teaspoons canola oil
2 cups chopped onions
6–8 cloves garlic
4 cups fresh mushrooms
2 cups stout, strong ale, or heavy dark beer
1 cup homemade beef stock (see page 21)

2 teaspoons fresh thyme or 1 teaspoon dried thyme
2 tablespoons chopped fresh parsley
$^1/_4$ teaspoon freshly grated nutmeg
1 pound egg noodles
2 tablespoons cornstarch
2 tablespoons wine vinegar

Brown the beef in the oil in a large skillet over medium heat, then add the onions and garlic. Cook until soft. Add the mushrooms, beer, stock, herbs, and spices. Simmer gently for 35 to 45 minutes, adding some water or stock as necessary to maintain the liquid.

Shortly before the sauce is ready, cook the noodles until they are tender (about 5 minutes). Drain.

Mix the cornstarch and vinegar, and stir it into the sauce. Cook to thicken, then toss with the noodles.

SERVES 4—680 cal.; 14g (19% of cal.) total fat; 3.7g (5%) saturated fat; 102g (60%) carbohydrate; 40mg cholesterol; and 152mg sodium per serving

Pasta with Artichoke Hearts

ARTICHOKE HEARTS SAUTÉED WITH HAM ARE COMMON SIDE DISHES ON SPANISH TABLES. IN THIS RECIPE, THE ADDITION OF SHERRY-FLAVORED HAM STOCK TRANSFORMS THE SIDE DISH INTO A PASTA SAUCE. IF YOU DON'T HAVE THE STOCK, SUBSTITUTE A RICHLY FLAVORED BEEF OR CHICKEN STOCK PLUS 2 TABLESPOONS OF DRY SHERRY OR MADEIRA.

1½ tablespoons olive oil
2 9-ounce packages frozen artichoke hearts, chopped
¼ pound cooked ham, minced
8–10 cloves of garlic, mashed
1 cup diced fresh or canned pimiento

1 pound linguini or similar long pasta
1 cup ham stock (page 24) diluted with 1 cup water or 2 cups rich beef stock plus 2 tablespoons sherry
¼–½ cup lemon juice
2 tablespoons grated Parmesan cheese

Heat the oil in a very large skillet and sauté the artichoke hearts, ham, garlic, and pimiento pieces until they are very hot.

Cook the pasta until it is al dente (about 7 to 11 minutes). Drain immediately.

Toss the pasta in the skillet, pour in the stock and water, and smaller amount of lemon juice. Toss together and taste for seasoning. Add more lemon juice, if desired, or a little sugar if too tart. Sprinkle in the cheese, toss, and serve.

SERVES 4—628 cal.; 10g (14% of cal.) total fat; 2.7g (4%) saturated fat; 105g (67%) carbohydrate; 23mg cholesterol; and 456mg sodium per serving

Tibetan Buckwheat Noodles

THIS RECIPE IS A HYBRID OF VARIOUS ORIENTAL CUISINES BUT EMPHASIZES FOODS AND FLAVORS FOUND IN TIBETAN COOKING. YOU CAN SERVE THE SAUCE OVER MILLET OR BUCKWHEAT KASHA AS WELL AS NOODLES.

2 teaspoons canola oil
1/2 pound lean, fat-trimmed boneless lamb, diced
6–8 cloves garlic, mashed
2 tablespoons minced gingerroot
2 teaspoons turmeric
1/2 teaspoon ground fenugreek (optional)

1/8–1/2 teaspoon mild to hot cayenne
2 cups chopped tomatoes
3 cups homemade beef or chicken stock (see pages 21 and 22)
2 teaspoons soy sauce
1 10-ounce package frozen spinach
14 ounces buckwheat noodles

Heat the oil in a large, covered skillet over medium heat. Brown the lamb, then add the garlic and spices and sauté for about 15 seconds. Add the tomatoes, stock, soy sauce, and spinach. Cover and simmer for about 20 minutes.

Cook the noodles until they are soft but not mushy (about 3 to 7 minutes). Drain and serve in large bowls with the sauce ladled over them.

SERVES 4—518 cal.; 9g (16% of cal.) total fat; 2.6g (5%) saturated fat; 83g (64%) carbohydrate; 48mg cholesterol; and 776mg sodium per serving

Buckwheat Noodles with Red-Cooked Beef

THIS IS ANOTHER HYBRID DISH BASED ON EARTHY-FLAVORED JAPANESE BUCKWHEAT NOODLES. IN THIS CASE, THEY'RE COATED WITH A SPICY CHINESE SAUCE.

1/2 pound lean, fat-trimmed boneless beef chuck, diced
4 cups homemade concentrated beef flavoring (see page 22)
2 cups chopped, peeled turnips
1 cup chopped onions
1/2 cup dry sherry
2 tablespoons soy sauce
2 teaspoons sugar

2 teaspoons sesame oil
1 teaspoon ground Szechuan peppercorns
1 whole or several pieces star anise
14 ounces Japanese buckwheat noodles
2 8-ounce cans sliced water chestnuts, drained
2 tablespoons chopped fresh cilantro

Put all the ingredients except the noodles, water chestnuts, and cilantro in a heavy stockpot. Cover and simmer for about 40 to 50 minutes.

Shortly before the sauce is ready, cook the noodles until they are soft but not mushy (about 3 to 7 minutes). Drain immediately.

Add the water chestnuts and cilantro to the sauce and remove and discard the star anise.

Serve the noodles in very large soup bowls and pour the sauce over them.

SERVES 4—640 cal.; 11g (15% of cal.) total fat; 3.7g (5%) saturated fat; 103g (64%) carbohydrate; 40mg cholesterol; and 575mg sodium per serving

CHAPTER 5

Steamed Grains: Rice and Couscous

Each day, steamed or boiled grains provide more of the world's calories than any other type of food. Some are served at every meal. Even at dinner, these grains are considered the central dish, to be spiked with the foods and sauces that tradition, whim, or one's pocketbook dictates.

This chapter offers a sampling of such dishes. Superficially, they may seem like dishes you've eaten in ethnic restaurants or read in other cookbooks, but these recipes differ in one important way. All emphasize the recipes' original sense of a grain fortuitously sauced with a little meat, instead of featuring the meat accompanied by a little grain. Try to apply this concept to other recipes in your favorite ethnic cookbooks. You'll often find it easy to reverse the roles of vegetables and meats. Keep the oil you use for stir-frying to a minimum (1 to 3 teaspoons per serving is plenty) as well.

Review the two versions of the Chinese restaurant staple, beef with broccoli (which becomes broccoli with beef) that appear below for simple ways to add flavor and texture at the same time you cut out fat. The first recipe resembles the dish you'll find in many Chinese restaurants. Almost half its calories come from fat. The adapted recipe is as tasty, but it cuts fat by two-thirds. The alterations are simple. In this recipe, the broccoli dominates and the beef becomes a flavoring. Water chestnuts make up for some of the lost texture. Shiitake mushrooms and beef stock add meaty flavor.

Beef and Broccoli with Rice

1 pound beef chuck	2 tablespoons dry sherry**
3 tablespoons canola oil	2 teaspoons cornstarch **
2 tablespoons fresh ginger*	2 teaspoons sugar**
4–6 cloves garlic*	4 cups broccoli slices
2 tablespoons soy sauce**	3/4 cup white rice
1/2 teaspoon Szechuan pepper*	

SERVES 4

NUTRITIONAL CONTENTS (PER SERVING)

Food*	Calories	Protein	Total fat	Saturated fat	Carbohydrate
		gram (% cal.)	gram (% cal.)	gram (% cal.)	gram (% cal.)
Beef	252	23 (17%)	17 (28%)	7.6 (13%)	—
Broccoli	38	4 (3%)	trace	—	7 (5%)
Rice	130	2 (2%)	trace	—	29 (21%)
Oil	93	—	11 (18%)	0.8 (1%)	—
Other**	28	trace	—	—	5 (4%)
Total	541	29	28	8.4	41
% of calories		22%	46%	14%	30%

*Ingredients with trivial calories aren't included.
**Ingredients with modest calories (including soy sauce, sherry, cornstarch, and sugar) are combined as *other*.

Adapted Broccoli and Beef with Rice

1½ cups white rice
½ pound trimmed beef chuck arm
2⅔ tablespoons soy sauce**
2⅔ tablespoons cornstarch**
1 tablespoon sugar**
2½ cups beef stock**
1 ounce dry shiitake mushrooms*

¼ cup sherry**
1 tablespoon canola oil
2 tablespoons fresh ginger*
4–6 cloves garlic*
½ teaspoon Szechuan pepper*
6 cups broccoli
1 can water chestnuts

SERVES 4

NUTRITIONAL CONTENTS (PER SERVING)

Food*	Calories	Protein	Total fat	Saturated fat	Carbohydrate
		gram (% cal.)	gram (% cal.)	gram (% cal.)	gram (% cal.)
Beef	84	12 (9%)	4 (6%)	1.6 (3%)	—
Broccoli	58	7 (5%)	1 (1%)	—	11 (8%)
Rice	259	5 (3%)	trace	—	58 (42%)
Oil	31	—	4 (6%)	0.2 (trace)	—
Water chestnut	29	trace	trace	—	6 (4%)
Mushroom	21	1 (1%)	trace	—	5 (3%)
Other**	76	3 (2%)	trace	—	12 (9%)
Total	558	28	9	1.8	92
% calories		20%	13%	3%	66%

*Ingredients with trivial calories aren't included.
**Ingredients with modest calories (including soy sauce, stock, sherry, cornstarch, and sugar) are combined as *other.*

Techniques

Although most of this chapter's recipes feature steamed (some call it boiled) rice, you can substitute almost any whole grain you prefer. All are easy to cook by the following method, which actually involves both boiling and steaming. Initially, they're simmered, but ultimately they steam in the remaining vapor trapped in their spongy matrix. Couscous is an exception. It is always best steamed over water, not simmered in it.

The simplest way to cook most grains is in a pot on top of the stove or in an electric rice cooker. The microwave oven does an effective job of cooking the most rapidly cooked grains. A pressure cooker is ideal for cooking those that take the longest time. Each method is detailed below, along with methods for steaming couscous.

Refer to the table on page 109 for approximate cooking times, necessary liquid, and ultimate volume. Note that the values are based on cooking 1 cup of dry grain.

STOVE-TOP STEAMED RICE AND WHOLE GRAINS

If you have a favorite and foolproof method of cooking rice and other grains, stick with it. If not, the following method should consistently produce a tender dish.

Rinse the grain or not as you prefer.

Put the grain in a covered saucepan. Add cold water or other liquid, using about the amount cited in the table on page 109. Use a little less if you rinsed the grain first. Bring the water to a boil over a high flame.

You can also bring the water to a boil first, then stir in the grain.

In either case, stir once with a fork, cover the pan, then reduce the heat to a very low setting.

Don't stir the grains once they begin cooking, or they will release starch and become gummy. Don't lift the pan lid unnecessarily. You may lose so much steam that the grain will be undercooked or stick to the pan.

Cook until the grains are tender. Check the table on page 109 for the approximate time it takes. To make sure it's cooked, lift a piece out with a fork, cover the pan immediately, and taste it. If it's still crunchy, cook a little longer. Drizzle a tablespoon or so of water over it if it has absorbed all the original liquid and threatens to stick to the pan. If excess water remains after it is cooked, remove the lid, raise the heat, and cook it just long enough to evaporate it.

For fluffier grains, let it rest in a warm place for a few minutes after it's cooked. Either turn the burner off or place an asbestos mat or flame tamer between the pan and a very low flame.

Cooking Basmati Rice

You can cook basmati rice by the above method, but if you want the grains to achieve their maximum length and tenderness, try this method instead.

Rinse the rice and check it for debris.

Put the rice in a heavy saucepan with about twice its volume of water. Soak for 20 minutes to one hour.

Bring the water to a boil over a high flame. Stir it a few turns with a fork, cover the pan, and reduce the heat to the lowest possible setting.

Cook for 15 to 20 minutes and test the rice to make sure it is tender. If not, continue cooking until it is soft and fluffy.

Turn the heat off and let the rice rest over the warm burner for an additional 5 to 10 minutes. It elongates more as it rests.

Cooking Grains in the Microwave Oven

The microwave is a great tool for cooking the most tender grains (amaranth, quinoa, bulgur, buckwheat kasha, and teff). The microwave technique for cooking couscous is given below.

Put the grain and liquid in a soufflé dish or similar microwave-safe container, and cook on high until the grain is tender, stirring it once with a fork about halfway through the process.

The times and liquid listed in the table on page 109 are very approximate. They can vary considerably, depending on the oven's maximum wattage and the amount of grain you're cooking. Refer to your manufacturer's directions as well as this book's cooking chart.

COOKING GRAINS IN A PRESSURE COOKER

The tough whole grains that take the longest time to cook on the stove top will cook in about half the time in a pressure cooker. It is perhaps the best way to cook rye, wheat, triticale berries, sorghum, Job's tears, and oat groats. It will also speed up the preparation of brown rice. Don't use it for wild rice, because the cooking time varies enormously from one batch to another.

Be sure to follow your manufacturer's directions on the minimum and maximum quantities your pressure cooker can hold, on cleaning the cooker, keeping the gaskets supple, and all the minutiae of pressure cooking. If the manufacturer's instructions counter any here, follow those directions, rather than these.

Put the grain and requisite liquid in the cooker, seal the lid, set the pressure gauge in place, and put on the stove.

Raise the heat to a high setting and keep it there until the gauge indicates it has reached full pressure.

Reduce the heat to the point that just maintains this pressure and cook for the specified time.

Cool down slowly, or cook a few extra minutes, then cool rapidly in a cold water bath.

ELECTRIC RICE COOKERS

These devices are costly and take up counter space. If you cook rice every night, they're probably worth the money; otherwise, I wouldn't bother.

They are simple to use. Just put the manufacturer's suggested quantities of rice and water in the inner cylinder, close it, flip the switch or timer, and wait until it's cooked.

STEAMING COUSCOUS

The critical aspect of couscous cookery is that the delicate grain is steamed over—*never in*—its accompanying stew, for it becomes mushy when simmered.

Traditionally, couscous is steamed in the top of a two-tiered pot called a couscousiere. Its bottom section resembles a kettle or stockpot with a slightly narrowed neck. The perforated bottom of the upper pan sits about a half inch below the rim of the lower pan. These pots are astoundingly expensive in America, and if you don't own one, you can steam the grain in a cheesecloth-lined colander instead. Be sure the bottom of the colander sits well above the liquid level in the lower pot.

Moistening the grain. Put the couscous in a large mixing bowl and pour about twice its volume of water over it. Swirl the grains in the water for a few seconds. Decant the liquid off the grain or drain it in a very fine sieve. Shake the dampened couscous back into the bowl and let it sit for at least ten minutes. During this time it will swell and become slightly sticky.

Steaming the grain. Drizzle the grain into the top portion of your couscous pot or a cheesecloth-lined colander. Put the top pot over the bottom pot containing the stew. Use water if you're making the stew in a different pot. Keep the upper pot uncovered. If the seam between the pots isn't tight, wrap it with cheesecloth to prevent steam escaping through the gap. Regulate the heat to make sure it produces a generous amount of steam, but don't let it boil so vigorously that the stew sticks to the pan.

Resting the grain. Remove the top pot and scrape the couscous back into the mixing bowl with a fork. Sprinkle a few tablespoons of cold water over the grain, then toss it with two forks, and as soon as it is cool enough to handle, break up any remaining lumps by rubbing them between your fingers. Gently toss it back in the pot's top section, seal with the cheesecloth, and steam, uncovered, a further twenty minutes. If you want to scent the grain with spices, orange flower water, or olive oil, rake the couscous back into the mixing bowl and rub the flavoring into the grain, using your fingers, but beware of its steam. Dribble the grain onto a large, deep platter and form it into a volcano shape. Scoop the stew's solids into the depression, and serve the sauce separately.

Microwave Steamed Couscous

Put the couscous and water in a large microwave-safe dish, using about 1²⁄₃ cups liquid for every cup of couscous. Cook, uncovered, on high for about six minutes. Remove and fluff with a fork. Drizzle with a little extra water if the grain seems too dry, but don't saturate it at this point. Return to the microwave and cook on high for two to four minutes more, until the couscous is steaming, lightly textured, and all liquid is absorbed. If you cook smaller quantities, decrease the cooking times by about 25 percent; if you double quantities, increase times by about 50 percent.

GRAINS—COOKING LIQUID AND TIME

	Stove-top*	***Microwave*****	***Pressure******	***Cooked***
Grain	cups (minutes)	cups (minutes)	cups (minutes)	volume (cups)
Amaranth	2–2¼ (20–30)	1¾ (15–20)	—	2¼
Barley, pearled	2½–3 (40–50)	—	—	3½
Buckwheat groats	2–3 (15–25)	—	—	3–4
Buckwheat kasha	2 (12–15)	2 (7–10)	—	3½
Millet	2½–3 (20–35)	2¼ (12–15)	—	4
Oat groats	2½ (40–60)	—	2½ (20–25)	3
Quinoa	2 (15–18)	1½ (16–18)	—	3¾
Rice, white, long grain	1¾–2 (15–20)	—	—	3–3½
Rice, white, converted	2–2¼ (18–25)	—	—	—
Rice, white, basmati	2 (20–30)	—	—	3–3¾
Rice, white, med. grain	1⅓–1¾ (15–20)	—	—	2½–3
Rice, white, short grain	1⅓–1⅔ (15–20)	—	—	2–2½
Rice, brown, long grain	2¼ (40–50)	—	1¾ (12–15)	3½
Rice, brown, med. grain	2–2¼ (40–50)	—	1¾ (12–15)	3
Rice, Indonesian, black	2¼–2¾ (40–50)	—	2½ (15–18)	3½
Rye berries	2¼–3 (45–75)	—	2½ (25)	3
Triticale berries	3–3½ (45–90)	—	2½ (25)	3½–4
Wheat, durum, berries	2½–3 (45–75)	—	3 (30)	3½
Wheat, medium bulgur	2–2½ (18–25)	—	—	3–3½
Wild rice	2½ (40–60)	—	—	3½–4

*If you cook much smaller quantities, increase the amount of water slightly, since a higher percentage will evaporate. Conversely, if you prepare more than 1 cup of grain, you can add slightly less water per cup of grain. Cooking times are independent of volume.

**Shortest time specified for 1 cup of grain cooked on high at 700 watts. Longer times for lower wattage. Adjust liquid and time as needed for different quantities of grain.

***Time indicated from the point full pressure is reached. In each case, the pressure cooker is allowed to cool slowly over a 15-minute period. Add an extra 3 to 5 minutes to these times if you plan to cool the cooker rapidly in a cold water bath. Increase or decrease liquid proportional to the amount of dry grain cooked. Cooking times aren't much affected by volume differences.

Chinese Broccoli Beef

THIS IS THE COMPLETE VERSION OF THE LEAN RECIPE THAT APPEARS ON PAGE 103.

1½ cups long grain white or brown rice

½ pound lean, fat-trimmed beef chuck

2⅔ tablespoons soy sauce

2⅔ tablespoons cornstarch

1 tablespoon sugar

2½ cups homemade beef stock (see page 21)

1 ounce dry shiitake mushrooms

¼ cup dry sherry

1 tablespoon canola oil

2 tablespoons minced fresh ginger

4–6 cloves garlic

½ teaspoon ground Szechuan pepper (optional)

6 cups sliced broccoli

1 8-ounce can water chestnuts

Cook the rice.

Slice the beef thinly and mix with half the soy sauce and cornstarch. Mix the rest of the soy sauce and cornstarch with the sugar and stock. Soak the mushrooms in the sherry.

Heat the oil in a large wok and stir-fry the beef until browned. Add the seasonings and broccoli and stir-fry until the broccoli is tender. Add the water chestnuts and cornstarch mixture and cook to thicken. Serve with the rice.

SERVES 4—558 cal., 8.4g (13% of cal.) total fat; 1.8g (3%) saturated fat; 92g (66%) carbohydrate; 40mg cholesterol; and ±650mg sodium per serving

Snow Peas with Scallops

WATER CHESTNUTS, WHICH RESEMBLE SCALLOPS, ADD TEXTURE AND THE APPEARANCE OF EXTRA FISH.

1½ cups long grain white rice
6 ounces fresh scallops
1 tablespoon canola oil
1 teaspoon sesame oil
6–8 cloves garlic, minced
2½ cups fresh snow peas or 2
   6-ounce packages frozen snow peas
2 8-ounce cans sliced water chestnuts,
   drained

2 tablespoons dry sherry
2 tablespoons minced fresh
   gingerroot
1½ tablespoons cornstarch
2 tablespoons oyster sauce
⅔ cup bottled clam broth
1 cup water
2 bunches scallions, sliced in
   ½-inch lengths (optional)

Cook the rice.

Slice the scallops into ¼-inch pieces, if thick.

Heat the oils in a wok over medium heat. Sauté the scallops and garlic until they are golden and fragrant. Add the snow peas and water chestnuts. Stir-fry until cooked.

Mix the remaining ingredients except the scallions, and add to the wok. Simmer until thickened, sprinkle with the scallions, and serve with the rice.

SERVES 4—477 cal.; 6g (11% of cal.) total fat; 1g (2%) saturated fat; 88g (74%) carbohydrate; 23mg cholesterol; and 527mg sodium per serving

Spicy Beef Shreds

SHIITAKE MUSHROOMS' TASTE AND TEXTURE GIVE THE ILLUSION OF EXTRA MEAT.

1½ cups long grain white or
    brown rice
2 large carrots
2 medium green bell peppers,
    cored and seeded
10 ounces flank steak
2 tablespoons soy sauce
3 tablespoons cornstarch
1 ounce dry shiitake mushrooms
¼ cup dry sherry

2 cups homemade beef stock
    (see page 21)
2 teaspoons sugar
1½ tablespoons canola oil
4–8 hot hontaka or other small hot
    pepper or ¼ teaspoon cayenne
2 tablespoons minced fresh gingerroot
6–8 cloves garlic, mashed
2 tablespoons hulled sesame seeds

Cook the rice.

Cut the carrots, green peppers, and steak into matchstick-sized pieces.

Put the steak bits in a small bowl and mix with the soy sauce and half the cornstarch. Set aside.

Break the dry mushrooms in pieces and soak in the sherry for a few minutes. Add the stock, sugar, and remaining cornstarch, and set aside.

Heat the oil over moderate heat in a large wok. Add the hot peppers and cook until they darken. Remove and discard.

Add the meat slivers to the wok and stir-fry until browned, then add the ginger, garlic, carrots, and green pepper. Stir-fry until the carrots begin to darken. Add the mushrooms and sauce mixture. Cook until thickened.

Sprinkle with the sesame seeds and serve immediately with the rice.

SERVES 4—538 cal.; 10g (17% of cal.) total fat; 3g (5%) saturated fat; 81g (60%) carbohydrate; 50mg cholesterol; and 888mg sodium per serving

Oyster–Sauced Greens

FRESH OYSTERS AND OYSTER SAUCE COMPLEMENT THESE PUNGENT GREENS.

2 cups long grain white or brown rice
2 tablespoons cornstarch
2 tablespoons sherry
1 tablespoon soy sauce
2 tablespoons Chinese oyster sauce
1/8–1/2 teaspoon mild or hot cayenne
2 cups fish fumet (see page 23) or
  chicken stock (see page 22)
2 teaspoons canola oil

1 teaspoon sesame oil
2 tablespoons minced fresh ginger
8–10 cloves garlic, minced
2 pounds collards, bok choy, or
  mustard greens, shredded
2 cups chopped tomatoes,
  preferably fresh
10 ounces fresh oyster meat, diced
1 1/2 tablespoons sugar

Cook the rice.

Mix the cornstarch, sherry, soy sauce, oyster sauce, and cayenne, then stir in the fish fumet or stock and set aside.

Heat the two oils in a wok over medium-high heat. Stir-fry the ginger and garlic for a few seconds, then add the greens and cook until they're wilted (about 3 to 6 minutes). Add the tomatoes, oysters, and sugar and cook until oysters are very hot. Add the liquid mixture and cook until thickened. Serve with the rice.

> **SERVES 4—584 cal.; 7g (11% of cal.) total fat; 1g (2%) saturated fat; 106g (73%) carbohydrate; ±50mg cholesterol; and 650mg sodium per serving**

Orange-Flavored Chicken

PEPPERY SPICES AND ORANGE PEEL SCENT THE OIL USED TO SAUTÉ THIS DISH'S VEGETABLES AND MEATS. USE AN ORANGE WITH FRAGRANT PEEL, IF POSSIBLE.

1½ cups long grain white or brown rice
Juice and peel of 2 oranges
4 small skinned, fat-trimmed, boned chicken thighs
⅓ cup dry sherry
2 teaspoons soy sauce
2 teaspoons cornstarch
1 tablespoon canola oil
1 teaspoon sesame oil

1 teaspoon Szechuan peppercorns
2 teaspoons minced gingerroot
1–2 hontaka or other small, dry, hot chili
2 8-ounce cans sliced water chestnuts, drained
2 8-ounce cans sliced bamboo shoots, drained
2 teaspoons sugar

Cook the rice.

Cut the orange peel into 20 to 30 pieces.

Dice the chicken, mix with the sherry and soy sauce, and marinate for a few minutes, then drain. Add the marinade to the orange juice. Roll the chicken pieces in the cornstarch.

Heat the oils in the wok over a moderate flame. Stir-fry the orange peel slices, Szechuan pepper, ginger, and chili until they darken slightly. Remove with a slotted spoon and discard. Save the flavored oil.

Add the chicken and sauté until golden, then add the bamboo shoots and water chestnuts. Cook until very hot, then add the sugar and the sherry/orange mixture. Cook until thickened and serve with the steamed rice.

SERVES 4—557 cal.; 12g (19% of cal.) total fat; 3.2g (5%) saturated fat; 93g (67%) carbohydrate; 48mg cholesterol; and 658mg sodium per serving

Variations. You can substitute slivers of beef or pork for the chicken. Of, if you prefer, use a firm fish. Don't overcook it.

Hot and Sour Fish

WHOLE STEAMED FISH GARNISHED WITH EMERALD SCALLIONS AND ORANGE LILY BUDS OR CARROT SLIVERS ARE A COMMON SIGHT ON CHINESE BANQUET TABLES. THIS DISH UTILIZES SIMILAR FLAVORS IN A SIMPLE SAUCE FOR RICE.

2 cups long grain white rice or long grain brown rice

10 ounces swordfish or other firm fish steak

1/2 cup dried lily buds or 2 large carrots

12 small, dry shiitake mushrooms

2 tablespoons dry sherry

2 tablespoons cornstarch

2 tablespoons vinegar

1 1/2 tablespoons soy sauce

2 cups fish fumet (see page 23) or chicken stock (see page 22)

1 tablespoon canola oil

1 1/2 teaspoons sesame oil

2 tablespoons minced fresh ginger

4 cloves garlic, mashed or finely chopped

1/8–1/4 teaspoon medium to hot cayenne pepper

1/2 pound snow peas or 1 6-ounce package frozen snow peas

Cook the rice.

Slice the fish steak into 1/4-inch-thick pieces.

Briefly soak the lily buds in water to cover, then discard liquid. If using carrots, cut them into matchstick-sized slivers.

Soak the mushrooms in the sherry for a few minutes. Remove the mushrooms, chop them, and set aside.

Save the sherry marinade and mix it with the cornstarch, vinegar, and soy sauce. Stir in the fish fumet or stock and set aside.

Heat the oils in a wok over a medium flame. Stir-fry the fish pieces until almost cooked. Add the ginger, garlic, and red pepper and stir-fry about 15 seconds.

Next add the snow peas, chopped mushrooms, and lily buds or carrots. Stir-fry until the carrots and peas are cooked.

Pour in the liquid mixture and cook until thickened.

Serve with the rice.

SERVES 4—561 cal.; 9g (14% of cal.) total fat; 1.7g (3%) saturated fat; 95mg (68%) carbohydrate; 28mg cholesterol; and 628mg sodium per serving

Yu Xiang Pork

USE ANY LEAN MEAT OR POULTRY IN THIS SPICY SZECHUAN DISH.

2 cups long grain white or brown rice
1 ounce wood ear fungus (optional)
2 tablespoons cornstarch
1/4 cup dry sherry
2 tablespoons soy sauce
2 tablespoons vinegar
1/2–3 teaspoons Chinese chili paste with garlic
2 teaspoons sugar
2 cups chicken or pork stock or water

1 1/2 tablespoons canola oil
1/2 pound lean, fat-trimmed, boneless pork, diced
6–8 cloves garlic, mashed
2 tablespoons minced fresh gingerroot
2 cups sliced fresh mushrooms
2 8-ounce cans sliced bamboo shoots, drained
2 8-ounce cans sliced water chestnuts, drained

Cook the rice.

Soak the wood ear fungus in water to cover for about 10 minutes, or until it is soft enough to shred. Discard the soaking liquid and any woody stem portions of the fungus.

Make a paste with the cornstarch, sherry, soy sauce, vinegar, chili paste, and sugar. Stir it into the stock, and set aside.

Heat the oil in a large wok over medium heat and sauté the pork pieces until golden brown.

Add the garlic and ginger and sauté for a few seconds, then add the mushrooms, wood ear shreds, bamboo shoots, and water chestnuts. Stir-fry over high heat for about 1 minute.

Add the sauce mixture and cook until thickened. Serve with the rice.

SERVES 4—664 cal.; 12g (17% of cal.) total fat; 3g (4%) saturated fat; 109g (66%) carbohydrate; 37mg cholesterol; and 600mg sodium per serving

Sweet and Sour Pork

FRESH PINEAPPLE MAKES THIS AN APPETIZING DISH. DON'T OVERDO THE SUGAR UNLESS YOU PREFER THE CLOYING VERSIONS SOME RESTAURANTS SERVE.

1½ cups long grain white rice
2 large carrots
2 large green bell peppers
2 bunches scallions, green and white portions
⅓ cup cider or white or rice wine vinegar
¼ cup dry sherry
3 tablespoons sugar
2 tablespoons cornstarch

1 tablespoon soy sauce
1½ cups homemade chicken stock (see page 22)
1½ tablespoons canola oil
½ pound lean, fat-trimmed boneless pork
2 tablespoons minced fresh ginger
1 teaspoon ground Szechuan peppercorns (optional)
2 cups diced fresh pineapple

Cook the rice.

Cut the carrots and bell peppers into slivers. Chop the scallions into 1-inch diagonal slices. Set all three aside.

Mix the vinegar, sherry, sugar, cornstarch, and soy sauce, then stir in the chicken stock and set aside.

Heat the oil in a wok over medium-high heat. Stir-fry the pork cubes until they begin to brown on the outside.

Add the ginger and Szechuan peppercorns and fry these for about 10 seconds.

Add the carrots and stir-fry until barely tender.

Toss in the green pepper and stir-fry for about one minute.

Add the scallions and pineapple and stir-fry until the pineapple is very hot.

Pour in the cornstarch mixture and heat it, stirring constantly, until the sauce is thickened.

Serve with the steamed rice.

SERVES 4—613 cal.; 12g (18% of cal.) total fat; 3.1g (5%) saturated fat; 103g (67%) carbohydrate; 37mg cholesterol; and 682mg sodium per serving

Variations. Prawns and duck make equally flavorful sweet and sour dishes. Be sure to trim the duck of all skin and fat.

General Tso's Chicken

THIS IS A LEAN RENDITION OF A DISH YOU'LL FIND IN MANY CHINESE RESTAURANTS.

4 small lean, skinned, boned chicken thighs
2 tablespoons cornstarch
1½ cups long grain white rice
2 cups homemade chicken stock (see page 22)
2 tablespoons soy sauce
2 tablespoons dry sherry
1 tablespoon hoisin sauce

1½ tablespoons canola oil
1½ teaspoons sesame oil
1 pound green beans cut in ½-inch lengths
2 tablespoons minced fresh gingerroot
2–4 hontaka or other hot pepper (optional)
2 cups thinly sliced celery
2 cups chopped onions or scallions

Cut chicken into cubes, roll them in half of the cornstarch. Set aside.

Cook the rice.

Mix the remaining cornstarch with the stock, soy sauce, sherry, and hoisin sauce. Set aside.

Heat the two oils in a large wok over medium heat and stir-fry the chicken until golden. Add the green beans, ginger, and hot pepper. Stir-fry for another minute, then add the celery and onions. Cook until barely tender and hot. Pour the sauce mixture into the wok and heat until thickened. Serve with the rice.

SERVES 4—604 cal.; 13g (20% of cal.) total fat; 3g (4%) saturated fat; 92g (61%) carbohydrate; 58mg cholesterol; and 917mg sodium per serving

Asparagus Beef

OYSTER SAUCE AMPLIFIES THE MEATY FLAVOR OF THE SMALL QUANTITY OF BEEF IN THIS STIR-FRIED DISH.

1 1/2 cups long grain white or brown rice

1/2 pound lean, fat-trimmed, boneless beef chuck

1 tablespoon soy sauce

2 tablespoons cornstarch

1 1/2 pounds fresh asparagus

1/2 cup water

1/4 cup dry sherry

2 tablespoons oyster sauce

1 1/2 tablespoons sugar

1 1/2 tablespoons canola oil

1–6 hontaka or other hot peppers or 1/8–1 teaspoon mild or hot cayenne

2 tablespoons minced fresh gingerroot

4–6 cloves garlic, mashed

2 cups sliced fresh mushrooms

2 8-ounce cans sliced water chestnuts, drained

Cook the rice.

Slice the beef into 1/16-inch-thick slivers. Roll them in the soy sauce and 1 tablespoon of the cornstarch.

Snap off and discard the lower ends of the asparagus and cut the tender tops into 1-inch lengths.

Mix the remaining cornstarch with the water, sherry, oyster sauce, and sugar. Set aside.

Heat the oil with the hot peppers over medium-high heat in a large wok until the peppers darken. Remove them and discard.

Add the ginger, garlic, and beef slices to the oil and sauté until meat is browned.

Add the asparagus and stir-fry until barely tender.

Toss in the mushrooms and stir-fry until they're soft.

Add the water chestnuts and the cornstarch/sherry mixture and heat just until thickened.

Serve with the rice.

SERVES 4—577 cal.; 12g (19% of cal.) total fat; 3.3g (5%) saturated fat; 90g (62%) carbohydrate; 40mg cholesterol; and 650mg sodium per serving

Bamboo Shoots and Pork

PORK AND BAMBOO SHOOTS ARE FREQUENTLY PAIRED IN CHINESE CUISINES. IN THIS DISH
THEY ARE COMBINED WITH GREEN BEANS IN A HOT AND SOUR SAUCE.

2 cups long grain white or brown rice
2 teaspoons canola oil
1 teaspoon sesame oil
1/2 pound lean, fat-trimmed pork, diced
2 tablespoons minced fresh gingerroot
4 cloves garlic, mashed
4 cups fresh green beans, cut in 1-inch lengths
2 8-ounce cans sliced bamboo shoots

1 1/2 cups homemade chicken stock (see page 22)
1/4 cup sherry
2 tablespoons rice or white wine vinegar
1 tablespoon soy sauce
2 tablespoons cornstarch
1 tablespoon sugar
1/4–2 teaspoons chili paste with garlic

Cook the rice.

Heat the oils in a large wok over moderate heat. Sauté the pork pieces in it until they're golden. Add the ginger and garlic and stir-fry for a few seconds, then add the green beans. Stir-fry until they begin to brown slightly, then toss in the bamboo shoots.

Mix the remaining ingredients together and pour into the wok. Heat just until thickened, then serve with the rice.

SERVES 4—594 cal.; 11g (16% of cal.) total fat; 3g (5%) saturated fat; 96g (65%) carbohydrate; 37mg cholesterol; and ±950mg sodium per serving

Moo Goo Gai Pan

CRUNCHY BABY CORNCOBS CONTRAST WITH THIS DISH'S SOFT CHICKEN AND RICE.

2 cups long grain white or brown rice
3 medium-sized, fat-trimmed, skinned, boned chicken thighs
3 cups homemade chicken stock (see page 22)
1/4 cup dry sherry
3 tablespoons cornstarch
2 tablespoons soy sauce
2 teaspoons sugar

2 teaspoons canola oil
1 teaspoon sesame oil
2 cups sliced fresh mushrooms or paddy straw mushrooms
2 15-ounce cans baby corn, drained and rinsed
4 large scallions, cut in 1/2-inch lengths

Cook the rice.

Dice the chicken and set it aside.

Mix the stock with the sherry, cornstarch, soy sauce, and sugar. Set aside.

Heat the two oils over a moderate flame. Stir-fry the chicken pieces until golden. Toss in the mushrooms and baby corn and stir-fry for about 1 minute or until they're very hot. Pour in the sauce and scallions and heat until thickened.

Serve with the rice.

SERVES 4—615 cal.; 8g (12% of cal.) total fat; 2.2g (3%) saturated fat; 109g (71%) carbohydrate; 40mg cholesterol; and 525mg sodium per serving

Spicy Tofu and Pork

YOU CAN MAKE THIS TOFU DISH WITHOUT MEAT, BUT KEEP IT SPICY, AS BEFITS ITS SZECHUAN PARENTAGE.

1½ cups long grain rice
6 ounces lean, fat-trimmed, boneless pork
1 20-ounce package firm tofu
2 teaspoons canola oil
2–4 hontaka or other small hot chili or ⅛–½ teaspoon hot cayenne pepper
1 teaspoon ground Szechuan pepper (optional)
2 cups thinly sliced mushrooms
4–6 cloves garlic, mashed

2 tablespoons minced fresh gingerroot
1½ tablespoons sugar
3 cups pork or chicken stock
1 tablespoon soy sauce
1½ cups fresh or frozen peas
2 8-ounce cans sliced water chestnuts, drained
¼ cup cornstarch
⅓ cup dry sherry
1 teaspoon sesame oil
½ cup chopped scallions

Cook the rice.

Chop the pork and tofu into ½-inch cubes.

Heat the oil with the hot chilis and Szechuan pepper in a large wok over medium heat. Remove and discard the chilis when dark.

Add the pork to the oil and stir-fry until golden.

Add the mushrooms, garlic, ginger, and sugar and stir-fry briefly.

Next add the stock, soy sauce, and tofu and cook for about 5 minutes.

Add the peas and water chestnuts and cook an additional 5 minutes.

Mix the cornstarch with the sherry and sesame oil and add it to the wok. Heat just until the sauce thickens.

Mix in the scallions and serve with the rice.

SERVES 4—652 cal.; 13g (18% of cal.) total fat; 3g (4%) saturated fat; 99g (61%) carbohydrate; 32mg cholesterol; and 403mg sodium per serving

Variations. A firm fish, even strongly flavored shark, is a good substitute for pork.

Beef Kew

SHIITAKE MUSHROOMS EXTEND THE FLAVOR AND CHEWY TEXTURE OF THE BEEF IN THIS BRIGHTLY COLORED DISH. USE FRESH TOMATOES IF POSSIBLE.

1½ cups long grain white or brown rice

⅔ pound flank or well-trimmed, lean round beef steak

1½ tablespoons cornstarch

10–15 small dry shiitake mushrooms

1 cup water

¼ cup dry sherry

1 tablespoon soy sauce

1½ tablespoons oyster sauce

1½ tablespoons sugar

1½ tablespoons canola oil

2 cups fresh snow peas, cut in 1-inch lengths, or 2 6-ounce packages frozen snow peas

2 teaspoons grated gingerroot

4 cloves garlic, mashed

2 8-ounce cans sliced water chestnuts, drained

3 cups coarsely chopped tomatoes

½ cup chopped scallions

Cook the rice.

Slice the beef into ¹/₁₆- to ⅛-inch-thick pieces, roll them in the cornstarch, and set aside.

Soak the mushrooms in the water for at least 10 minutes. Chop them coarsely and set them aside. Save the soaking liquid and add the sherry, soy sauce, oyster sauce, and sugar to it. Set it aside as well.

Heat the oil in a large wok over a moderate heat. Stir-fry the beef slices until they are browned.

Add the snow peas, ginger, and garlic, and stir-fry until they are hot and limp.

Next add the chopped mushrooms and water chestnuts and stir-fry until the mushrooms are cooked.

Add the tomatoes and cook just until they are very hot.

Pour the liquid mixture in and cook until slightly thickened.

Sprinkle the scallions over the beef and serve with the rice.

SERVES 4—598 cal.; 10g (15% of cal.) total fat; 3g (5%) saturated fat; 96g (64%) carbohydrate; 50mg cholesterol; and 650mg sodium per serving

Chinese-Style Brussels Sprouts with Pork

BRUSSELS SPROUTS ARE ONE OF THE HEALTHIEST VEGETABLES AVAILABLE. THEY ARE ALSO MANY PEOPLE'S LEAST FAVORITE. THIS DISH COULD CHANGE THEIR MINDS. USE ONLY TINY YOUNG BRUSSELS SPROUTS, ABOUT THE SIZE OF WHOLE WALNUTS. THOSE THAT ARE OLDER AND LARGER CAN BE SULFUROUS AND BITTER.

2 cups long grain white rice
1/2 pound lean, fat-trimmed pork
1 pound tiny fresh brussels sprouts
2 cups orange juice
Grated peel of 1 orange (optional)
1/4 cup dry sherry
1 tablespoon soy sauce
2 tablespoons cornstarch

2 teaspoons oyster sauce
2 teaspoons sugar
2 teaspoons vinegar
1/8–1/4 teaspoon mild to hot cayenne
2 teaspoons canola oil
1 teaspoon sesame oil
4–5 cloves garlic, mashed or
chopped

Cook the rice.

Chop the pork into 1/4- to 1/2-inch cubes.

Trim and quarter the brussels sprouts and set aside.

Mix the remaining ingredients, except the oils and garlic, and set aside.

Heat the oils over moderate heat in a large wok. Toss in the pork and stir-fry until golden.

Add the garlic and brussels sprouts and stir-fry until the latter are barely tender.

Pour the liquid mixture in and cook until slightly thickened.

Serve with the rice.

SERVES 4—662 cal.; 11g (15% of cal.) total fat; 3g (4%) saturated fat; 111g (67%) carbohydrate; 37mg cholesterol; ±550mg sodium per serving

Variations. Prawns or strongly flavored, boneless fish, or skinless, fat-trimmed duck can replace the pork. If you really hate brussels sprouts, substitute asparagus.

Chinese Eggplant and Pork

THIS DISH, AS IT'S PREPARED IN MANY SZECHUAN RESTAURANTS, IS VERY SPICY. IF YOU PREFER LESS FIERY FOOD, SUBSTITUTE SOME MILD CALIFORNIA CHILI POWDER FOR THE CHILI PASTE (OR HOT CAYENNE) SUGGESTED BELOW.

2 cups long grain white or brown rice
1/2 pound lean, boneless pork
4 Chinese eggplants, peeled, or
    2 medium-sized eggplants, peeled
2 teaspoons canola oil
1 teaspoon sesame oil
2 tablespoons minced fresh gingerroot
6–8 cloves garlic, minced
3 cups sliced fresh mushrooms
2 tablespoons hulled sesame seeds

3 cups homemade chicken stock
    (see page 22)
1/4 cup cornstarch
1/3 cup dry sherry
2 tablespoons soy sauce
1/4–3 teaspoons chili paste with
    garlic or 1/8–1/2 teaspoon hot
    cayenne pepper
1/2 cup chopped scallions, green
    and white portions

Cook the rice.

Cut the pork into 1/2-inch cubes and the eggplant into 3/4-inch cubes. Set both aside.

Heat the two oils in a large, covered wok over moderate heat and stir-fry the pork cubes until browned.

Toss in the ginger, garlic, and eggplant cubes. Cook until the latter are soft.

Add the mushrooms and sauté them for about 2 to 4 minutes or until they become limp and darken.

Sprinkle in the sesame seeds, then pour the stock into the wok, raise the heat, and bring the liquid barely to a boil.

Mix the cornstarch with the sherry and soy sauce. Pour this mixture into the wok and continue cooking just until the sauce thickens slightly.

Add chili paste or cayenne to taste.

Sprinkle the scallions over the mixture and serve immediately with the rice.

SERVES 4—655 cal.; 13g (18% of cal.) total fat; 3.6g (5%) saturated fat; 105g (62%) carbohydrate; 37mg cholesterol; and 700mg sodium per serving

Hearty Stir-Fried Vegetables

LEAN BEEF HEART FLAVORS THIS SIMPLE STIR-FRIED VEGETABLE MÉLANGE. USE FLANK STEAK, ROUND, OR WELL-TRIMMED CHUCK IF YOU DON'T LIKE HEART.

1½ cups long grain white or
  brown rice
10 ounces fat-trimmed beef heart
¼ cup dry sherry
1½ tablespoons soy sauce
1½ tablespoons oyster sauce
1½ tablespoons cornstarch
2 teaspoons sugar
2 teaspoons Chinese red vinegar or
  rice wine vinegar
1½ cups water

1 tablespoon canola oil
1 teaspoon sesame oil
3–4 hot hontaka or other hot chili
  pepper (optional)
4–6 cloves garlic, mashed
2 tablespoons minced fresh gingerroot
2 large carrots, thinly sliced
2 cups green beans, cut in 1-inch
  lengths
2 8-ounce cans sliced water chestnuts,
  drained

Cook the rice.

Cut the beef heart into long, thin strips, then cut crosswise to make 1½-inch-long matchstick-sized pieces.

Mix the sherry, soy sauce, oyster sauce, cornstarch, sugar, and vinegar together in a bowl, then mix in the water and set it aside.

Heat the two oils in a large wok over a moderate heat. Toss in the hot chili peppers and sauté until they darken. Remove and discard chilis.

Add the beef strips and stir-fry until they begin to brown.

Add the garlic and ginger, and after a few seconds, add the carrots and green beans. Stir-fry these until they begin to darken, but are still crisp (about 2 minutes).

Add the water chestnuts and cook for about 30 seconds.

Pour the sauce mixture in and cook just until it is very hot and thickened.

Serve immediately with the rice.

SERVES 4—522 cal.; 8g (14% of cal.) total fat; 2.3g (4%) saturated fat; 88g (67%) carbohydrate; 100mg cholesterol; and 900mg sodium per serving

Lamb-Scented Greens

THE NEXT TWO RECIPES FEATURE LAMB AS A FLAVORING FOR PUNGENT STIR-FRIED VEGETABLES.

1½ cups long grain rice
2 teaspoons canola oil
½ pound lean, fat-trimmed, boneless lamb, diced
1½ tablespoons minced fresh gingerroot
4 cloves garlic, mashed
4 cups sliced fresh mushrooms
2 8-ounce cans sliced water chestnuts, drained
2 8-ounce cans sliced bamboo shoots, drained
2 pounds fresh bok choy, collards, or mustard greens
½ cup water
¼ pound cornstarch
¼ cup dry sherry
2 tablespoons soy sauce

Cook the rice.

Heat the oil in a large wok over moderate heat, and brown the lamb in it. Add the ginger and garlic, then the mushrooms, and stir-fry until limp.

Add the water chestnuts and bamboo shoots and stir-fry for 2 minutes, then stir in the bok choy. Cover the wok and cook over medium-high heat, stirring occasionally, until it is limp and much reduced in volume (about 3 to 5 minutes).

Mix the water with the cornstarch, sherry, and soy sauce and add to the vegetables. Cook until thickened and serve with the rice.

SERVES 4—659 cal.; 11g (15% of cal.) total fat; 2.7g saturated fat; 112g (68%) carbohydrate; 48mg cholesterol; and 939mg sodium per serving

Broccoli with Hoisin Sauce and Lamb

2 cups long grain white or brown rice
1/2 cup dry sherry
2 tablespoons cornstarch
1 1/2 tablespoons soy sauce
2 teaspoons hoisin sauce
2 cups homemade beef or chicken stock (see pages 21 and 22)
1 1/2 tablespoons canola oil
1/2 pound lean, fat-trimmed lamb shoulder, diced

4 cups coarsely chopped fresh broccoli (about 1 pound)
4–6 cloves garlic, mashed
1/8–1 teaspoon medium or hot cayenne
4 cups sliced mushrooms (about 1 pound)
1 10-ounce package firm-style tofu, cut in cubes

Cook the rice.

Mix the sherry, cornstarch, soy sauce, and hoisin sauce, then stir in the stock. Set aside.

Heat the oil in a large wok over a medium flame. Stir-fry the lamb until the pieces are browned. Add the broccoli, garlic, and cayenne. Stir-fry until it begins to darken but is still crisp (about 1 to 3 minutes).

Add the mushrooms and tofu and stir-fry for about 1 to 2 minutes longer.

Pour in the cornstarch mixture and cook until thickened. Serve with the rice.

SERVES 4—663 cal.; 13g (18% of cal.) total fat; 2.9g (4%) saturated fat; 100g (60%) carbohydrate; 48mg cholesterol; and 753mg sodium per serving

Indonesian Curry

SWEET CORN AND PRAWNS FLAVOR THIS CURRY.

1½ cups long grain white rice
2 tablespoons cornstarch
2 teaspoons turmeric
2 teaspoons ground coriander
2 teaspoons ground, dried ginger
⅛–1 teaspoon mild to hot cayenne
4 cups fish stock or clam broth
1½ tablespoons canola oil
⅔ pound prawns, cut in ½-inch
  lengths
½ cup chopped fresh shallots or
  5–6 cloves garlic, mashed

3 cups fresh or frozen corn kernels
¼ cup crushed roasted, unsalted,
  peanuts, or 3 tablespoons unsalted
  peanut butter
2 tablespoons ketjap manis, or
  1 tablespoon soy sauce plus
  1 tablespoon brown sugar
1–3 tablespoons lime juice or
  white wine vinegar

Cook the rice.

Mix the cornstarch and spices with a little of the broth. Set aside.

Heat the oil in a wok over medium heat. Stir-fry the prawns until they are a golden/pink, then add the shallots and stir-fry for a few seconds. Add the corn, peanuts, ketjap manis, the cornstarch mixture, and the broth. Simmer until the corn is cooked and the sauce is thick. Add lime juice to taste, and serve with the rice.

SERVES 4—581 cal.; 12g (19% of cal.) total fat; 1.5g (2%) saturated fat; 92g (62%) carbohydrate; 115mg cholesterol; and ±1,000mg sodium per serving

Cauliflower Curry

1½ cups basmati or long grain rice

⅔ pound swordfish or
    other firm fish

2 tablespoons flour

1½ tablespoons canola oil

2 cups chopped onions

2–3 cloves garlic, mashed

2 teaspoons sugar

2 teaspoons ground coriander

2 teaspoons fennel seed, preferably
    ground

1 teaspoon turmeric

½ teaspoon ground cardamom

⅛–1 teaspoon medium-hot chili
    powder

4 cups cauliflower segments
    (about 1 pound)

3 cups chopped tomatoes

Cook the rice.

Cut the fish into ½-inch cubes and roll the pieces in the flour.

Heat the oil over a moderate heat in a covered skillet or wok. Stir-fry the fish cubes until golden. Add the onions, garlic, sugar, and spices. Cook for 1 minute, then add the cauliflower and tomatoes. Stir and cover the pan.

Cook just until the cauliflower can be pierced with a fork and the fish is cooked through (about 4 to 5 minutes). Serve immediately with the rice.

SERVES 4—500 cal.; 9g (16% of cal.) total fat; 1.7g (3%) saturated fat; 81g (65%) carbohydrate; 30mg cholesterol; and 120mg sodium per serving

Red Beans and Rice

THIS IS A SIMPLE AND LEAN RENDITION OF A CLASSIC CAJUN DISH.

2 cups long grain white rice
2 teaspoons olive oil
2 cups chopped onions
2 cups cooked kidney beans or
   1 1/2 16-ounce cans kidney beans,
   drained
1/2 pound low-fat, smoked turkey
   sausage, diced
1 large green bell pepper, chopped

1 large sweet red pepper, chopped
1 cup beer
2 teaspoons chopped fresh thyme or
   1 teaspoon dried thyme
1/8–1/2 teaspoon medium or
   hot cayenne
2 cups chopped radish leaves or
   mustard greens

Cook the rice.

Heat the oil over a moderate heat in a large, heavy saucepan. Add the onions and sauté until limp.

Add the beans, sausage, peppers, beer, thyme, and cayenne. Cover and simmer for 20 minutes. Mash a few of the beans to thicken the sauce.

Add the greens and simmer for 2 to 3 minutes longer, then serve with the rice.

SERVES 4—648 cal.; 9g (13% of cal.) total fat; 2.5g (3%) saturated fat; 110g (68%) carbohydrate; ±60mg cholesterol; and 605mg sodium per serving

Spicy Chickpeas

LAMB FLAVORS THIS SAVORY ETHIOPIAN SAUCE. HERE IT ACCOMPANIES RICE. YOU CAN SERVE IT WITH MILLET OR POTATOES IF YOU PREFER.

1½ cups long grain white or brown rice
½ pound lean, boneless, fat-trimmed lamb, diced
1 teaspoon ground fenugreek (optional)
1 teaspoon cinnamon
½ teaspoon cardamom
½ teaspoon ajwain (optional)
⅛–1 teaspoon cayenne
¼ teaspoon cloves
¼ teaspoon freshly grated nutmeg

2 teaspoons canola oil
2 cups chopped onions
8–10 cloves garlic, mashed
3 cups cooked chickpeas (garbanzo beans) or 2 15-ounce cans garbanzo beans, drained
2½ cups homemade beef stock (see page 21)
4 cups chopped collard or mustard greens (about 1 pound)
⅔ cup unflavored, nonfat yogurt
2 teaspoons honey

Cook the rice.

Mix the lamb with the spices.

Heat the oil over moderate heat in a large covered skillet. Brown the lamb, then add the onions and garlic. Cook until the onions are fragrant.

Add the chickpeas and stock. Cover the pan and simmer for about 30 minutes.

Add the greens and cook for another 10 minutes.

Mix the yogurt with the honey and add it to the lamb. Cook just until the mixture is very hot. Don't let it boil or it will curdle.

Serve with the rice.

SERVES 4—666 cal. 11g (15% of cal.) total fat; 2.4g (3%) saturated fat; 108g (65%) carbohydrate; 50mg cholesterol; and ±400mg sodium per serving

West African Rice and Crab

DISHES OF RICE ACCOMPANIED BY LOCAL VEGETABLES AND FISH ARE FAVORITES IN MUCH OF WEST AFRICA'S COASTAL AREA. THIS DISH, DERIVED FROM THE SENEGALESE TIEBOU DIENN, IS CHARACTERIZED BY OKRA, PEANUTS, AND PEPPER. SUBSTITUTE GREEN BEANS IF YOU DISLIKE OKRA.

2 cups long grain white or brown rice
2 cups chopped tomatoes
2 cups chopped onion
2 cups fresh or frozen okra
1/4 cup lemon juice
2 tablespoons brown sugar

2 teaspoons chopped fresh ginger
2 teaspoons mild to medium hot red pepper or paprika
1/2 pound cooked crabmeat
1/4 cup peanut butter

Cook the rice.

Put the remaining ingredients, except the crab and peanut butter, in a saucepan and simmer over medium heat until the vegetables are cooked (about 10 minutes).

Add the crab and peanut butter and simmer for 2 more minutes.

Serve over the rice.

SERVES 4—632 cal.; 10g (14% of cal.) total fat; 2.1g (3%) saturated fat; 109g (70%) carbohydrate; 38mg cholesterol; and 537mg sodium per serving

Couscous with Cardoons and Lamb

MANY MEDITERRANEAN CUISINES PAIR LAMB AND CARDOONS OR ARTICHOKES, TYING THEIR MUSKY AND HERBACEOUS FLAVORS TOGETHER WITH SALTY OLIVES AND TART LEMON JUICE. IF CARDOONS (THE ARTICHOKE'S LEAFY RELATIVE) AREN'T AVAILABLE, SUBSTITUTE A PACKAGE OF FROZEN ARTICHOKE HEARTS OR AN EQUAL AMOUNT OF SLICED CELERY AND/OR FENNEL. USE A RICH STOCK TO GIVE THE SAUCE A MEATIER FLAVOR.

2 cups couscous
4 cups water
$1/2$ pound lean, fat-trimmed, boneless lamb
2 teaspoons extra virgin olive oil
3 cups chopped sweet red onion
4 cups coarsely chopped cardoons or 3 9-ounce packages frozen artichoke hearts

$1/4$ cup chopped green olives
2 cups homemade beef or chicken stock (see pages 21 and 22)
Juice and grated peel of 2 lemons
1 tablespoon chopped fresh or dried oregano
1 teaspoon cinnamon
$1/8$–$1/2$ teaspoon mild to hot cayenne
1–2 tablespoons sugar

Put the couscous in a large bowl and pour the water over it. Swirl the grains in the water, then pour the liquid off the couscous. Let dampened couscous sit for at least 10 minutes.

Dice the lamb and brown it with the oil in the bottom of your couscousiere or cheesecloth-lined colander over a moderate flame. When golden, add the onion and cook until fragrant. Add the cardoons, olives, stock, lemon juice, lemon peel, spices, and 1 tablespoon of the sugar.

Put the moistened couscous in the top of the couscousiere or cheesecloth-lined colander. Set it over the lamb stew and bring the liquid to a boil over a medium-high heat. Reduce the flame to a point that maintains a strong, steam-producing simmer but not a vigorous boil. Steam for 20 minutes.

Remove the top pot and scrape the couscous back into the bowl with a fork.

Sprinkle a few tablespoons of cold water over the grain, then toss it with two forks. As soon as it is cool enough to handle, break up any lumps by rubbing them between your fingers. Gently return the couscous to the top section of the couscousiere. Steam, uncovered 10 to 20 minutes more.

Taste the stew and add more sugar if necessary to balance the lemon.

Dribble the grain onto a large, deep platter and form it into a volcano shape. Scoop the stew's solids into the depression, and serve the sauce separately.

SERVES 4—609 cal.; 12g (18% of cal.) total fat; 2.6g (4%) saturated fat; 95g (62%) carbohydrate; 48mg cholesterol; and 525mg sodium per serving

Scallop Couscous

SERVE WITH A SALAD OF CARROTS, BEETS, OR MIXED GREENS.

2¼ cups semolina or
  whole wheat couscous
⅔ pound scallops
Juice of 1 large orange
1 clove garlic, minced
Pinch of saffron (optional)
2 teaspoons chopped fresh basil or
  fresh spearmint
1½ tablespoons olive oil
2 teaspoons ground coriander

1 teaspoon turmeric
½ teaspoon ground cumin
½ teaspoon ground cinnamon
½ teaspoon ground dry ginger
¼ teaspoon freshly grated nutmeg
2 cups chopped onions
2 cups chopped tomatoes
2 cups water
1 teaspoon orange flower water
  (optional)

Moisten the couscous. (See page 107.)

Put the scallops, orange juice, garlic, saffron, and basil in a glass or noncorrosive bowl and marinate for at least 20 minutes.

Warm the oil and spices over low heat in the bottom of a couscousiere or large pot. Raise the heat and add the onion. Cook until limp, then add the tomatoes and water.

Put the moistened grain in the top of the couscousiere or colander. Set it on top of the stew. Keep the flame hot enough to produce plenty of steam but avoid burning the stew.

After 15 to 20 minutes, fluff the grain, then steam for about 10 to 15 minutes further, adding more water if necessary to keep the stew liquid.

Add the scallop/orange mixture to the vegetables and simmer until the scallops are cooked (about 3 to 5 minutes).

Sprinkle the orange flower water over the grain and toss to mix, then serve as directed on page 107.

SERVES 4—599 cal.; 7g (11% of cal.) total fat; 1.3g (2%) saturated fat; 102g (68%) carbohydrate; 25mg cholesterol; and 208mg sodium per serving

Variation. You can substitute bits of firm fish or other shellfish for the scallops.

Tunisian Duck Couscous

DUCK IS SPLENDID WHEN COOKED WITH TURNIPS. SO IS CHICKEN. USE EITHER.

2½ cups seminola or
   whole wheat couscous
5 cups water
2 teaspoons olive oil
4 small skinned, fat-trimmed duck or
   chicken thighs
4 cups coarsely chopped celery
2 cups coarsely chopped onions

2 cups coarsely chopped turnips
2 cups chopped tomatoes
2 cups homemade chicken stock
   (see page 22)
⅓ cup chopped olives
1 tablespoon chopped fresh parsley
½ teaspoon or more harissa or
   ⅛–1 teaspoon hot cayenne

Put the couscous in a large bowl and pour the water over it. Swirl the grains in the water, then pour the liquid off the couscous. Let dampened couscous sit for at least 10 minutes.

Heat the oil in the bottom pan of the couscousiere or heavy kettle over a medium flame. Sauté the duck until golden, then add the vegetables, stock, olives, and parsley.

Put the moistened couscous in the top of the couscousiere. Fit the top over the bottom pan and raise the heat to bring the liquid to a boil. Regulate the heat to maintain a brisk flow of steam.

After about 20 minutes, remove the top pot and scrape the couscous back into the bowl with a fork. Sprinkle a few tablespoons of cold water over the grain, then toss it with two forks. As soon as it is cool enough to handle, break up any lumps by rubbing them between your fingers. Gently return the couscous to the top section of the couscousiere. Add water to the stew, if needed, to keep it liquid, then resuspend the top over the bottom pan.

Steam for 10 to 20 minutes longer, then add a little harissa or cayenne. Taste and add more as you wish.

Dribble the grain onto a large, deep platter and form it into a volcano shape. Scoop the stew's solids into the depression, and serve the sauce separately.

SERVES 4—676 cal.; 13g (17% of cal.) total fat; 3.5g (5%) saturated fat; 106g (65%) carbohydrate; 60mg cholesterol; and 350mg sodium per serving

Lamb Couscous

CARROTS SWEETEN THIS COUSCOUS.

2 cups semolina or
  whole wheat couscous
2 teaspoons olive oil
1/2 pound diced, lean, fat-trimmed
  boneless lamb shoulder
1 cup chopped onions
1 cup chopped carrots
2 teaspoons ground coriander
1 teaspoon turmeric
1/2 teaspoon cinnamon
1/2 teaspoon ground dried ginger

1/4 teaspoon freshly ground black
  pepper
1/8–1/2 teaspoon mild or medium
  hot cayenne
11/2 cups cooked garbanzo beans
  or 1 can garbanzo beans, drained
2 cups chopped tomatoes
2 cups homemade lamb, beef, or
  chicken stock
2 cups chopped zucchini

Put the couscous in a large bowl and pour the water over it. Swirl the grains in the water, then pour the liquid off the couscous. Let dampened couscous sit for at least 10 minutes.

Heat the oil in the bottom section of a couscousiere over a moderate flame Sauté the lamb cubes in it until browned, then add the onion and cook until limp.

Add the carrots and spices. Cook until the spices are fragrant (about 1 minute), then add the remaining ingredients except the zucchini.

Put the moistened grain in the couscousiere top and set it over the stew. Regulate the heat so that the liquid produces a gentle steam, and cook for about 20 minutes.

Remove the top pot and scrape the couscous back into the bowl with a fork. Sprinkle a few tablespoons of cold water over the grain, then toss it with two forks. As soon as it is cool enough to handle, break up any lumps by rubbing them between your fingers. Gently return the couscous to the top section of the couscousiere. Add the zucchini and more water, if necessary, to the stew, replace the top section, and steam for about 20 minutes longer.

Dribble the grain onto a large, deep platter and form it into a volcano shape. Scoop the stew's solids into the depression, and serve the sauce separately.

SERVES 4—688 cal.; 12g (16% of cal.) total fat; ±2.7g (4%) saturated fat; 104g (60%) carbohydrate; 48mg cholesterol; and 367mg sodium per serving

Sardinian Couscous

THIS RECIPE IS A REMNANT OF THE MOSLEMS' BRIEF OCCUPATION OF SARDINIA.

2 cups semolina or whole wheat couscous	3 cups tomatoes
4 cups water	3 cups chopped celery
2 2½-ounce cans anchovies	⅓ cup raisins
2 teaspoons olive oil	1 cup dry white wine
2 cups chopped onions	1 tablespoon sugar
	2 teaspoons fennel seeds

Put the couscous in a large bowl and pour the water over it. Swirl the grains in the water, then pour the liquid off the couscous. Let dampened couscous sit for at least 10 minutes.

Drain the anchovies, discarding the oil. Pat remaining oil off the anchovies with paper towels, rinse to remove excess salt, chop, and set aside.

Heat the olive oil in the bottom pan of the couscousiere or kettle over medium heat. Sauté the onion until limp and fragrant. Add the anchovies and remaining ingredients, except the couscous and bring to a simmer over moderate heat.

Put the moistened grain in the couscousiere top and steam over the sauce. Add water as needed as the sauce thickens.

After steaming 15 minutes, remove the top pot and scrape the couscous back into the bowl with a fork. Sprinkle a few tablespoons of cold water over the grain, then toss it with two forks. As soon as it is cool enough to handle, break up any lumps by rubbing them between your fingers. Gently return the couscous to the top section of the couscousiere. Steam a further 15 minutes.

Dribble the grain onto a large, deep platter and form it into a volcano shape. Scoop the stew's solids into the depression, and serve the sauce separately.

SERVES 4—622 cal.; 6g (9% of cal.) total fat; 1.3g (2%) saturated fat; 112g (72%) carbohydrate; and ±900mg sodium per serving

CHAPTER 6

Pilafs and Similar Pretoasted Grain Dishes

Surely the Arabs invented pilafs, for virtually all cuisines touched by Islam produce at least one form of these appealing toasted grain dishes. That religion's early westward expansion into Spain and southern Italy produced paellas and risottos. Later northern expansion to the Caucasus and Balkan regions resulted in plov. To the east, polo became the Persian and Afghan versions, while in India the Mogul rulers introduced pilau. Even our own South Carolinian perloo is a likely descendent of this ancient class of dishes.

Try a few recipes in this chapter to see how lean a pilaf can be. Then, for variety, search out other lean recipes or adapt fatter dishes as needed. To insure their lean status, watch out particularly for the amount and kind of meat. Choose the leanest possible cut that's compatible with the dish, trim it well, and restrict portions to two ounces per serving. Whenever possible, replace red meats with leaner poultry or fish. Rely on meat stocks for flavor and make up for meat's texture with crisp, pleasing vegetables. Keep oil to a minimum. One to two teaspoonfuls is plenty to sauté both meats and rice or other grains. Watch out for other high-fat ingredients like cheese and nuts. If possible, restrict these to one tablespoonful per serving.

141

For an example of how easily you can cut out fat, check the two paella recipes on the following pages. The traditional version has 39 percent fat calories. The adapted version substitutes a bevy of the many vegetables used in classic paellas for most of the meat and ends up with slightly more than 7 percent fat. Although the textural interest shifts to vegetables, the dish's flavor retains the savor of sweet shellfish and spices.

Techniques

Most pilafs are easy to make if you follow this simple method.

Toasting the grain. Mix the grain and oil in a heavy skillet to coat each grain. Slowly toast over low to moderate heat, stirring frequently so it won't burn. Continue cooking until the grains develop a faint, toasted aroma and begin to change appearance. Whole grains will darken slightly while refined grains, like white rice, should become slightly transparent around the edges, opaque in the center, and a pale golden color.

Alternatively, you can heat the oil over low to moderate heat until it looks shiny and lively but isn't yet smoking. Then add the grain, stir well, and sauté until it changes its appearance and aroma, as mentioned above.

If you combine two grains in the same pilaf, note the times required to cook each. If they cook within the same time, you can sauté and cook them together. If one grain cooks in substantially less time, sauté it first, scrape it out of the pan, and set it aside. Then sauté the longer-cooking grain, pour in the liquid, and add the grain that takes less time to cook partway through the cooking period.

Additional ingredients. Meats can be sautéed separately and then added to the toasted grain, or you can sauté them in the same pan along with or before the grain. Nuts, fruits, vegetables, and spices are usually added after the grain is sautéed, either with the liquid or toward the end of the cooking.

Adding liquids. As soon as the grain is barely toasted, add your liquid. If your dish contains lots of flavorful ingredients, you can add plain water. With fewer or milder ingredients, you should add flavorful liquids such as meat, fish, or poultry stocks, wine, citrus or tomato juices.

After you've added the liquid, stir the grains as little as possible or they'll break up, release starch, and become sticky. If necessary, you can stir one or two turns with a fork. Cover the pan and raise the heat to bring the liquid barely to a boil. Reduce the heat to low and cook until the grain is tender.

The quantity of liquid you'll need depends on the grain. Most require slightly less when cooked as a pilaf than when steamed on the stove top. Consult the table on page 109 as a loose guide. You may need slightly more liquid if you cook the pilaf in a wide pan than in a narrow one, or on a rather high heat.

If you include large amounts of juicy fresh fruits or vegetables (like canned tomatoes), you should reduce the initial amount of other liquid you add by about $1/3$ to $2/3$ of the volume of fruit or vegetables. Add the normal amount of liquid if the vegetables don't release much water.

If necessary, you can add a little extra liquid toward the end of the cooking period. Be sure to drizzle it over the grain and, if you must, stir with a fork.

If there is extra liquid left when the pilaf is cooked, you can vaporize the excess simply by raising the heat slightly (with the pan lid removed). Don't let the pilaf burn.

The time needed to cook a pilaf is roughly the same time (once you've added liquid) needed to steam the same grain on the stove top.

Traditional Paella

1 pound prawns with shell
4 bay leaves*
18 medium-sized clams with shells
4 tablespoons olive oil
1½ pounds boneless chicken thighs
4 pound chorizo sausage
1½ cups Spanish or Italian rice
Juice of two lemons*

¾ cup chopped onion
4 cloves garlic, mashed*
1 tablespoon Hungarian paprika*
Pinch of saffron threads (optional)*
⅜ cup dry white wine
1 tablespoon fresh or dry thyme*
¾ cup fresh or frozen peas

SERVES 6

This chart shows why you'll want to keep meat and oil to a minimum. Together, they supply virtually all this dish's hefty 39 percent fat calories.

NUTRITIONAL CONTENTS (PER SERVING)

Food*	Calories	Protein	Total fat	Saturated fat	Carbohydrate
		gram (% cal.)	gram (% cal.)	gram (% cal.)	gram (% cal.)
Prawns	51	10 (6%)	1 (1%)	0.1 (trace)	1 (1%)
Clams	23	3 (2%)	trace	0.1 (trace)	1 (1%)
Oil	82	—	9 (13%)	0.9 (1%)	—
Chicken	150	20 (13%)	7 (10%)	2.5 (4%)	—
Sausage	123	7 (4%)	11 (16%)	3.9 (6%)	—
Rice	173	3 (2%)	trace	—	38 (24%)
Onion	8	trace	—	—	2 (1%)
Wine	12	—	—	—	1 (1%)
Peas	13	1 (1%)	—	—	2 (1%)
Total	635	44	28	7.5	45
% of calories		28%	40%	11%	29%

*Ingredients with trivial calories aren't included.

Adapted Paella

1 pound prawns with shells
7 cups water
1 tablespoon olive oil
3 cups Spanish rice or Arborio rice
1½ cups chopped onions
4 cloves garlic, mashed*
1 tablespoon Hungarian paprika*
Pinch of saffron (optional)*
⅜ cup dry white wine

1 tablespoon minced thyme*
4 bay leaves*
36 medium-sized clams
3 9-ounce packages frozen artichoke
   hearts
1½ cups peas
3 fresh sweet red peppers
Juice of 2 lemons*

Serves 6

NUTRITIONAL CONTENTS (PER SERVING)

Food*	Calories	Protein	Total fat	Saturated fat	Carbohydrate
		gram (% cal.)	gram (% cal.)	gram (% cal.)	gram (% cal.)
Artichoke	45	3 (2%)	—	—	11 (7%)
Prawns	51	10 (7%)	1 (1%)	0.1 (trace)	1 (1%)
Clams	46	6 (4%)	1 (1%)	0.2 (trace)	2 (1%)
Oil	20	—	2 (3%)	0.3 (1%)	—
Rice	346	6 (4%)	trace	—	77 (51%)
Onion	15	trace	trace	—	3 (2%)
Wine	12	—	—	—	trace
Pepper	16	1 (1%)	trace	—	4 (3%)
Peas	26	2 (1%)	trace	—	5 (3%)
Total	601	29	±5	0.6	108
% of calories		20%	±7%	1%	71%

*Ingredients with trivial calories aren't included.

Paella

THIS IS THE COMPLETE VERSION OF THE RECIPE THAT APPEARS ON PAGE 144.

1 pound prawns with shells
7 cups water
1 tablespoon olive oil
3 cups Spanish Granza or
   Italian Arborio rice
1½ cups chopped onions
4 cloves garlic, mashed
1 tablespoon Spanish or
   sweet Hungarian paprika
Pinch of saffron (optional)

⅜ cup dry white wine
1 tablespoon chopped fresh or
   dried thyme
4 bay leaves
36 medium-sized fresh clams
3 9-ounce packages artichoke hearts
1½ cup fresh or frozen peas
3 large pimientos or red bell peppers
Juice of 2 lemons

Preheat the oven to 375 degrees.

Clean the prawns and set aside. Put the prawn shells in a saucepan with the water and simmer for 15 minutes. Strain and save the liquid. Discard the shells.

Heat the oil in a paella pan or very large skillet and sauté the rice, onions, garlic, paprika, and saffron. When the rice is transparent around the edges, add the strained liquid, wine, and herbs. Bring to a boil, then put in the 375 degree oven until the rice is nearly tender (about 15 minutes).

Remove from the oven and decorate the top with the prawns, clams, artichoke hearts, peas, and pepper slices. Return to the oven and bake until the rice is tender and the fish and vegetables are cooked (about 10 to 15 minutes). Remove and dribble the lemon juice over the paella.

SERVES 6—601 cal.; 5g (7% of cal.) total fat; ±0.6g (1%) saturated fat; 107g (71%) carbohydrate; 120mg cholesterol; and ±575mg sodium per serving

Arroz con Pollo

VARIATIONS OF THIS SAVORY DISH APPEAR ON TABLES THROUGHOUT THE HISPANIC WORLD.

2 teaspoons olive oil
4 small, skinned, fat-trimmed
  chicken thighs
2 cups long grain white rice
2 cups chopped onions
2 teaspoons ancho chili powder or
  sweet Hungarian paprika
2 teaspoons chopped fresh or
  dried thyme

4 cups chicken stock (see page 22)
1 cup chopped tomato
1 medium-sized bell pepper,
  thinly sliced
2 cups fresh or frozen peas
1/4 cup chopped fresh parsley

Heat the oil in a large, heavy, covered skillet over medium heat. Sauté the chicken until golden, then add the rice. Cook until the grains clarify around the edges, then add the onions, paprika, and thyme and sauté for a minute longer.

Add the stock and tomato, cover, and bring to a boil. Reduce the heat to low and cook for about 15 minutes.

Decorate the top with the pepper slices and peas, cover, and cook until the chicken is done and the rice is tender. Sprinkle with parsley and serve.

SERVES 4—650 cal.; 11g (15% of cal.) fat; 2.7g (4%) saturated fat; 106g (65%) carbohydrate; 60mg cholesterol; and 295mg sodium per serving

Mogul Pilaf

PREPARE THIS PILAF WITH FRESH MINT AND DILL FOR AN IRANIAN TASTE, OR SUBSTITUTE 1½ TABLESPOONS OF GARAM MASALA FOR AN INDIAN TOUCH.

½ pound lean, fat-trimmed, boneless lamb
1 tablespoon plus 1 teaspoon olive oil
1½ cups basmati or long grain white rice
2 cups chopped onions
4 large carrots, thinly sliced
3 cups beef or chicken stock (see pages 21 and 22)

½ teaspoon cinnamon
2 cups fresh or frozen peas
2 tablespoons chopped fresh English mint or spearmint
2 tablespoons chopped fresh dillweed
2 tablespoons sugar
1–2 tablespoons lemon juice

Cut the lamb into ½-inch cubes. Heat the oil over moderate heat in a large, heavy, covered skillet. Brown the lamb in it, then add the rice. Stir to coat the grains with oil and sauté for about 1 minute. Add the onions and cook until they become soft and transparent.

Add the carrots, stock, and cinnamon. Cover, bring to a boil, then reduce the heat to low and cook until the rice is tender (about 20 minutes).

Sprinkle the remaining ingredients over the rice, adding water if needed, and cook 5 minutes longer.

SERVES 4—573 cal.; 11g (17% of cal.) total fat; 2.5g (4%) saturated fat; 94g (66%) carbohydrate; 48mg cholesterol; and 232mg sodium per serving

Perloo

2 cups long grain white rice
1 tablespoon plus 1 teaspoon canola
  or safflower oil
2 cups chopped onions
3 cups chopped fresh or
  canned tomatoes*
1½ cups chopped green pepper or
  2 small peppers

¼ teaspoon ground mace or
  freshly grated nutmeg
¼ teaspoon medium or hot cayenne
3–4 bay leaves
¼ cup chopped pecans
1–2 cups water
½ pound peeled and cleaned
  shrimp or prawns

Sauté the rice and oil in a heavy, covered skillet over medium heat until the rice is transparent around the edges. Add the onion and cook until soft.

Add the tomatoes, pepper, spices, and pecans. Add the water as well, using the small amount if using canned tomatoes and the larger amount if using fresh. Cover and bring the liquid to a boil. Reduce the heat to the lowest setting and simmer for about 10 minutes.

When the rice is tender, top with the shrimp. Cover and heat until they are pink and cooked. Remove bay leaves and serve.

SERVES 4—573 cal.; 11g (17% of cal.) total fat; 1.3g (2%) saturated fat; 95g (67%) carbohydrate; 87mg cholesterol; and 100mg sodium per serving

*The sodium content will be about 600mg per serving if you use canned tomatoes.

Turkish Pilaf

THIS RECIPE FOR THE TRADITIONAL TURKISH IC PILAV BECOMES LEAN BY SUBSTITUTING CHICKEN GIZZARDS AND HEARTS AND A PINCH OF OLIVE OIL FOR THE USUAL GOOSE LIVER AND GENEROUS BUTTER.

1 tablespoon plus 1 teaspoon olive oil
1/2 pound chicken gizzards and/or
   hearts, minced
2 cups long grain white or brown rice
2 cups chopped onion
8–10 cloves garlic, mashed
1/4 cup chopped pine nuts or
   walnuts

1/2 teaspoon cinnamon
4 cups homemade chicken stock
   (see page 22)
1/2 cup raisins
1/2 cup chopped fresh parsley
1/4 cup chopped fresh or
   dried English mint or spearmint

Heat the oil in a heavy, covered skillet over medium heat. Sauté the meat briefly, then add the rice and sauté for one minute. Add the onion, garlic, pine nuts, and cinnamon and cook until the onion is transparent.

Add the remaining ingredients, cover, bring the liquid to a boil, then reduce the heat to the lowest setting. Cook until the liquid is absorbed and the rice is tender (about 15 to 20 minutes). If using brown rice, add water as necessary to keep the pilaf moist and cook at least 20 minutes longer.

SERVES 4—659 cal.; 15g (20% of cal.) total fat; 3g (4%) saturated fat; 107g (65%) carbohydrate; 125mg cholesterol; and 150mg sodium per serving

Dirty Rice

1 tablespoon plus 1 teaspoon olive oil
1/2 pound chicken hearts and/or
   gizzards, diced
2 cups long grain white rice
2 cups chopped onion
2 cups chopped celery
2 medium green or red bell peppers,
   chopped

4 cups homemade chicken stock
   (see page 22)
1/2 cup chopped fresh parsley
1/2 teaspoon ground allspice
1/8–1/4 teaspoon mild to hot
   cayenne pepper

Heat the oil in a heavy, covered skillet over medium heat. Sauté the meat until lightly browned, then add the rice. Sauté for a minute, then add the onion and cook until soft.

Add the remaining ingredients, stir once, cover the pot, and bring to a boil. Reduce the heat to the lowest setting and cook until the rice is tender (about 15 minutes).

SERVES 4—542 cal.; 10g (17% of cal.) total fat; 2.3g (4%) saturated fat; 91g (67%) carbohydrate; 125mg cholesterol; 129mg sodium per serving

Orzo Pilaf

RICE-SHAPED PASTAS LIKE GREEK ORZO OR ITALIAN RISO MAKE TENDER YET CHEWY PILAFS.

4 medium-sized, fresh artichokes
½ pound lean, boneless, fat-trimmed lamb shoulder
2 teaspoons olive oil
2 cups rice-shaped pasta
4–6 cloves garlic, mashed
2 cups tomatoes, chopped
4 cups water
2 tablespoons chopped Calamata or other flavorful olive
2 tablespoons minced fresh oregano or 1 tablespoon dried oregano

1 teaspoon minced fresh rosemary or ½ teaspoon dried rosemary
2 teaspoons sugar
2 teaspoons minced fresh mint or fresh parsley
1½ tablespoons mayonnaise
½ cup nonfat, unflavored yogurt
1 teaspoon minced fresh lemon thyme or fresh tarragon
Juice of 1 lemon

Trim the artichokes cutting off as much of the stem as possible. Clip off the thorny tips with scissors. Steam them in a rack over boiling water until tender (about 35 to 45 minutes). You can simmer them directly in water, in which case they will be tender within 20 to 35 minutes. Drain and cool briefly, then cut in half, remove the bristly "choke", and set aside.

Chop the lamb into ½-inch cubes. Heat the oil in a heavy skillet over a moderate flame. Sauté the lamb in it until brown, then reduce the flame and add the pasta. Sauté, stirring constantly, until it becomes slightly golden (about 2 to 5 minutes). Add the garlic and cook for a few seconds.

Add the tomatoes, water, olives, oregano, rosemary, and sugar. Bring to a boil, then reduce the heat to low and simmer, stirring occasionally, until the orzo is almost tender (about 12 to 18 minutes). Add more water if it begins to stick.

While it cooks, mix the mayonnaise, yogurt, lemon thyme or tarragon, and lemon juice together in a small serving bowl and set aside.

When the pasta is tender, arrange the artichoke halves cut sides down on the pilaf with the bases toward the center of the pan. Sprinkle the lemon juice over the pilaf and serve it with the yogurt as a dipping sauce for the artichokes.

SERVES 4—630 cal.; 14g (20% of cal.) total fat; 3.5g (5%) saturated fat; 96g (61%) carbohydrate; 52mg cholesterol; and 335mg sodium per serving

Variations. You can make this pilaf with long grain white or brown rice. Brown Texmati is particularly good. Use the same quantity of water for the brown varieties, and allow about 25 minutes extra cooking time. For white rice, use about ¾ cup less water. It will cook in about the same time as the pasta.

Barley Pilaf with Lamb Kabobs

EARTHY BARLEY AND LAMB ARE A NATURAL FLAVOR MATCH.

1/2 pound lean, fat-trimmed
  boneless lamb
1/2 cup dry red wine
4–5 bay leaves
1/4 teaspoon crushed juniper berries
  or 1/2 teaspoon ground allspice
1 1/2 cups pearl barley
1 tablespoon plus 1 teaspoon olive oil
4–6 cloves garlic, mashed
4 cups homemade beef or chicken
  stock (see pages 21 and 22)

2 cups diced carrots
2 teaspoons chopped fresh thyme or
  1 teaspoon dried thyme
24 medium-sized mushroom caps
24 cherry tomatoes
3 cups fresh or frozen peas
2 tablespoons chopped fresh parsley
  to garnish (optional)

Cut the lamb into 16 cubes and mix them with the wine, bay leaves, and juniper berries. Marinate in the refrigerator for at least 30 minutes.

Mix and cook the barley, oil, and garlic in a large, heavy, covered skillet over medium heat. When the barley is lightly toasted, add the stock, carrots, and thyme. Cover and bring to a boil. Reduce the heat to low and cook until tender (about 45 minutes).

While the barley cooks, preheat the broiler. Drain the lamb cubes, saving the marinade, and thread the meat onto 4 bamboo skewers, interspersing the lamb with the mushrooms and tomatoes.

When the barley is barely tender, stir the peas into it. Cover and cook 10 minutes longer.

At the same time, broil the lamb until cooked, turning the skewers once and basting them with the reserved marinade.

Drizzle any drippings in the broiler pan over the barley, then sprinkle it with the parsley. Serve pilaf and kabobs very hot.

SERVES 4—596 cal.; 12g (18% of cal.) total fat; 3.3g (5%) saturated fat; 89g (60%) carbohydrate; 48mg cholesterol; and 205mg sodium per serving

Variations. You can substitute buckwheat kasha or a medium grade of bulgur, both of which cook much faster than barley. Reduce the preliminary cooking step from 45 minutes to about 10 minutes. In addition, cut the stock to about 2½ to 3 cups, adding the smaller amount to begin with, and more as needed when you add the peas.

Jambalaya

YOU CAN PREPARE THIS SOUTHERN DISH EITHER AS A THICK SAUCE POURED OVER RICE OR PILAF-STYLE, AS IN THIS RENDITION.

1/4 pound cleaned shrimp or prawns
13/4 cups long grain rice
1 tablespoon plus 1 teaspoon olive oil
1 cup chopped onion
4–5 cloves garlic, mashed
2 cups chopped fresh tomatoes
2 cups packed, chopped fresh kale or similar greens
1 cup chopped green bell pepper
1/4 pound fat-trimmed raw or cooked ham

2 cups richly flavored homemade chicken stock or diluted ham stock (see pages 22 and 24)
2 tablespoons dry sherry
2 teaspoons chopped fresh thyme or 1 teaspoon dried thyme
1/2 teaspoon freshly ground black pepper
1/2–2 teaspoons ground mild to hot red pepper
2 tablespoons chopped pimiento

Preheat the oven to 375 degrees. If the shrimp are large, chop them into 1/2-inch pieces. Set aside.

Mix the rice and oil in a paella pan, skillet, or shallow casserole that can be used on top of the stove and in the oven. Sauté over a moderate heat until the grains become slightly transparent around the edges. Add the onions and garlic and cook until soft.

Stir in the other vegetables, ham, stock, sherry, herbs, and spices and raise the heat to just bring the mixture to a boil. Reduce the heat to the lowest setting and simmer for 15 minutes. Add water if it sticks to the pan.

Put the shrimp and pimiento on top and bake until the fish are cooked through (about 5 to 10 minutes), and serve immediately.

SERVES 4—495 cal.; 8g (15% of cal.) total fat; ±1g (2%) saturated fat; 82g (66%) carbohydrate; 95mg cholesterol; and 103mg sodium per serving

Variations. If you'd rather serve this as a sauce over rice, steam 1³/₄ cups of rice in about 3¹/₂ cups of water until tender (about 15 to 20 minutes). To make the sauce, sauté the onion and garlic in the oil in a large saucepan, add the remaining ingredients, including an extra cup each of tomatoes and stock. Simmer at least 15 minutes and serve, poured over the rice.

Jollof Rice

VERSIONS OF THIS DISH, NAMED FOR THE JOLLOF TRIBE, ARE PREPARED THROUGHOUT MUCH OF COASTAL WEST AFRICA. VARY THE AMOUNT AND TYPE OF CAYENNE TO SUIT YOUR TOLERANCE FOR HOT CHILIS.

1/2 pound lean, fat-trimmed, boneless beef chuck
1/8–1 teaspoon mild to hot cayenne
2 teaspoons mild California chili powder
2 teaspoons canola oil
2 cups chopped onion
2 tablespoons minced fresh gingerroot
6–8 cloves garlic, mashed
1 teaspoon ground cardamom
1 1/2 cups long grain white rice

2 cups sliced carrots
3 cups chopped tomatoes
1 1/2 cups homemade beef stock (see page 21) or chicken stock (see page 22)
2 teaspoons sugar
Juice of 1 lemon
4 cups green beans, sliced
2 cups sliced okra or zucchini
2 tablespoons chopped fresh cilantro or parsley

Cut the beef into 1/4-inch cubes and roll them in a mixture of the cayenne and chili.

Heat the oil in a large, heavy, covered skillet, over medium heat. Sauté the meat quickly, preferably with an exhaust fan venting any cayenne fumes. As soon as the meat is browned, add the onions, ginger, garlic, and cardamom. Sauté for about 20 seconds, then add the rice. Sauté it for about a minute, scraping up any coagulated meat juices on the bottom of the pan.

Add the carrots, tomatoes, and stock. Cover the pan, raise the heat to bring the liquid to a boil, then reduce it to a low setting and simmer for about 10 minutes.

Stir the sugar, lemon juice, and green beans in with a fork, then lay the okra or zucchini pieces on top, cover the pan, and cook 10 minutes longer, adding water if the rice is sticking to the pan.

As soon as the rice is tender, sprinkle with the cilantro or parsley and serve.

SERVES 4—567 cal.; 9g (14% of cal.) total fat; 3.4g (5%) saturated fat; 94g (66%) carbohydrate; 47mg cholesterol; and 83mg sodium per serving

Variations. You can replace the beef with chicken, lamb, or any firm (preferably boneless) fish or shellfish. If you prefer brown rice to white, add a little extra stock and cook it at least 30 minutes longer.

Quinoa Pilaf with Baked Chicken Legs

ALTHOUGH VANILLA SEEMS INEXTRICABLY LINKED TO DESSERTS, A DROP ADDS A WOODY NOTE
TO FISH AND POULTRY TO ACCENTUATE THEIR MEATY FLAVORS. HERE IT DEEPENS THE TASTE
OF THE BAKED CHICKEN'S JUICE, WHICH IS EVENTUALLY DRIZZLED OVER THIS MILD PILAF.

4 small, skinned, fat-trimmed chicken
  drumsticks
1/2 teaspoon vanilla extract
2 cups chopped onions
2 1/2 cups quinoa
2 teaspoons olive oil
4 cloves garlic, mashed
3 cups homemade chicken stock
  (see page 22)

2 10-ounce packages frozen chopped
  spinach, thawed
2 7-ounce cans sliced water
  chestnuts, rinsed and drained
2 teaspoons sugar
Pinch of freshly grated nutmeg
1/4 cup dry white wine

Preheat the oven to 400 degrees. Rub the chicken pieces with the vanilla and
put them in a small baking dish with 1/2 cup of the onions. Cover with foil and
bake until they're cooked through (about 30 to 40 minutes).

While chicken bakes, check the quinoa for bits of grit, rinse it, and drain it
well.

Heat the oil in a heavy, covered skillet over moderate heat. Add the quinoa,
remaining onions, and garlic and cook until the onion is limp. Stir in the remaining ingredients, except the wine. Cover the pan, and raise the heat slightly.
As soon as the liquid comes to a boil, reduce the heat to low and simmer for
about 15 to 20 minutes.

When most of the liquid has been absorbed and the quinoa has cooked, remove the lid and continue to cook until any unabsorbed liquid has evaporated.

Remove the baking pan from the oven. Place the chicken thighs on top of the
quinoa. Add the wine to the onions and juice in the baking pan. Stir to loosen
coagulated juices, then scoop the mixture over the chicken and quinoa. Serve
immediately.

SERVES 4—628 cal.; 14g (20% of cal.) total fat; 3.5g (5%) saturated fat; 95g (61%) carbohydrate; 46mg cholesterol; and 115mg sodium per serving

Variations. You can make this pilaf with millet or rice as well as quinoa. In either case, reduce the grain to 2 cups, and increase the stock to 4 cups for rice and about 5 cups for millet. White rice cooks in about the same time as quinoa. Brown rice and millet will take about 30 minutes longer.

Golden Pilaf

TURMERIC AND SHRIMP BRIGHTEN THIS LEMON-FLAVORED PILAF.

10 ounces cleaned prawns or shrimp
2 cups long grain rice
1 tablespoon plus 1 teaspoon olive oil
1 teaspoon turmeric
3–4 cloves garlic, minced or mashed

2 cups sliced fennel bulb
2 cups water
1½ cups clam broth
Juice and grated peel of 2 lemons
2 teaspoons sugar

If using large prawns, cut them into ½-inch lengths and set aside.

Put the rice, oil, turmeric, and garlic in a covered skillet, stir to coat the grains, then heat over moderate heat. When the rice is transparent around the edges, add the fennel, water, clam broth, lemon juice, lemon peel, and sugar. Cover the pan and bring to a boil. Reduce the heat to low and cook for 10 minutes.

Sprinkle the fish over the top, cover, and cook until the rice is tender and fish cooked.

SERVES 4—475 cal.; 6g (11% of cal.) total fat; 1.2g (2%) saturated fat; 82g (69%) carbohydrate; 103mg cholesterol; and ±400mg sodium per serving

Rice and Lentil Pilaf

THIS PILAF IS A SPICED-UP VERSION OF MEGEDARRA, A CLASSIC (AND USUALLY VEGETARIAN)
MIDDLE EASTERN DISH OF RICE AND LENTILS.

1/2 cup lentils
2 cups water
1 tablespoon plus 1 teaspoon olive oil
1/3 pound chopped, fat-trimmed ham
2 cups rice
2 cups chopped onions
2 tablespoons sweet Hungarian
  paprika

2 tablespoons ground coriander
2 teaspoons ground cumin
4 cups chicken stock (see page 22)
1/4 cup dry sherry
2 9-ounce packages frozen artichoke
  hearts
Juice of 2 lemons

Simmer the lentils and water in a small saucepan for about 15 minutes.

Heat the oil in a large, heavy, covered skillet over moderate heat. Sauté the
ham until the pieces are lightly browned, then add the rice and sauté until the
grains are slightly golden. Add the onions and cook until limp.

Drain the lentils and add them to the rice, along with the spices, stock, and
sherry. Decorate the top with the artichoke hearts, cover the pan, and simmer
until the rice and lentils are tender (about 20 minutes). Drizzle the lemon juice
over the top and serve.

SERVES 4—667 cal.; 9g (12% of cal.) total fat; 2.1g (3%) saturated fat;
114g (68%) carbohydrate; 24mg cholesterol; and 537mg sodium per
serving

Wild Rice Pilaf

CURRANTS AND GRAPES ADD A TOUCH OF SWEETNESS TO THIS FRAGRANT PILAF.

1 tablespoon plus 1 teaspoon olive oil
1/2 pound chicken gizzards or hearts, thinly sliced
2 cups wild rice
1/2–1 teaspoon fragrant curry powder
2–4 cloves garlic, mashed

2 cups sliced mushrooms
1/2 cup golden currants
5 cups homemade chicken stock (see page 22)
1 1/3 cups red or green seedless grapes

Heat the oil over a moderate heat in a heavy, covered skillet. Sauté the gizzard pieces until golden, then add the wild rice and sauté for 2 to 3 minutes longer. Add the curry powder, garlic, and mushrooms and sauté for one minute longer, then add the currants and stock.

Cover the pan and bring the liquid to a boil. Reduce the heat to moderate and simmer briskly until the grains begin to open (about 40 to 50 minutes). Check the wild rice occasionally and add extra water if it is sticking to the pan. If there is excess liquid after the wild rice is cooked, remove the lid, raise the heat, and boil off the excess.

After the grains have opened and are soft but still a little chewy, add the grapes and cook for another 3 to 4 minutes. Serve immediately.

SERVES 4—623 cal.; 11g (16% of cal.) total fat; 2.8g (4%) saturated fat; 102g (65%) carbohydrate; 130mg cholesterol; and 79mg sodium per serving

CHAPTER 7

Fried Grains and Noodles

For Americans, fried rice belongs in the realm of Chinese cuisine, but the range of this delicious mélange actually extends across most of the Orient. Because so many cuisines embrace this dish, you can produce versions with quite different flavors by incorporating the individual spices and vegetables each country favors. For variety, you can substitute precooked wheat, rye, or triticale berries. You can fry up precooked noodles to make classic dishes like Indonesian bamie goreng, Chinese lo mein, and Japanese yaki soba.

All the recipes in this chapter are very lean. None exceed 20 percent calories from fat. This isn't true of many similar recipes you'll find in ethnic cookbooks written for American tastes. In them, fat often supplies 30 percent to 60 percent of the calories. Don't shy away from them, though. You can easily modify most with no loss of flavor. If possible, reduce the amount of oil to a minimum: one to one and a half teaspoons per main-dish serving is usually plenty.

For an example of how simply you can modify most dishes, review the two versions of Chinese fried rice on the following pages. With a few simple adjustments, the fat is reduced from 49 percent to 15 percent.

Chinese Fried Rice

THIS RECIPE IS ALMOST IDENTICAL TO ONE IN A POPULAR CHINESE COOKBOOK. GLANCE AT THE CHART THAT FOLLOWS TO SEE WHICH FOODS SUPPLY MOST OF THE FAT.

1 cup long grain white rice*
6 tablespoons canola oil*
8 ounces diced pork shoulder*
8 ounces minced shrimp*

4 cloves garlic, minced*
1 cup frozen peas
4 medium-sized eggs
2 tablespoons soy sauce*

SERVES 4

NUTRITIONAL CONTENTS (PER SERVING)

Food*	Calories	Protein		Total fat		Saturated fat		Carbohydrate	
		gram	(% cal.)	gram	(% cal.)	gram	(% cal.)	gram	(% cal.)
Rice	173	3	(2%)	trace		—		39	(25%)
Oil	192		—	21	(30%)	3.0	(4%)		—
Pork	108	12	(8%)	7	(9%)	2.3	(3%)		—
Shrimp	51	10	(6%)	1	(1%)	—		1	(1%)
Peas	29	2	(1%)	trace		—		5	(3%)
Eggs	81	6	(4%)	6	(8%)	1.9	(3%)		trace
Total	634	33		35		7.2		45	
% of calories			21%		48%		10%		29%

*Ingredients with trivial calories not included.

Adapted Chinese Fried Rice

IN THIS RECIPE, ASSERTIVELY FLAVORED VEGETABLES AND GINGER REPLACE MUCH OF THE MEAT. THEY NOT ONLY ENLIVEN FLAVOR AND TEXTURE, BUT ADD A BUNDLE OF VITAMINS AND MINERALS AS WELL.

2 cups rice
4 teaspoons oil
2 tablespoons fresh ginger*
6 ounces shrimp
8 cloves garlic*
2 tablespoons soy sauce*

2 cups frozen peas
3 cups bean sprouts
4 cups shredded mustard greens
1 cup diced sweet red pepper
2 extra large eggs

SERVES 4

NUTRITIONAL CONTENTS (PER SERVING)

Food*	Calories	Protein	Total fat	Saturated fat	Carbohydrate
		gram (% cal.)	gram (% cal.)	gram (% cal.)	gram (% cal.)
Rice	346	6 (4%)	trace	—	77 (54%)
Oil	42	—	5 (8%)	0.5 (1%)	—
Shrimp	39	8 (6%)	1 (2%)	0.1 (trace)	1 (1%)
Peas	57	4 (3%)	trace	—	9 (6%)
Bean sprouts	24	2 (1%)	trace	—	5 (3%)
Greens	8	1 (1%)	trace	—	1 (1%)
Pepper	10	trace	—	—	2 (1%)
Egg	45	4 (2%)	3 (5%)	1.0 (2%)	trace
Total	571	25	9	±1.6	95
% of calories		17%	15%	3%	66%

*Ingredients with trivial calories aren't included.

Techniques

Most fried grains cook very rapidly, so be sure to have all ingredients prepared before you start frying any of them.

Stir-fried Grains

A large wok is the ideal pan to stir-fry whole grains. It is big, broad, and deep enough to allow you to toss the ingredients with abandon. Be sure to keep the wok hot enough to seal in meat and vegetable juices.

Cooking the grain. Cook the rice or other grain as directed in chapter 5. You can use freshly cooked or leftover rice, noodles, or other grains. If you cook them in advance, they tend to be sticky. Be sure to break the clumps apart before frying.

Heating the oil. Put a small amount of oil in a large wok or heavy skillet and heat it over medium heat until it looks lively. Tilt the pan to coat as much of the bottom and sides as possible and put it back on the burner until it just begins to fume but not smoke.

Cooking meats and vegetables. Toss in your meat bits and stir-fry them until they're cooked on the surface. (If you're using precooked meat, add it later with the rice.) Then throw in your vegetables, first adding those requiring the longest cooking.

Adding the grain. Toss in the cooked grain and stir-fry until it is lightly toasted or fried.

Adding liquids. Drizzle any liquid flavorings over the cooked mélange, stir to mix, and heat just long enough to warm and blend the whole.

Chinese Fried Rice

THIS IS THE COMPLETE VERSION OF THE LEAN RECIPE THAT APPEARS ON PAGE 166.

2 cups long grain white rice
4 teaspoons canola oil
2 tablespoons minced fresh ginger
6 ounces shrimp
8 cloves garlic, minced
2 cups fresh or frozen peas

3 cups bean sprouts
4 cups shredded mustard greens or
   similar greens
1 cup diced sweet red pepper
2 extra large eggs
2 tablespoons soy sauce

Steam the rice.

Heat the oil and ginger in a large wok over medium heat. Sauté the shrimp and garlic.

Toss in the vegetables and stir-fry until hot and wilted.

Add the rice and stir-fry briefly.

Beat the eggs with the soy sauce and pour over rice. Cook until eggs are set.

SERVES 4—571 cal.; 9.3g (15% of cal.) total fat; ±1.6g (3%) saturated fat; 95g (66%) carbohydrate; 230mg cholesterol; and 690mg sodium per serving

Nasi Goreng

NASI GORENG IS INDONESIA'S TRADITIONAL FRIED RICE DISH. MOST RECIPES SUGGEST USING LONG GRAIN WHITE RICE, BUT TEXMATI AND SIMILAR LONG GRAIN BROWN RICE STRAINS GIVE THE DISH A NUTTY NUANCE. NUMEROUS VARIATIONS OF THIS DISH ARE POSSIBLE. IF YOU DON'T LIKE THE CHICKEN GIZZARDS, SEE THE SUGGESTED VARIATIONS BELOW.

2 cups long grain brown or white rice
2 tablespoons canola oil
1/4 pound diced chicken gizzards
  and hearts
1/2 cup chopped shallots or onion
1 tablespoon ground coriander
1/4–2 teaspoons mild or hot chili
  powder
2 teaspoons caraway seeds
2 teaspoons cinnamon
2 large carrots, slivered
2 medium-sized zucchinis, sliced

2 cups sliced celery (4 medium
  stalks)
4 cups sliced broccoli
2 medium-sized green peppers,
  chopped
1 cup sliced radishes
1/3 pound cooked crabmeat
2 tablespoons chopped fresh mint
1/4 cup ketjap manis or 3 tablespoons
  Chinese soy sauce mixed with
  2 tablespoons brown sugar

Cook the rice.

Heat the oil in a large wok and sauté the chicken meat first. Add the shallots or the onions, spices, and carrots and stir-fry until the carrots are almost tender. Add and stir-fry the remaining vegetables for a minute, then add the crab and cooked rice and fry briefly.

Toss in the mint, and drizzle the ketjap manis over the fried rice. Stir, then serve immediately.

Serves 4—642 cal.; 12g (17% of cal.) total fat; 2g (3%) saturated fat; 104g (65%) carbohydrate; 90mg cholesterol; and ±1,000mg sodium per serving

Variations. Use any shellfish, boneless fish, lean pork, or poultry, along with copious amounts of other vegetables (peas, lima beans, green beans, etc.) to replace those given above. For a vegetarian version, substitute firm tofu cubes for the meat(s), adding them to the wok at the last minute.

Yaki Soba

PORK COMPLEMENTS THE EARTHY FLAVOR OF THESE FRIED JAPANESE BUCKWHEAT NOODLES.

1 pound dry soba (Japanese buckwheat noodles)
1 bunch radishes with leaves (about 1 pound)
1½ tablespoons canola oil
½ pound fat-trimmed, lean, boneless pork, diced
2 tablespoons minced fresh ginger

2 cups chopped onions
4 cups cauliflower segments
2 cups snow peas cut in 1-inch lengths
2 tablespoons sherry
1½ tablespoons soy sauce
1½ tablespoons vinegar

Boil the noodles in a large kettle of water until they are al dente (about 3 to 6 minutes). Drain as soon as they're cooked, and rinse with cold water.

Rinse the radishes and their greens well and slice both thinly.

Heat the oil in a large wok and stir-fry the pork and ginger, followed by the onion. Cook the cauliflower and snow peas just until hot, but still crisp. Add the noodles and stir-fry until very hot. Toss in the radishes and their leaves and stir-fry for a few seconds.

Mix the sherry, soy sauce, and vinegar. Pour over the noodles, then serve.

SERVES 4—675 cal.; 14g (19% of cal.) total fat; 3.3g (4%) saturated fat; 104g (62%) carbohydrate; 37mg cholesterol; and 690mg sodium per serving

Fried Rice with a Korean Flavor

SESAME, GARLIC, AND RED PEPPER DOMINATE THE FLAVOR OF THIS FRIED RICE. CHOOSE A MILD CAYENNE OR CALIFORNIA CHILI POWDER IF YOU PREFER A MILDER TASTE.

2 cups long grain white or brown rice
2 10-ounce packages frozen spinach
1/2 pound lean, fat-trimmed boneless beef
1/2 pound snow peas or 1 6-ounce package frozen snow peas
1 teaspoon canola oil
2 tablespoons minced fresh gingerroot
12–15 cloves garlic, mashed
1/8–1/2 teaspoon mild to hot cayenne or other red pepper and/or mixture of these
1 tablespoon sesame oil
1 1/2 tablespoons soy sauce

Cook the rice.

Whack the block of spinach into large pieces. Slice the beef into 1/16-inch-thick slices. Chop the snow peas into 1-inch lengths.

Heat the canola oil in a large wok and sauté the beef strips and spices. Add the snow peas and sauté for about 1 minute, then add the spinach. Cook until it is hot and most of the liquid is vaporized.

Add the sesame oil, then stir in the cooked rice and sauté until the rice is very hot and slightly golden. Stir in the soy sauce and serve immediately.

SERVES 4—541 cal.; 10g (17% of cal.) total fat; 3.2g (5%) saturated fat; 89g (66%) carbohydrate; 40mg cholesterol; and 686mg sodium per serving

Pancit Guisado

USE FRESH CHINESE NOODLES OR REGULAR EGG NOODLES IN THIS PHILIPPINE DISH.

1/4 pound lean, fat-trimmed, boneless pork

2 tablespoons Chinese soy sauce

1 tablespoon sweet Hungarian paprika or other mild, sweet paprika

1/8–1 teaspoon medium hot cayenne (optional)

1 1/2 pounds fresh wheat noodles or 1 pound dried egg noodles

1 tablespoon plus 1 teaspoon canola oil

1/4 pound shelled prawns or shrimp

2 cups chopped onions

2 cups chopped fresh broccoli

2 cups bean sprouts

2 cups chopped fresh tomatoes

4 cups shredded fresh spinach, loosely packed

Juice of 1 large lemon

2 tablespoons Thai or Philippine fish sauce

2 tablespoons brown sugar

Mince the pork and put it in a bowl with 1 teaspoon of the soy sauce, 1/2 teaspoon of the paprika, and all of the cayenne. Set it aside to blend the flavors.

Boil the noodles in a large kettle of water until barely tender (about 2 to 4 minutes for fresh noodles or 4 to 9 minutes for dried noodles). Drain immediately, rinse with cold water, and drain thoroughly.

Heat the oil in a very large wok and stir-fry the pork until it browns. Add the shrimp, stir-fry for 30 seconds, then add the onions and broccoli. Stir-fry about 2 minutes, then add the noodles and cook until very hot. Next add the bean sprouts, tomatoes, and spinach and cook until the vegetables are wilted. Add the remaining ingredients, mix, and serve.

SERVES 4—680 cal.; 15g (20% of cal.) total fat; 3.3g (4%) saturated fat; 106g (62%) carbohydrate; 99mg cholesterol; and 900mg sodium per serving

Chicken Lo Mein

1 pound dry egg noodles or
  1½ pounds fresh Chinese noodles
3 small, skinned, boned, fat-trimmed
  chicken thighs
1 tablespoon canola oil
1 teaspoon sesame oil
2 large carrots, thinly sliced
4 cloves garlic, mashed or chopped

2 tablespoons minced fresh ginger
½ pound bean sprouts, rinsed
1 cup homemade chicken stock
  (see page 22)
2 tablespoons oyster sauce
1½ tablespoons soy sauce
2 teaspoons sugar

Cook the noodles in boiling water as directed on package (about 4 to 9 minutes for dried noodles or 2 to 4 minutes for fresh noodles). Drain them immediately.

Chop the chicken into ¼- to ½-inch cubes.

Heat the oils in a large wok and stir-fry the chicken until it is opaque.

Add the carrots, garlic, and ginger and fry about 2 minutes, then add the noodles, cooking them about 2 more minutes. Add the bean sprouts and cook until very hot.

Mix the stock, oyster sauce, soy sauce, and sugar together and pour it in. Heat thoroughly and serve.

SERVES 4—644 cal.; 14g (20% of cal.) total fat; 2.2g (3%) saturated fat; 96g (60%) carbohydrate; ±50mg cholesterol; and ±900mg sodium per serving

Bamie Goreng

BAMIE GORENG IS INDONESIA'S BEST-KNOWN VERSION OF FRIED NOODLES. TRADITIONALLY, THEY ARE SERVED WITH SLICES OF HARD-BOILED EGG. THIS RECIPE LEAVES THE EGGS OUT.

½ large (or 1 whole small) chicken breast, skinned
1 teaspoon turmeric
1 teaspoon sereh (lemon grass) powder (optional)
½ teaspoon cinnamon
¼–1 teaspoon medium hot chili powder
1 pound dry egg noodles
1 tablespoon plus 1 teaspoon canola or safflower oil

2 cups thinly sliced carrots
¼ cup minced shallots or onions
2 tablespoons minced fresh gingerroot
2 cups green beans cut in 1-inch lengths
2 cups thinly sliced zucchini
1 pound bok choy, chopped
1 tablespoon soy sauce
2 tablespoons ketjap manis
¼ cup chopped fresh cilantro or flat-leafed parsley

Bone the chicken and cut the meat into ½-inch cubes. Roll them in the turmeric, sereh, cinnamon, and chili.

Cook the noodles until tender (about 4 to 9 minutes). Drain, rinse with cold water, and set aside.

Heat the oil in a large wok and stir-fry the chicken cubes until golden. Add the carrots, shallots, and ginger, cook 1 minute, then add the green beans and zucchini. Cook until the beans are tender, then add the bok choy and noodles. Stir-fry until very hot. Stir in the last ingredients and serve.

SERVES 4—669 cal.; 13g (17% of cal.) total fat; 3.5g (5%) saturated fat; 102g (61%) carbohydrate; 45mg cholesterol; and 843mg sodium per serving

Fried Rice with a Mexican Flair

2 cups long grain white rice
3 cups water
½ cup clam broth or fish fumet
  (see page 23)
1 tablespoon plus 1 teaspoon olive oil
½ pound cleaned shrimp
10 cloves garlic, minced

¼ cup chopped Spanish green
  olives, stuffed with pimientos
2 cups chopped fresh tomatoes
2 tablespoons capers
2 teaspoons California or similar
  mild chili powder

Simmer the rice in the water and clam broth until moisture is absorbed and rice is tender.

Heat the oil in a wok or very large skillet and sauté the shrimp until they are pink. Add the garlic and rice and stir-fry for about 1 minute, then add the remaining ingredients. Stir-fry just until very hot, then serve.

SERVES 4—507 cal.; 9g (16% of cal.) total fat; 1.3g (2%) saturated fat; 93g (70%) carbohydrate; 56mg cholesterol; and 371mg sodium per serving

Fried Rice Stick Noodles

Fresh basil strikes a pleasing note in these Thai noodles.

14 ounces rice stick noodles
1 1/2 tablespoons canola oil
10 ounces cleaned prawns, cut in
   1/2-inch lengths
4 cups sliced zucchini or
   other summer squash
2 cups chopped onions
2 cups chopped fresh tomatoes
1 cup chopped fresh sweet red pepper

1/4 cup chopped fresh Thai basil or
   sweet basil
2 tablespoons Thai fish sauce or
   1/4 teaspoon anchovy paste
1 1/2 tablespoons brown sugar
1 teaspoon cinnamon
1/2 teaspoon tamarind concentrate or
   juice of 1 lemon (optional)
1/8–1/2 teaspoon mild or hot cayenne

Snap the noodles into small pieces and put them in a large bowl. Pour boiling water over them and let them soak several minutes, then drain.

Heat the oil in a large wok and stir-fry the prawns first, adding the zucchini and onions when the prawns are pink. Add the noodles, stir-fry until golden, then add the remaining ingredients in the order listed. Heat thoroughly and serve.

SERVES 4—550 cal.; 6g (10% of cal.) total fat; 0.9g (1%) saturated fat; 103g (72%) carbohydrate; 105mg cholesterol; and ±600mg sodium per serving

CHAPTER 8

Pizzas and Similar Grain-Wrapped Foods

Long before John Montague, the Fourth Earl of Sandwich, invented a genre of bread-wrapped treats that bears his name, the world's humbler folk enjoyed similar grain-enveloped foods. Sandwiches may come first to Americans' minds, but pizzas run a close second. This open-faced sandwich, which seems uniquely Italian, also appears in French and Middle Eastern cuisines as pissaladière and lamah. China's dim sum repertoire features many grain-coated appetizers, like steamed buns, pot stickers, wontons, and spring rolls. Mexican cooks contribute enchiladas, tamales, burritos, and quesadillas. Empanadas are Caribbean favorites, not too different in character from Cornish pasties and Russia's piroshkis. Pita pocket bread, long a Middle Eastern staple, is now an American favorite. French crepes or buckwheat galettes may embrace the simplest leftovers or elegant fare. The same is true for Russian buckwheat blinis, as delectable with scraps of ham as traditional caviar. Some breads, notably Indian chapatis and Ethiopian injera, are even used as edible spoons.

Although the recipes in this chapter all contain no more than 20 percent fat, you shouldn't assume that all, or even most, pizza or enchilada recipes are equally lean. Certainly pizzas slathered with mozzarella and sausage, cheese enchiladas soused with sour cream, or empanadas encased in pastry, aren't. While they're fine for infrequent indulgences, you can easily create leaner versions for everyday fare.

For inspiration, look through cookbooks devoted to pizzas, Mexican or Italian cuisines, or check those on the foods of China (for dim sum), the Middle East (for pocket breads), the Caribbean (empanadas), and Russia (piroshkis). To keep these lean, look for the main sources of fat.

Pastry crusts. Use a pizza dough instead.

Sour cream. Use nonfat sour cream. You won't notice much difference in these spicy dishes.

The amount and kind of meat. Use the smallest amount possible, and substitute trimmed chicken or fish for pork or beef. Add extra vegetables and/or beans (as appropriate to the cuisine) for substance, texture, and flavor.

Cheese. Use a small amount of reduced-fat mozzarella on pizzas. Save your cheese-fat indulgences for another time—and a really fine cheese.

The two pizza recipes that follow show how a few judicious substitutions can reduce the fat by more than half.

Pepperoni and Cheese Pizza

ALTHOUGH THIS RECIPE PRODUCES A LEANER PIZZA THAN YOU'LL GET IN YOUR SUPERMARKET OR CORNER TAKE-OUT PIZZERIA, IT STILL CONTAINS 37 PERCENT FAT.

1 recipe pizza dough (see page 180)
1 recipe basic tomato sauce
 (see page 78)

1/2 cup sliced mozzarella cheese
1/2 pound pepperoni, thinly sliced

SERVES 4

NUTRITIONAL CONTENTS (PER SERVING)

Food	Calories	Protein		Total fat	Saturated fat	Carbohydrate
		gram (% cal.)		gram (% cal.)	gram (% cal.)	gram (% cal.)
Dough	472	13	(6%)	5 (5%)	±0.5 (1%)	92 (43%)
Sauce	58	2	(1%)	2 (2%)	±0.2 trace	9 (4%)
Cheese	90	6	(3%)	7 (7%)	4.0 (4%)	trace
Pepperoni	243	11	(5%)	22 (23%)	8.1 (8%)	2 (1%)
Total	863	32		36	12.8	103
% of calories		15%		37%	13%	48%

Pizza Dough

USE THIS BASIC DOUGH FOR PIZZAS, CALZONES, AND EVEN THE EMPANADAS, PASTIES, AND PIROSHKIS THAT ARE USUALLY WRAPPED IN RICH PASTRY CRUSTS.

1⅓ cup warm (110 degrees F) water

1 package (about 2½ teaspoons) dry yeast

1 tablespoon olive oil

1 teaspoon sugar

¼ teaspoon salt

4 cups flour

2 tablespoons cornmeal or semolina to dust baking stones or a little olive oil to grease metal pans

Put the warm water in a very large mixing bowl and sprinkle the yeast over it.

After a few minutes, stir the yeast until it is dissolved, then add the oil, sugar, and salt.

Slowly beat in the flour, kneading the last bits in by hand. Turn the dough out onto a floured board and knead it for 4 to 5 minutes. If you use a food processor or mixer to knead the dough, follow the manufacturer's instructions.

Put the kneaded dough in an oiled mixing bowl, cover, and set it in a warm place to rise.

When the dough has doubled in volume, punch it down, divide in two, and lay one piece on a floured board.

Roll it into a 12- to 14-inch circle. Lay the circle on a baking stone dusted with cornmeal or on a large, oiled cookie sheet. Crimp the edges up slightly like a pie.

Cover the dough with a damp towel and set it aside in a warm place to rise for an additional 15 to 30 minutes. Repeat with the second ball of dough.

While it rises, preheat the oven to 425 degrees. Set it a little lower (about 400 degrees) if you use a dark metal baking sheet and find the crust burns at 425.

Spread the topping over the crust and bake until the crust is golden, usually about 20 to 30 minutes.

MAKES 2 10- to 12-inch pizza crusts (4 large servings)—472 cal.; 5g (10% of cal.) total fat; 0.5g saturated fat; 92g (78%) carbohydrate; 0 cholesterol; and 137mg sodium per serving

Adapted Pizza

THIS RECIPE USES EQUALLY TYPICAL TOPPINGS, YET THE FAT IS REDUCED BY MORE THAN HALF BY CUTTING THE CHEESE (AND USING A REDUCED-FAT TYPE), AND BY SUBSTITUTING A TINY AMOUNT OF PUNGENT ANCHOVIES FOR THE PEPPERONI.

1 recipe pizza dough (page 180)
1 recipe basic tomato sauce (page 78)
2 ounces reduced-fat mozzarella

1 2-ounce can anchovy filets
1½ cups sliced mushrooms
2 cups sliced onions

To prepare this pizza, follow the directions for any of the next pizzas, using the above toppings.

SERVES 4

NUTRITIONAL CONTENTS (PER SERVING)

Food	Calories	Protein	Total fat	Saturated fat	Carbohydrate
		gram (% cal.)	gram (% cal.)	gram (% cal.)	gram (% cal.)
Anchovy	25	3 (2%)	1 (1%)	0.4 (1%)	—
Dough	472	13 (8%)	5 (7%)	0.5 (1%)	92 (60%)
Sauce	58	2 (1%)	2 (3%)	—	9 (6%)
Cheese	35	3 (2%)	2 (3%)	1.4 (2%)	trace
Mushroom	12	1 (1%)	trace	—	2 (1%)
Onion	16	trace	trace	—	3 (2%)
Total	618	22	10	2.3	106
% of calories		14%	14%	4%	69%

Sunny Pizza

SEA BASS IS A GOOD FISH TO USE ON PIZZAS BECAUSE IT TOLERATES HIGH BAKING TEMPERA-
TURES BETTER THAN MOST FISH. THE SUN-DRIED TOMATOES, WHICH LEND A SMOKY, ROASTED
NUANCE, BURN MORE READILY. ADD THEM AT THE LAST MINUTE.

1 recipe pizza dough (see page 180)
1 recipe basic tomato sauce
  (see page 78)
1 ounce dry or ²/₃ cup rehydrated
  sun-dried tomatoes

Cornmeal or olive oil to coat
  baking pans
¹/₂ pound sea bass
1 cup thinly sliced fennel
20–30 large fresh basil leaves

Prepare the dough and tomato sauce then reduce the sauce to about 3 cups by
boiling and stirring constantly to prevent sticking.

Put the sun-dried tomatoes in a small bowl and cover with warm water.

Preheat the oven to 425 degrees. Roll the dough, place on baking stones
dusted with cornmeal or oiled pans, and let it rest for 15 to 30 minutes, then
spoon the sauce over them.

Remove any bones from the sea bass and cut it into ¹/₂-inch slices. Sprinkle
the fish and fennel over the tops. Bake until the crusts are golden, or for about
20 to 35 minutes.

Drain and chop the tomatoes. Decorate the pizzas with these and the basil
leaves. Return to the oven and bake 2 minutes longer. Let the pizzas cool for a
minute before cutting.

SERVES 4—595 cal.; 8g (12% of cal.) total fat; ±1.1g (2%) saturated fat;
104g (70%) carbohydrate; 23mg cholesterol; and ±590mg sodium per
serving

Swiss Chard Pizza

SWISS CHARD COOKED WITH LEMON AND OLIVE OIL IS A CLASSIC ITALIAN SIDE DISH. HERE
THE SAME COMBINATION EMBELLISHES A PIZZA.

1 pizza dough recipe (see page 180)
Cornmeal or olive oil to coat
 baking pans
1½ tablespoons olive oil
2 pounds (10 cups) shredded Swiss
 chard
15–20 cloves of garlic, peeled and
 thinly sliced
Juice of 1 lemon

½ cup dry red wine (optional)
¼ pound chopped ham or
 hot Italian sausage
2–4 teaspoons sugar
Pinch of freshly grated nutmeg
2 cups sliced mushrooms
1 cup sliced onions
2 tablespoons grated Parmesan cheese

Prepare and roll the pizza dough. Lay it on baking stones dusted with cornmeal
or large, oiled cookie sheets.

Heat the oil in a large skillet over a moderate flame. Add the chard and garlic and sauté briefly. Stir, cover the pan, reduce the heat, and cook, stirring occasionally, for at least 10 minutes. Add the lemon juice, wine, ham, sugar, and
nutmeg. Cover and cook until the chard is soft and reduced to about 5 to 6
cups. Don't let it burn.

Preheat the oven to 425 degrees.

Spread the chard over the pizza doughs, cover with the mushrooms and
onions, then dust the tops with the cheese. Bake 20 to 30 minutes, until the
crust is golden.

SERVES 4—689 cal.; 14g (18%) total fat; 3.1g (4%) saturated fat; 107g
(62%) carbohydrate; 19mg cholesterol; and 833mg sodium per serving

Artichoke Pizza

ARTICHOKE HEARTS AND ANCHOVIES DECORATE THIS PIZZA. THE LATTER ARE VERY SALTY. SUBSTITUTE FRESH FISH OR SHELLFISH IF YOU'RE ON A SODIUM-RESTRICTED DIET. THE RESULTING PIZZA WILL HAVE HALF THE SODIUM SHOWN BELOW.

1 recipe pizza dough (see page 180)
Cornmeal or olive oil to coat
  baking pans
1 recipe basic tomato sauce
  (see page 78)

2 9-ounce packages frozen
  artichoke hearts
2 2-ounce cans anchovy fillets
2 cups thinly sliced red onion

Prepare the dough and place on baking stones dusted with cornmeal or on oiled pans.

Reduce the tomato sauce to about 3 cups over medium-high heat. Cool slightly.

Preheat the oven to 425 degrees.

Thaw the artichoke hearts and chop coarsely. Drain the anchovies and pat any residual oil off the fillets with paper towels.

Spoon the sauce over the prepared doughs. Decorate the tops with the anchovies, artichokes pieces, and onion slices. Bake 20 to 30 minutes, until the crust is golden.

SERVES 4—655 cal.; 8g (11% of cal.) total fat; 1.2g (2%) saturated fat; 121g (74%) carbohydrate; low cholesterol; 1,070mg sodium per serving

Mushroom and Mussel Pizza

FRESH MUSSELS ARE A SEASONAL ITEM. USE ANY OTHER SHELLFISH IF MUSSELS AREN'T AVAILABLE.

1 recipe pizza dough (see page 180)
Cornmeal or olive oil to coat
  baking pans
1 recipe basic tomato sauce
  (see page 78)

²/₃ pound fresh shucked or
  cooked mussels
4 cups sliced mushrooms
1 cup diced onions

Prepare the dough and place on baking stones dusted with cornmeal or on oiled pans.

Reduce the tomato sauce to about 3 cups over medium-high heat. Cool slightly.

Preheat the oven to 425 degrees.

Clean the mussels as needed and set them aside in the refrigerator.

Spoon the sauce over the prepared doughs, then distribute the mushroom slices and onions over the tops and bake for 15 minutes.

Remove from the oven carefully, place the mussels over the top, and return to the oven. Bake until the crust is golden and the mussels are cooked (an additional 5 to 15 minutes).

SERVES 4—642 cal.; 8g (11% of cal.) total fat; 1.2g (2%) saturated fat; 111g (69%) carbohydrate; 22mg cholesterol; and 359mg sodium per serving

Black and White Pizza

Cleaning squid is a messy job, but it's worth the effort. If you haven't the time or stomach for it, buy it precleaned or use baby scallops instead.

1 recipe pizza dough (see page 180)
Cornmeal or olive oil to coat
  baking pans
1 recipe basic tomato sauce
  (see page 78)

1 pound of whole squid or
  ²/₃ pound cleaned squid
4 cups thinly sliced zucchini
1 cup thinly sliced white onions
¹/₄ cup chopped black olives

Prepare the dough and place on baking stones dusted with cornmeal or on oiled pans.

Reduce the tomato sauce to about 3 cups over medium-high heat. Cool slightly.

Preheat the oven to 425 degrees.

To clean the squid, run a knife into its body cavity opposite the quill side. Slit it open and discard all the interior material. Pull out the quill and discard it as well. Chop the tentacles off and save them, but discard the head. Rinse the cleaned bodies and tentacles and slice them thinly. If you bought the squid precleaned, simply rinse and slice.

Spoon the sauce over the prepared pizza doughs. Lay the squid strips on tops, then add the zucchini, onions, and olives. Bake 20 to 30 minutes, until the crusts are golden.

Serves 4—652 cal.; 10g (14% of cal.) total fat; 1.2g (2%) saturated fat; 111g (68%) carbohydrate; 168mg cholesterol; and 314mg sodium per serving

Sardine Pissaladière

THIS PIZZA, HAILING FROM THE FRENCH MEDITERRANEAN REGION, IS TRADITIONALLY MADE
WITH ANCHOVIES AND IS SERVED AS A SNACK. THIS VERSION CALLS FOR EQUALLY ASSERTIVE
SARDINES. USE EITHER.

1 recipe pizza dough (see page 180)
Cornmeal or olive oil to coat
   baking pans
4 cups chopped fresh tomatoes
2 cups chopped onions
3–4 cloves garlic, mashed
Juice of 1 lemon

1½ tablespoons sugar
1 teaspoon chopped fresh or
   dried rosemary
1 cup sardines, canned in tomato
   sauce (or fresh, if available)
¼ cup halved olives

Prepare the dough and place on baking stones dusted with cornmeal or on oiled pans.

Put the tomatoes, onions, garlic, lemon juice, sugar, and rosemary in a large, heavy skillet and cook the mixture over moderate heat until most of the liquid has evaporated. Cool slightly.

Preheat the oven to 425 degrees.

Spread the tomato sauce over the prepared doughs.

Cut the sardines into narrow strips. Decorate the pizza tops with the strips and the olives. Bake 20 to 30 minutes, until the crust is golden. Serve hot or warm.

SERVES **4 as a large main course or 12 to 16 as an appetizer—706 cal.; 13g (17%) total fat; 2.6g (3%) saturated fat; 113g (64%) carbohydrate; 81mg cholesterol; and 543mg sodium per large serving**

Lamah

This pizza is made throughout much of the Middle East, often in the form of hors d'oeuvres rather than as a large pizza.

1 recipe pizza dough (see page 180)
Cornmeal or olive oil to coat
 baking pans
1/2 pound lean, fat-trimmed,
 boneless lamb shoulder
2 teaspoons olive oil
2 cups chopped onions
3–4 cloves garlic, mashed

2 teaspoons ground cumin
1 teaspoon ground allspice
1/4 teaspoon mild or hot cayenne
 pepper (optional)
4 cups chopped tomatoes
1 1/2 tablespoons sugar
1/4 cup chopped fresh parsley

Make the pizza dough and place on baking stones dusted with cornmeal or on oiled pans.

Mince the lamb as finely as possible.

Brown the minced lamb lightly in the oil in a heavy skillet, then add the onions, garlic, and spices and cook until the onion is limp. Add the chopped tomatoes and sugar and scrape up any bits of meat stuck to the pan. Cook, stirring occasionally, over medium heat until the sauce is reduced and the tomato juice evaporated.

Stir in the parsley and set the sauce aside in the refrigerator if you aren't ready to use it within 15 minutes.

Preheat the oven to 425 degrees.

Spread the sauce over the doughs and bake 20 to 30 minutes, until the crusts are golden.

SERVES 4 as a main course or 12 to 16 as an appetizer—679 cal.; 13g (17%) total fat; 2.9g (4%) saturated fat; 112g (66%) carbohydrate; 48mg cholesterol; and 322mg sodium per large serving

Sardine Calzone

ITALIAN CALZONES ARE ESSENTIALLY PIZZAS WITH ONE-HALF THE DOUGH FOLDED OVER THE OTHER HALF. IF SARDINES ARE TOO FISHY FOR YOU, SUBSTITUTE ANY FAVORITE PIZZA FILLING.

2/3 cup warm (110 degrees) water
2/3 cup warm (110 degrees)
   nonfat milk
1 package (about 2 1/2 teaspoons)
   dry yeast
1 teaspoon sugar
1/4 teaspoon salt
3 1/2 cups unbleached white flour
2 teaspoons olive oil

1 1/3 cups (about 10 ounces)
   tomato-packed sardines
5 cups sliced fresh mushrooms
1/2 cup chopped fresh basil
6–8 cloves garlic, mashed
Juice and grated peel of 1 lemon
Cornmeal or olive oil to coat
   baking sheets

Put the warm water and milk in a very large mixing bowl and sprinkle the yeast over it.

After a few minutes, stir the yeast until it is dissolved, then add the sugar and salt.

Slowly beat in the flour, kneading the last bits in by hand. Turn the dough out onto a floured board and knead it for 4 to 5 minutes.

Put the kneaded dough in an oiled mixing bowl, cover, and set it in a warm place to rise.

When the dough has doubled in volume, punch it down, divide it in four pieces and roll each piece into a 12-inch circle on a floured board.

Preheat the oven to 450 degrees.

Spread the upper surface of each circle with 1/2 teaspoon of the oil.

Mix the sardines, mushrooms, basil, garlic, lemon juice, and lemon peel. Put 1/4 of this filling on half of the oiled surface of each of the dough circles, leaving about 1 inch free around each edge. Moisten the edge of the dough with water and fold the opposite sides of the dough over the fillings and crimp the edges together securely.

Put the calzones on a baking stone dusted with cornmeal or on a lightly oiled baking sheet and let them rise again for about 20 minutes.

Bake for about 10 minutes, then reduce the heat to 400 degrees and bake an additional 15 to 25 minutes until the crust is golden and the filling is extremely hot.

Remove the calzones from the oven and let them cool for 2 to 3 minutes before serving.

SERVES 4—600 cal.; 13g (20% of cal.) total fat; 2.8g (4%) saturated fat; 92g (61%) carbohydrate; 45mg cholesterol; and 485mg sodium per serving

Beef Empanada

OLIVES, SHERRY, AND SWEET/SOUR FLAVORS OF DRIED FRUIT AND VINEGAR ACCENTUATE THE MEATY FLAVOR OF THESE LATIN AMERICAN TURNOVERS.

1¹/₃ cup warm (110 degrees) nonfat milk

1 package (about 2¹/₂ teaspoons) dry yeast

2 teaspoons sugar

1¹/₂ tablespoons olive oil

¹/₄ teaspoon salt

3¹/₂–4 cups flour

¹/₂ pound lean, fat-trimmed, boneless beef rump, minced

2 teaspoons ground cinnamon

1 cup chopped onion

1¹/₂ cups chopped potatoes

1¹/₂ cups chopped tomatoes

4 large pitted prunes, chopped

¹/₃ cup chopped pitted olives

¹/₄ cup dry sherry

¹/₄ cup raisins

2 tablespoons rice wine vinegar or malt vinegar or lime juice

1¹/₂ tablespoons chopped fresh oregano or 2 teaspoons dried oregano

2 teaspoons capers (optional)

Cornmeal or olive oil to coat baking sheets

2 tablespoons nonfat milk

Put the warm milk in a very large mixing bowl and sprinkle the yeast over it.

After a few minutes, stir the yeast until it is dissolved, then add the sugar, 2 teaspoons of the oil, and the salt.

Slowly beat in the flour, kneading the last bits in by hand. Turn the dough out onto a floured board and knead it for 4 to 5 minutes.

Put the kneaded dough in an oiled mixing bowl, cover, and set it in a warm place to rise.

Mix the beef and cinnamon and set it aside in the refrigerator to blend the flavors.

After the dough has risen, punch it down, divide it in four pieces, and roll each on a floured board into thin 10- to 11-inch circles. Cover the circles with a towel and let them rise while you prepare the filling.

Preheat the oven to 425 degrees.

Heat the remaining oil over a moderate heat in a heavy, covered skillet. Brown the beef lightly, then add the onion, potatoes, tomatoes, and prunes. Cover the pan and cook until the potatoes are soft. Add a little water if necessary to keep the mixture from sticking to the pan. If any liquid remains after the potatoes are cooked, remove the lid, raise the heat, and evaporate the excess, stirring constantly so it doesn't stick.

Stir in the olives, sherry, raisins, vinegar, oregano, and capers and cook for about 30 seconds to heat them through.

Place equal amounts of the mixture on half of each dough circle, keeping at least ³⁄₄ inch of the dough's edge free of filling.

Moisten the edge of the dough with water and fold the free side over the filling. Crimp the edges together firmly.

Lay the empanadas on a large baking stone sprinkled with the cornmeal or on baking sheets greased with oil. Slash the tops to let steam escape, and brush with the milk.

Bake in the preheated oven until the crust is golden, or about 20 to 25 minutes. Remove from the oven and let them cool for 2 to 3 minutes before serving.

Serves 4—684 cal.; 11g (14% of cal.) total fat; 2.5g (3%) saturated fat; 118g (69%) carbohydrate; 40mg cholesterol; and 521mg sodium per serving

Mushroom Piroshki

DILL AND YOGURT ACCENTUATE THE EARTHY FLAVORS OF MUSHROOM AND BEEF IN THESE TRADITIONAL RUSSIAN TURNOVERS. USE FRESH DILL, IF POSSIBLE.

1 1/3 cups warm (110 degrees) nonfat milk

1 package (about 2 1/2 teaspoons) dry yeast

2 teaspoons sugar

2 teaspoons olive oil

1/4 teaspoon salt

3 1/2–4 cups flour

1/2 pound lean, fat-trimmed, boneless beef rump

1 1/2 tablespoons canola oil

2 cups finely chopped onion

4 cups minced fresh mushrooms

1/4 cup shredded radish greens (optional)

1/4 cup flour

1/2 cup unflavored nonfat yogurt or nonfat sour cream

1/4 cup chopped fresh parsley

1 1/2 tablespoons chopped fresh or dried dillweed

Cornmeal or olive oil to coat baking pans

2 tablespoons nonfat milk

Put the warm milk in a very large mixing bowl and sprinkle the yeast over it.

After a few minutes, stir the yeast until it is dissolved, then add the sugar, olive oil, and salt.

Slowly beat in the flour, kneading the last bits in by hand. Turn the dough out onto a floured board and knead it for 4 to 5 minutes.

Put the kneaded dough in an oiled mixing bowl, cover, and set it in a warm place to rise.

After dough has doubled in size, punch it down and divide it into 4 pieces. Roll each piece out on a floured board into a 10-inch circle.

Preheat the oven to 425 degrees.

Mince the beef as fine as possible.

Lightly brown the beef in the canola oil in a large skillet. Add the onion and cook until it is soft. Add the mushrooms and cook for about 1 minute.

Stir in the remaining ingredients except the cornmeal and milk. Cook just long enough to heat through.

Put one-quarter of the filling on half of each circle, leaving at least ¾ inch at the edge free of filling. Moisten the edge of the dough with water. Fold the dough over the filling and crimp the edges together firmly.

Lay the piroshkis on a large baking stone dusted with the cornmeal or on a large cookie sheet greased with the oil. Slash the tops to allow steam to escape and brush with milk.

Bake until the crust is golden and the interior cooked (about 20 to 25 minutes). Let them cool for a minute before serving.

SERVES 4—654 cal.; 13g (18% of cal.) total fat; 3.5g (5%) saturated fat; 101g (62%) carbohydrate; 40mg cholesterol; and 385mg sodium per serving

Pork and Bean Burrito

THE PRUNES GIVE AN UNRECOGNIZABLE BUT ELUSIVE SWEET COUNTERPOINT TO THE FILLING.

½ pound lean, fat-trimmed,
   boneless pork
2 cups chopped onions
1 cup chopped, pitted prunes
2 cups water
1¾ cups cooked pinto beans or
   1 16-ounce can pinto beans
¼ cup dry red or white wine
1 teaspoon chopped fresh or dried
   epasote or 1 tablespoon chopped
   fresh cilantro

2 teaspoons ground cumin
½–2 teaspoons mild or hot ground
   chili
1 teaspoon ground cinnamon
1 tablespoon wine or cider vinegar
4 9- to 10-inch flour tortillas

Simmer the pork, onions, and prunes with the water in a saucepan for about 30 minutes. Remove the pork, set aside to cool slightly, then shred the meat.

Raise the heat under the pan and evaporate most of the water. Mash the prunes and onions, then mix in the shredded pork.

Simmer the beans with the wine, spices, herbs, and vinegar for a few minutes, then mash this mixture.

Warm the tortillas on a dry griddle or heavy skillet.

Spread a thin layer of the bean mixture over most of the tortillas' surfaces. Put a long strip of the pork mixture along the center of each. Fold the tortilla sides over the filling. Keep warm until serving.

SERVES 4—540 cal.; 11g (18% of cal.) total fat; 2.9g (5%) saturated fat; 84g (62%) carbohydrate; 37mg cholesterol; and 507mg sodium per serving

CHAPTER 9

Grain Salads

Around the world, whenever temperatures soar, cooks turn to cold grains. The Italians prepare pasta or rice salads, the Japanese and Chinese respectively relish cold buckwheat and wheat noodles, while Middle Easterners are justifiably proud of their bulgur salad, tabouli. Most are very easy to prepare, so serve them often as summer main-course items, and year round for picnics and brownbag lunches.

Virtually all grain salads can be very lean, as long as you use a low-fat dressing. Be cautious about the amount of oil, mayonnaise, or sour cream suggested. Use a really good extra-virgin olive oil. It will add many times as much flavor as a common oil. Good vinegars are also worth the money. You don't need much to get a splendid flavor.

The two versions of macaroni salad that follow show how easy it is to cut out lots of fat. The first recipe resembles one found in a best-selling American cookbook. Almost half its calories are derived from fat. The adapted recipe is at least as tasty but has only 11 percent fat. This drastic reduction in fat is accomplished by increasing the pasta and vegetables, replacing the ham with poached fish, and instead of a sour cream dressing, the low-fat version uses one based on nonfat yogurt and the fish's poaching liquid.

Techniques

Plan ahead when you make these salads. Many taste best from 2 to 24 hours after they're made. This gives the pasta or other grain time to absorb the dressing without loosing the freshness of any of its fruits or vegetables.

Most grains should be cooked until they become al dente. At this toothsome stage they remain distinct and pleasantly chewy. Some grains, like white rice and most pastas, cook within 5 to 10 minutes. Other grains take longer—up to an hour for triticale and similar coarse, whole grains. Avoid using all sticky grains in salads.

Use one of these simple procedures, depending on the basic grain.

PARBOILING GRAINS AND PASTA

Bring a large kettle of water to a boil. Use at least 10 to 12 cups of water for 2 cups of grain or 3/4 to 1 pound of pasta.

Drizzle the grain or pasta into the water. Stir it occasionally with a fork or slotted spoon. Boil them until they are barely tender and chewy, which is the al dente stage. Most grains reach this stage about 10 to 15 minutes faster than if they're steamed on the stovetop. You can approximate the required times by subtracting those values from the times given in the table on page 109.

Don't overcook grain and pasta or they will loose their individuality and pleasing texture.

Drain the grain or pasta in a large sieve or colander. Rinse briefly with cold water to arrest the cooking and remove excess starch, then drain again. Lift the grains a few times with a fork so they don't settle into each other, then put it into a bowl, mix with the salad's remaining components, and chill for several hours.

REHYDRATING GRAINS

A few grains such as couscous, fine bulgur, and buckwheat kasha become tender when simply moistened. Specific directions for these are given in individual recipes.

LEFTOVER COOKED GRAINS

You can use most leftover cooked grains in salads, though they tend to be stickier than freshly cooked grains. Break apart any clumps of these before you add the other ingredients. If necessary, you can plunge them into a bowl of cold water, crumble the clumps with your fingers, and drain very thoroughly.

Leftover grains may require more dressing to moisten, so be ready to make extra if necessary.

Macaroni and Ham Salad

8 ounces elbow macaroni
1 pound cooked ham
2 cups celery
1 cup olives
1 cup fresh parsley*

½ cup chopped chives*
2 tablespoons olive oil
6 tablespoons sour cream
¼ cup lemon juice*

SERVES 4

NUTRITIONAL CONTENTS (PER SERVING)

Food*	Calories	Protein		Total fat		Saturated fat		Carbohydrate	
		gram	(% cal.)	gram	(% cal.)	gram	(% cal.)	gram	(% cal.)
Pasta	210	7	(5%)	1	(1%)	—		44	(29%)
Ham	188	24	(15%)	9	(13%)	3.8	(6%)	—	
Celery	5	trace		—		—		1	(1%)
Olives	104	1	(1%)	11	(16%)	1.2	(2%)	2	(1%)
Sour cream	39	trace		4	(6%)	2.4	(3%)	1	(1%)
Oil	63	—		7	(10%)	0.8	(1%)	—	
Total	609	32		32		8.2		48	
% of calories			22%		46%		12%		32%

*Ingredients with trivial calories aren't shown.

Adapted Macaroni Salad

1 pound elbow macaroni
1/2 pound sea bass
2 tablespoons white wine
4 cups celery
1/4 cup olives
1 cup parsley*

1/2 cup chives*
1 cup pimiento
1 1/3 cups nonfat yogurt
1/2 cup lemon juice*
1 1/3 tablespoons mayonnaise

SERVES 4

NUTRITIONAL CONTENTS (PER SERVING)

Food*	Calories	Protein	Total fat	Saturated fat	Carbohydrate
		gram (% cal.)	gram (% cal.)	gram (% cal.)	gram (% cal.)
Fish	45	8 (5%)	1 (1%)	0.2 (trace)	2 (1%)
Wine	6	—	—	—	trace
Pasta	420	15 (10%)	1 (1%)	—	87 (60%)
Celery	18	1 (1%)	trace	—	4 (3%)
Olives	26	trace	3 (5%)	0.3 (1%)	trace
Pimiento	10	trace	—	—	2 (1%)
Yogurt	37	4 (3%)	trace	—	6 (4%)
Mayonnaise	20	—	2 (3%)	0.4 (1%)	—
Total	582	28	7	0.9	101
% of calories		19%	11%	2%	69%

*Ingredients with trivial calories not shown.

Macaroni Salad

THIS IS THE COMPLETE VERSION OF THE RECIPE THAT APPEARS ON PAGE 200.

1 pound elbow macaroni
1/2 pound sea bass or halibut
2 tablespoons white wine
4 cups diced celery
4 tablespoons chopped olives
1 cup chopped fresh parsley
1/2 cup chopped fresh chives or scallion tops

1 cup diced fresh or pickled pimiento
1 1/3 cups nonfat yogurt or nonfat sour cream
1/2 cup lemon juice
1 1/3 tablespoons mayonnaise

Cook the pasta until tender (about 4 to 8 minutes).

Simmer the fish in wine until cooked. Cool slightly, remove any bones, and shred.

Put the pasta and fish in a large bowl. Mix the remaining ingredients and stir them into the pasta. Chill before serving.

SERVES 4—582 cal.; 7.3g (11% of cal.) total fat; ±0.9g (2%) saturated fat; 101g (69%) carbohydrate; 32mg cholesterol; and 678mg sodium per serving

Variation. Replace the cooked fish with 1 6-ounce can of albacore tuna and add 2 or 3 tablespoons of capers.

Pasta and Smoked Turkey Salad

LEFTOVER SMOKED OR BARBECUED TURKEY ADDS THE PERFECT NOTE TO THIS SALAD. USE SMOKED SALMON, OR LEFTOVER COOKED CHICKEN, IF YOU PREFER.

1 pound pasta shells
2 cups chopped fresh tomatillos or 2 11-ounce cans tomatillos, drained and crushed
2 small serrano chilies
2/3 cup water
1/3 pound cooked, smoked turkey thigh, diced

2 cups chopped celery
1 cup nonfat plain yogurt
3–4 cloves garlic, minced
2 tablespoons chopped cilantro
1 1/2 tablespoons olive oil
2 tablespoons rice vinegar
2 teaspoons sugar
1 teaspoon ground California chili

Cook the pasta until it is al dente (about 6 to 11 minutes). Drain, rinse with cold water. Put in a large bowl.

Simmer the tomatillos and chilies with the water until soft (about 3 to 5 minutes). Mix in the remaining ingredients, and toss with the pasta.

Chill several hours before serving.

SERVES 4—572 cal.; 7g (11% of cal.) total fat; ±1.2g (2%) saturated fat; 97g (68%) carbohydrate; 25mg cholesterol; and ±660mg sodium per serving

Peppered Pasta Salad

Any sweet-flavored fish (like monkfish) or shellfish works well in this salad. If you have any poached or baked leftovers, you can use them and eliminate the baking step. English mint or spearmint gives a cooling counterpoint to the fish's flavor.

½ pound sea bass or other sweet fish
1 pound shell or corkscrew pasta
1 sweet red pepper, minced
1 green bell pepper, minced
1 cup nonfat, unflavored yogurt

¼ cup finely chopped fresh mint
2 tablespoons olive oil
2–3 tablespoons rice wine vinegar
2 teaspoons balsamic vinegar
Freshly ground black pepper, to taste

Bake the fish in a 425-degree oven until it's cooked through (about 10 to 15 minutes). Cool slightly, remove any bones, then shred.

Cook the pasta in a kettle of boiling water until it is al dente (about 7 to 11 minutes). Drain, drench it with cold water, then drain again.

Put the pasta and fish in a bowl. Mix the remaining ingredients and toss with the pasta and fish. Chill at least 2 hours before serving.

SERVES 4—585 cal.; 10g (15% of cal.) total fat; 1.4g (2%) saturated fat; 95g (65%) carbohydrate; 23mg cholesterol; and 81mg sodium per serving

Pasta Salad with Kumquats and Ham

THIS SALAD FEATURES ORANGE-FLAVORED KUMQUATS. USE ORANGE SEGMENTS IF KUMQUATS AREN'T AVAILABLE.

1/2 pound uncooked, lean, fat-trimmed ham or 6 ounces cooked ham, diced
1 pound shell, corkscrew, or wheel-shaped pasta
2 2/3 cup thinly sliced fresh kumquats (about 20 medium)
2 cups diced, peeled Jerusalem artichokes (sunchokes)

1 cup nonfat, unflavored yogurt
1/4 chopped fresh basil or lemon balm
1/4 cup rice vinegar
2 tablespoons olive oil
2–3 teaspoons sugar

If using uncooked ham, put it in a small saucepan with a few tablespoons of water and simmer it until it is cooked through (about 5 to 10 minutes). Cool, then dice.

Cook the pasta until it is al dente (about 6 to 11 minutes). Drain, rinse with cold water, and put in a large bowl.

Add the ham, kumquats, and Jerusalem artichokes to the pasta.

Mix the remaining ingredients and toss with the pasta. Taste for seasoning, adding extra sugar as needed, and chill for at least 2 hours before serving.

SERVES 4—655 cal.; 13g (18% of cal.) total fat; 2.7g (4%) saturated fat; 103g (63%) carbohydrate; ±30mg cholesterol; and 659mg sodium per serving

Pungent Pasta Salad

THREE WATER-DWELLERS (DUCK, WATERCRESS, AND WATER CHESTNUTS) PROVIDE THIS SALAD'S TEXTURE AND PUNGENCY. SERVE OVER SHREDDED ROMAINE OR BUTTER LETTUCE.

2 small, skinned, fat-trimmed duck thighs, or 3 medium-sized skinned, fat-trimmed chicken thighs
1/4 cup water
2 tablespoons soy sauce
1/4 cup rice wine vinegar
2 tablespoons chopped fresh ginger

1 1/2 tablespoons sesame oil
1 pound spinach-flavored shells or corkscrew pasta
2 8-ounce cans sliced water chestnuts, drained
2 cups coarsely chopped watercress leaves

Simmer the duck with the water, soy sauce, vinegar, ginger, and oil until it is cooked (about 20 minutes). Cool briefly, then dice. Save the poaching liquid to use as a dressing.

Cook the pasta until it is al dente (about 7 to 11 minutes). Drain and rinse with cold water.

Put the pasta, duck meat, water chestnuts, and watercress in a large bowl. Toss with the cooled poaching liquid, and chill for at least 2 hours.

SERVES 4—650 cal.; 12g (17% of cal.) total fat; 3g (4%) saturated fat; 104g (64%) carbohydrate; 60mg cholesterol; and 895mg sodium per serving

Pasta Salad with Grapes and Duck

This recipe also features duck and two of its classic accompaniments, grapes and oranges. Use chicken if it's more convenient.

2 medium-sized, skinned, fat-trimmed duck thighs or 2 large, skinned, fat-trimmed chicken thighs
1/4 cup dry red wine
1/4 cup water
1 teaspoon chopped fresh or dry thyme
3/4 pound orzo (rice-shaped) or small semolina or whole wheat pasta shells

2 cups halved seedless red grapes
1 1/2 cups diced celery
1 8-ounce can diced water chestnuts, drained
Juice of 2 oranges (about 1 1/3 cups)
2 tablespoons rice vinegar
1 tablespoon olive oil

Simmer the duck with the wine, water, and thyme until cooked through (about 15 to 20 minutes). Cool briefly, then dice. Reserve the poaching liquid.

Cook the pasta until it is al dente (about 6 to 9 minutes). Drain, rinse, and put in a large bowl.

Add the meat, grapes, celery, and water chestnuts to the pasta. Combine the poaching liquid with the orange juice, vinegar, and olive oil to make a dressing. Add the dressing, toss to mix, and chill before serving.

Serves 4—525 cal.; 9g (15% of cal.) total fat; 2.3g (4%) saturated fat; 89g (67%) carbohydrate; ±45mg cholesterol; and 125mg sodium per serving

Pasta Salad with a Taste of Turkey

WALNUTS AND SWEET MARJORAM ADD SUBTLE, EXTRA NOTES TO THIS TURKEY-SPIKED SALAD.

1/2 pound boneless, skinned turkey
thigh or breast meat

1 cup turkey or chicken stock

1/4 cup dry sherry

1 pound macaroni, small or medium
shells or similar pasta

2 medium-sized apples, peeled, cored,
and chopped

1/4 cup diced walnuts

1 cup nonfat, unflavored yogurt

2–4 tablespoons vinegar

1 1/2 tablespoons olive oil

1 teaspoon chopped fresh or
dried marjoram

1 clove of garlic, mashed, or
1 tablespoon chopped chives

Simmer the turkey with the stock and sherry until it is cooked through. Cool the meat slightly, then shred. Save the liquid for the dressing.

Cook the pasta until it is al dente (about 5 to 11 minutes). Drain and rinse with cold water.

Put the pasta in a large bowl with the turkey, apples, and walnuts. Mix the remaining ingredients, including the broth, and pour over the salad. Taste for seasoning and add more vinegar, if needed. Chill at least 2 hours and serve cold.

SERVES 4—684 cal.; 13g (17% of cal.) total fat; 2g (3%) saturated fat; 107g (63%) carbohydrate; 47mg cholesterol; and 150mg sodium per serving

Whole Wheat Pasta Salad

This salad calls for catfish, but cooked sea bass, salmon, or tuna are equally good.

1/2 pound fresh or cooked catfish
1 pound whole wheat pasta
3 cups chopped fresh tomatoes
2 cups diced cucumber
1 bunch scallions, white and green portions, thinly sliced

1/4 cup chopped black olives
1 cup nonfat, unflavored yogurt
2 tablespoons olive oil
2–4 tablespoons rice vinegar

If the fish is fresh, bake (or poach in a little water) until cooked through. Cool briefly. Remove any skin or bones. Shred the fish.

Cook the pasta until it is al dente (about 7 to 12 minutes). Drain, rinse with cold water.

Put the pasta, fish, and vegetables in a large bowl. Mix the remaining ingredients and toss with the pasta. Chill 2 hours or longer.

Serves 4—642 cal.; 13g (18% of cal.) total fat; 1.8g (3%) saturated fat; 102g (64%) carbohydrate; 33mg cholesterol; and 255mg sodium per serving

Pasta and Fennel Salad

TOMATOES, FISH, FENNEL, ORANGE, AND CAPERS, ALL INGREDIENTS TYPICAL OF SOUTHERN FRENCH CUISINE, DISTINGUISH THIS SALAD.

1/3 pound salmon steak
1/4 cup water
1 pound semolina or whole
   wheat-based corkscrew or
   shell-shaped pasta
2 cups diced fresh tomatoes

2 cups thinly sliced fresh fennel
Peel and juice of 2 oranges
2 tablespoons capers
2 tablespoons olive oil
2 tablespoons rice vinegar
2 teaspoons balsamic vinegar

Simmer the salmon with the water until it is cooked through. Cool slightly, remove skin and bones, and shred the meat. Save the poaching liquid.

Cook the pasta until it is al dente (about 7 to 11 minutes). Drain and rinse with cold water.

Put the pasta, fish, tomatoes, and fennel in a large bowl.

Grate the orange peel and add it to the pasta.

Mix the remaining ingredients, including the orange juice and poaching liquid, and toss with the pasta. Chill before serving.

SERVES 4—615 cal.; 12g (18% of cal.) total fat; 4.2g (3%) saturated fat; 102g (66%) carbohydrate; ±40mg cholesterol; and ±300mg sodium per serving

Pasta and Shrimp Salad

RADISHES AND THEIR PUNGENT GREENS ADD ZEST TO THIS SALAD. LEAVE THE LATTER OUT IF THEY'RE MUSHY, OR SUBSTITUTE WATERCRESS. IF YOU START WITH PRECOOKED (RATHER THAN RAW) FISH, ADD IT TO THE COOKED PASTA, ALONG WITH THE OLIVE OIL.

3/4 pound bows or similarly shaped pasta
6 ounces cleaned shrimp
1 1/2 teaspoons olive oil
1 cup unflavored, nonfat yogurt
1 1/2 tablespoons mayonnaise
3–4 tablespoons balsamic or red wine vinegar
1/2 teaspoon powdered mustard

2 cups chopped fresh tomatoes
3 cups thinly sliced celery
3 cups thinly sliced radishes
1 1/2 cups shredded radish greens
1 bunch chopped scallions, white and green parts
2–3 tablespoons chopped fresh basil
1/2 teaspoon freshly ground black pepper

Cook the pasta until it is al dente (about 5 to 11 minutes). Drain the pasta and rinse with cold water, then put it in a large bowl.

Sauté the shrimp in the oil until cooked. Remove the pan from the heat and add the yogurt to it. Scrape up any shrimp bits stuck to the pan. Mix in the mayonnaise, vinegar, and powdered mustard.

Add the vegetables, basil, and black pepper to the pasta, then fold in the shrimp dressing. Chill several hours before serving.

SERVES 4—476 cal.; 9g (17% of cal.) total fat; 1.4g (3%) saturated fat; 77g (65%) carbohydrate; 59mg cholesterol; and 229mg sodium per serving

Variations. Use any sweet, mild-flavored fish or shellfish such as sea bass or scallops. You can also use wheat, rye, triticale berries, or white or brown rice, adjusting cooking times as appropriate.

Heart-Wise Pasta Salad

Two hearts—beef and artichoke—flavor this salad. Use well-trimmed leftover roast beef, ham, or cooked fish, if you prefer, and add the olive oil to the dressing.

1 pound shells or bow-shaped pasta
2 cups chopped fresh tomatoes
2 medium-sized cucumbers, peeled and diced
1 9-ounce package frozen artichoke hearts, thawed
1 cup sliced red or other sweet onion
1/4 cup chopped olives
2 tablespoons capers

1/2 pound fat-trimmed beef heart
1 1/2 tablespoons olive oil
1/4 cup dry white wine
2 tablespoons wine vinegar
1 1/2 tablespoons Dijon-style mustard
2 teaspoons sugar
2 tablespoons chopped fresh basil or Italian parsley

Cook the pasta until it is al dente (about 6 to 11 minutes), drain and rinse with cold water. Put in a large bowl and add the vegetables to it.

Cut the beef heart into matchstick-sized strips. Heat the oil in a skillet and brown the meat over moderate heat. Remove the pan from the heat and add the wine. Scrape up any coagulated meat juices, then add the meat and wine to the pasta.

Mix the remaining ingredients and toss with the pasta and vegetables. Chill well and serve.

Serves 4—656 cal.; 11g (15% of cal.) total fat; 2.3g (3%) saturated fat; 109g (66%) carbohydrate; 79mg cholesterol; and 357mg sodium per serving

Pasta and Chicken Salad

FLAVORS OF THE MIDDLE EAST—SESAME, CUMIN, FRESH PARSLEY AND MINT—DOMINATE THIS SALAD. IF YOU HAVE LEFTOVER CHICKEN AND STOCK, YOU CAN ELIMINATE THE FIRST COOKING STEP.

3 medium-sized, skinned, fat-trimmed chicken thighs
2/3 cup water or homemade chicken stock (see page 22)
1/2 cup unflavored nonfat yogurt
Juice of 2 large lemons
1 1/2 tablespoons tahini (sesame paste)
10–12 cloves garlic, mashed
1 teaspoon ground cumin
1/2 cup chopped fresh parsley

1/4 cup chopped fresh mint
1 pound macaroni or small shell-shaped pasta
2 cups chopped, peeled cucumber
2 cups chopped fresh tomatoes
2 cups chopped green bell pepper
2–3 large scallions, white and green portions, chopped
1–3 teaspoons sweet Hungarian or other mild paprika

Simmer the chicken with the water until the meat is cooked (about 20 minutes). Cool the meat, then shred it. Save the poaching liquid and mix it with the yogurt, lemon juice, tahini, garlic, cumin, parsley, and mint.

Cook the pasta until it is al dente (about 6 to 10 minutes). Drain and rinse with cold water. Put in a large bowl, add the chicken and vegetables, then toss with the yogurt dressing. Dust with the paprika, then chill.

SERVES 4—641 cal.; 11g (15% of cal.) total fat; 2.5g (4%) saturated fat; 105g (66%) carbohydrate; 46mg cholesterol; and 205mg sodium per serving

Variations. You can use cooked white or brown rice or soaked fine bulgur in place of pasta.

Bulgur Salad

BUTTER-FLAVORED SEA BASS GIVES AN ADDED DIMENSION TO TABOULI AND LIFTS IT TO MAIN-DISH STATUS.

½ pound sea bass
1½ cups water
¼ cup dry white wine
2½ cups coarse bulgur wheat
3½ cups chopped fresh tomatoes
2 bunches scallions, white and
  green portions, minced

Juice of 2 lemons
½ cup chopped fresh parsley
¼ cup chopped fresh mint
1½ tablespoons olive oil

Poach the fish in the water and wine until it's barely cooked (about 2 to 6 minutes). Remove the fish from the broth. Save the both.

Remove any bones from the fish, then shred.

Put the bulgur in a large bowl; pour the poaching liquid over it. Add the remaining ingredients, including the fish. Mix salad and chill until very cold.

SERVES 4—512 cal.; 8g (14% of cal.) total fat; 1.3g (2%) saturated fat; 87g (68%) carbohydrate; 23mg cholesterol; and 61mg sodium per serving

Ham and Rye Salad

THIS SALAD FEATURES THE CLASSIC SANDWICH DUO, HAM AND RYE.

2 cups rye berries
1/3 pound lean, fat-trimmed cooked
   ham, diced
6 cups shredded fresh spinach
2 cups chopped fresh tomatoes
1/2 cup diced red or other
   sweet onion

2 tablespoons wine vinegar
1 1/2 tablespoons olive oil
1 teaspoon sugar
Dash of freshly ground black pepper

Cook the rye berries in about 4 cups of water until they are al dente (about 30 minutes). Drain and rinse with cold water.

Put the rye in a large bowl and add the ham and vegetables.

Mix the vinegar, oil, sugar, and pepper together and pour it over the salad. Toss briefly and chill at least 2 hours before serving.

SERVES 4—518 cal.; 10g (17% of cal.) total fat; 2.4g (4%) saturated fat; 86g (66%) carbohydrate; 22mg cholesterol; and 514mg sodium per serving

Variations. Precooked pastas, especially bows or small shell-shaped pasta, are good substitutes for rye in this salad. Make up twice the dressing and toss in an extra tomato for good measure.

Rye and Melon Salad

THIS SALAD BLENDS LOW-FAT PARTNERS (RYE, CRAB, AND MELON) WITH HIGH-FAT AVOCADO. OVERALL, THE DISH REMAINS A LEAN 18 PERCENT FAT.

2 cups rye berries
1 large cantaloupe
1 medium-sized avocado
1/2 pound cooked crab
Juice of 1 or 2 lemons

1/4 cup dry white wine
2 tablespoons minced fresh lemon verbena or fresh basil
2 teaspoons honey

Cook the rye berries in about 4 cups of water until they're well cooked but still chewy (about 25 to 35 minutes). Drain and rinse with cold water. Put in a large bowl.

Remove skin and seeds from the cantaloupe and avocado. Cut the cantaloupe into 1/2-inch cubes. Cut the avocado into smaller slivers. Add to the rye berries.

Mix the remaining ingredients, using lemon juice to taste, then add to the rye. Chill well before serving.

SERVES 4—544 cal.; 11g (18% of cal.) total fat; 2g (3%) saturated fat; 91g (67%) carbohydrate; 50mg cholesterol; and 216mg sodium per serving

Variations. You can use any cooked mild fish or shellfish instead of crab. Alternative grains include parboiled triticale, wild rice, Texmati rice, quinoa, and presoaked couscous.

Arborio Rice and Tuna Salad

This salad takes very little time to make as long as you use canned tuna. Lemon juice and peel cut its tinny taste. If possible, use Arborio rice, which retains a chewy texture, but any long grain white or brown rice will do as well.

2 cups Arborio rice
2 6-ounce cans water-packed tuna, drained
Juice and peel of 3 large lemons
2–4 tablespoons chopped fresh sweet herbs (basil, chervil, tarragon, lemon balm, or lemon verbena)

2 tablespoons olive oil
4–5 cloves garlic, mashed

Parboil the rice until it is al dente (about 8 to 12 minutes). Drain, rinse briefly with cold water, then put in a large bowl.

Mix the other ingredients with it and chill at least 2 hours before serving.

Serves 4—525 cal.; 11g (18% of cal.) total fat; 1.6g (3%) saturated fat; 80g (61%) carbohydrate; 30mg cholesterol; and 405mg sodium per serving

Wild Rice, Papaya, and Duck Salad

DUCK'S GAMELIKE FLAVOR IS AN IDEAL MATE FOR WILD RICE'S NUTTY TASTE. AS LONG AS IT'S
WELL-TRIMMED, DUCK IS QUITE LEAN. SUBSTITUTE CHICKEN OR TURKEY THIGH MEAT IF
PREPARING DUCK IS TOO MUCH TROUBLE.

1½ cups wild rice
2 small, lean, skinless, boneless duck
   thighs or 3 medium-sized,
   fat-trimmed, skinless chicken thighs
½ cup water
1 medium-sized fresh papaya,
   chopped
2 8-ounce cans sliced water chestnuts
   drained

2 cups chopped fresh mushrooms
¼ cup chopped walnuts
Juice of 2 limes
2 tablespoons sugar
2 tablespoons rum
4 cups well-washed, shredded, fresh
   spinach leaves

Parboil the wild rice until it is barely tender (about 25 to 40 minutes). Drain
and rinse with cold water. Put in a large bowl.

Poach the duck (or chicken) in the water until it is cooked through (about
25 to 30 minutes). Cool the meat slightly, then shred. Pour the broth over the
wild rice.

Add the meat to the wild rice along with the papaya, water chestnuts, mushrooms, and walnuts. Sprinkle the lime juice, sugar, and rum over it. Toss and
chill.

Serve over a bed of the spinach.

SERVES 4—540 cal.; 9g (15% of cal.) total fat; 2.6g (4%) saturated fat;
83g (61%) carbohydrate; 36mg cholesterol; and 105mg sodium per
serving

Variations. Parboiled quinoa, basmati rice, Texmati rice, or rye are good alternative grains in this salad.

Tuna-Flavored Couscous Salad

COUSCOUS IS ONE OF THE MOST DELICIOUS GRAINS TO USE IN SALADS, AND, AS THIS RECIPE SHOWS, IT TAKES VIRTUALLY NO TIME TO PREPARE. SERVE THIS SIMPLE DISH OVER A BED OF SHREDDED ROMAINE OR OTHER LEAF LETTUCE.

2²/₃ cups semolina or whole wheat couscous

1 6-ounce can water-packed albacore tuna, drained

4 cups chopped fresh tomatoes

¹/₄ cup chopped olives

Juice of 2 or 3 lemons

2 tablespoons chopped fresh parsley

2 tablespoons chopped fresh basil

2 tablespoons chopped fresh chives

Put the couscous in a noncorrosive bowl and stir ²/₃ cup of ice water into it with a fork. When all this is absorbed, add more water, a tablespoon at a time, until there appears to be a little excess. Usually you'll need a total of about 1¹/₂ cups.

Mix in the remaining ingredients and chill for at least 2 hours before serving.

SERVES 4—594 cal.; 9g (14% of cal.) total fat; 2.4g (4%) saturated fat; 97g (65%) carbohydrate; 30mg cholesterol; and 479mg sodium per serving

Variations. You can replace the tuna with any mild, cooked, flaky fish like crab, sole, sea bass, or cod, and the couscous with fine bulgur or parboiled quinoa. Add chopped celery, fennel, and/or sweet red onions for extra texture and taste.

Quinoa Salad with Scallops

FRESH TOMATOES AND BASIL ADD ZEST TO THE DELICATELY FLAVORED SCALLOPS AND QUINOA.

2¼ cups quinoa
½ pound scallops
⅓ cup dry white wine
2 cups chopped fresh tomatoes

Juice of 1 to 2 lemons
2 tablespoons olive oil
2 tablespoons chopped fresh basil

Check the quinoa for grit, rinse it, and simmer in a large pot of water until the grains are barely tender (about 10 to 15 minutes). Decant the hot liquid off the grain and add ice cubes or cold water to arrest the cooking. Drain through a very fine sieve, then put in a large bowl.

Simmer the scallops in the wine in a small saucepan over a moderate flame until they're cooked through (about 1 to 2 minutes for tiny scallops, 3 to 4 minutes for large ones). Set aside to cool.

Add the scallops to the quinoa along with the remaining ingredients. Chill at least 2 hours before serving.

SERVES 4—517 cal.; 11g (19% of cal.) total fat; ±2.5g (4%) saturated fat;77 g (60%) carbohydrate; 20mg cholesterol; and 146mg sodium per serving

Variations. Use millet, Texmati rice, Arborio rice, small pastas, or presoaked couscous or bulgur if quinoa isn't available.

Fragrant Pear and Bulgur Salad

FRESH BASIL'S SWEET SPICINESS BRIDGES THE GAP BETWEEN BULGUR AND CHICKEN'S EARTHY TASTES AND THE FRUITY FLAVORS OF PEAR AND ORANGE. USE FINE OR MEDIUM GRADE BULGUR.

2 large or 4 small skinless,
  fat-trimmed chicken thighs
1/2 cup water
1/4 cup dry white wine
2 1/2 cups bulgur
4 medium-sized pears, peeled,
  cored, and diced

1 cup orange juice
1/2 cup minced fresh basil
2–4 tablespoons rice or white
  wine vinegar
1 1/2 teaspoons olive oil

Poach the chicken in the water and wine until it is cooked. Set the meat aside to cool, then shred. Save the juice.

Put the bulgur in a large bowl, pour in the poaching liquid, and add the diced pears, orange juice, basil, the smaller amount of vinegar, and oil.

Add the chicken shreds, taste for seasoning, and add more vinegar as needed. Chill at least 2 hours and serve cold.

SERVES 4—584 cal.; 11g (17% of cal.) total fat; 2.3g (4%) saturated fat; 98g (67%) carbohydrate; 46mg cholesterol; and 75mg sodium per serving

Sunny Millet Salad

FRESH GINGER AND PINEAPPLE GIVE SPICY NOTES TO THIS BRIGHT YELLOW SALAD.

2 cups millet
2 teaspoons canola or olive oil
1/2 pound tiny scallops
2 cups fresh pineapple cubes
2 large cucumbers, peeled and cubed
1 cup diced red or other sweet onion

1/4 cup unflavored, nonfat yogurt
2 tablespoons mayonnaise
2 teaspoons lemon juice
2 tablespoons minced fresh gingerroot
2 tablespoons chopped fresh parsley
2 teaspoons sugar

Parboil the millet until the grains begin to split but are still chewy (about 16 to 20 minutes). Drain, rinse with cold water, and put in a large bowl.

Heat the oil in a small skillet over moderate heat and sauté the scallops until they're golden and cooked through. Chop if they're large.

Add the scallops and the remaining ingredients to the millet. Stir and chill for several hours before serving.

SERVES 4—566 cal.; 12g (19% of cal.) total fat; 2.5g (4%) saturated fat; 96g (68%) carbohydrate; 25mg cholesterol; and 107mg sodium per serving

Variations. Use quinoa, or white, brown, or wild rice if you prefer them to millet.

Speckled Rice Salad

THIS SALAD COMBINES BLACK AND WHITE RICE. IF YOU CAN'T FIND THE INDONESIAN BLACK RICE, SUBSTITUTE LONG GRAIN BROWN, BROWN BASMATI, OR WILD RICE. SANSHO PEPPER ADDS AN ELUSIVE LEMONY FLAVOR. SUBSTITUTE A LITTLE GRATED LEMON PEEL IF YOU WISH.

4 small lean, skinless chicken thighs
1/2 cup water
1/3 cup dry sherry
1 tablespoon soy sauce
2 teaspoons sugar
1 tablespoon plus 1 teaspoon sesame oil
1/4 teaspoon sansho pepper (optional)

1 cup black Thai or Indonesian rice or other dark rice
1 cup long grain white rice
2 pounds fresh asparagus
2 tablespoons chopped fresh chives or 1/4 cup chopped scallion tops

Poach the chicken in the water and sherry until it is cooked through (about 20 minutes). Cool the meat slightly, then shred. Save the poaching liquid, adding the soy sauce, sugar, oil, and sansho to it.

Parboil the two types of rice in separate pots of water until each is barely tender. The white rice should cook in about 7 to 12 minutes. The black rice will take twice as long. Check each frequently.

Drain and rinse each with cold water as soon as they're cooked.

Snap off and discard the tough asparagus ends. Cut the tops into 1/2- to 1-inch lengths and cook them for about 1 minute in a small amount of water. Drain them as soon as they are barely tender.

Mix the drained rice and asparagus with the chicken and its poaching liquid and the chives. Chill at least 1 1/2 hours before serving.

SERVES 4—575 cal.; 10g (16% of cal.) total fat; 2.6g (4%) saturated fat; 91g (63%) carbohydrate; 46mg cholesterol; and 488mg sodium per serving

Tea-Scented Salad

This recipe is loosely adapted from one for ocha-zuki (rice steeped in hot green tea) given in Elizabeth Andoh's *At Home with Japanese Cooking*. While traditionally eaten as a hot snack, this recipe is served as a cold salad, appropriate for light summer dinners or year-round lunches. Serve with rye or pumpernickel bread and a mixed green or tart fruit salad.

2 cups medium grain white rice
2 teaspoons green tea (Gunpowder or Dragonwell)
1 teaspoon miso or 1/2 teaspoon salt (optional)
1/2 teaspoon wasabi powder or 1/4–1 teaspoon prepared horseradish (optional)

2 teaspoons sesame oil
3–6 tablespoons lime or lemon juice
1 ripe, medium-sized avocado
2/3 pound cooked shrimp
1 cup sliced radishes
1/2 cup chopped scallions or 2 tablespoons chopped fresh chives

Parboil the rice until it is barely tender (about 6 to 9 minutes). Stir it once or twice as it cooks so it won't stick to the pan, but don't stir it so often as to force the rice to release much starch. Drain and rinse immediately with cold water.

Add about 2/3 cup boiling water to the tea and infuse it for at least 5 minutes. Strain and discard the tea leaves.

Mix the tea with the miso, wasabi, sesame oil, and the smaller quantity of lime juice. Stir briefly to mix.

Peel the avocado and cut about two-thirds of it into slices. Set aside. Mash the remainder and add that portion to the tea dressing.

Put the drained rice in a large bowl and stir in the cooked shrimp, radishes, and scallions.

Add the avocado slices and pour the dressing over the rice. Taste it for seasoning and add more lime juice if necessary. Serve lukewarm, or cover tightly and chill it for a few hours and serve cold.

Serves 4—500 cal.; 10g (18% of cal.) total fat; 2.1g (4%) saturated fat; 81g (65%) carbohydrate; 87mg cholesterol; 363mg sodium per serving

Variations. Salmon is delicious in this salad, but has a higher fat content than shrimp. Wild rice or rye berries are also good substitutes for the rice.

Rice Salad with Two Tomatoes

SUN-DRIED TOMATOES ADD A SMOKY NOTE TO THIS RICE SALAD.

½ chicken breast, boned and
   skinned
½ cup water
2 tablespoons dry sherry
2 cups long grain white rice
4 halves sun-dried tomatoes
1 pound fresh asparagus

1 cup chopped fresh tomatoes
2 tablespoons chopped Spanish
   green or black oil-cured olives
1½ tablespoons olive oil
Juice of 2 lemons
2 teaspoons sugar

Poach the chicken breast with the water and sherry until the meat is cooked through (about 10 to 15 minutes). Cool the meat slightly, then shred. Save the liquid for the dressing.

Cook the rice and sun-dried tomatoes in a large volume of water until the rice is almost tender. Drain and rinse with cold water. Pull the sun-dried tomatoes out of the rice and dice them.

Break off and discard the tough asparagus bottoms, and simmer the tops in a little water until barely tender. Chop and put in a large bowl.

Add the rice, chicken, both kinds of tomatoes, and the olives. Mix the broth with the remaining ingredients and toss with the salad. Taste for seasoning, adding a little pepper or more sugar or lemon juice as needed. Chill at least 2 hours and serve cold.

SERVES 4—512 cal.; 8g (14% of cal.) total fat; 1.2g (2%) saturated fat; 92g (72%) carbohydrate; 17mg cholesterol; and 270mg sodium per serving

A Capered Salad

TANGY GREEN FLECKS OF FRESH TARRAGON, OLIVES, AND CAPERS FLAVOR THIS SALAD. SERVE OVER A BED OF LETTUCE FOR LUNCH OR WITH A SALAD OF PUNGENT GREENS AND CRUSTY BREAD FOR A SIMPLE DINNER.

2 cups Arborio or long grain rice
1½ tablespoons olive oil
½ pound tiny scallops
¼ cup chopped olives

Juice of 2 lemons
1½ tablespoons preserved capers
2–3 teaspoons chopped fresh tarragon

Parboil the rice until it's barely tender (about 8 to 12 minutes). Drain and rinse the rice with cold water, then put it in a large bowl.

Heat the oil in a small skillet over moderate heat. Sauté the scallops until they're golden and cooked through (about 2 to 4 minutes).

Add the scallops to the rice along with the remaining ingredients, using lemon juice to taste. Chill for several hours before serving.

SERVES 4—458 cal.; 8g (16% of cal.) total fat; 1.2g (2%) saturated fat; 79g (69%) carbohydrate; 20mg cholesterol; 445mg sodium per serving

Variations. You can replace the scallops with prawns, monkfish, sea bass, or tuna, and the rice with parboiled quinoa or soaked couscous.

Curried Chicken Salad

THE FLAVORS AND TEXTURES OF ALMONDS, APPLES, AND INDIAN SPICES PROVIDE A CONTRAST TO THIS OTHERWISE SOFT AND MILD SALAD. IF YOU HAVE A PREMIXED CURRY POWDER YOU LIKE, YOU CAN USE IT (TO TASTE) IN PLACE OF THE SEVEN SPICES.

SERVE THE SALAD OVER A BED OF SHREDDED LEAF LETTUCE MIXED WITH PUNGENT GREENS LIKE ROCKET OR RADICCHIO.

3 medium chicken thighs, skinned and boned
1½ cups white basmati or brown Texmati rice
1 teaspoon coriander
1 teaspoon black mustard seed
1 teaspoon cumin seed
½ teaspoon caraway seed
½ teaspoon turmeric
½ teaspoon ginger powder

⅛–½ teaspoon mild to hot cayenne
2 tablespoons brown sugar
2 cups chopped tart peeled apple
⅓ cup slivered almonds
¼ cup dark raisins
1–1½ cups nonfat, unflavored yogurt
¼–½ cup chopped fresh English mint, spearmint, or fresh cilantro

Poach the chicken in small amount of water until it is cooked through (about 15 to 25 minutes). Set it aside to cool, then shred the meat.

Parboil the rice until it is barely tender (about 15 minutes for white basmati rice and 35 minutes for brown rice). Drain, rinse with cold water, and put in a large bowl.

Toast the spices in a dry, heavy skillet over medium heat until the seeds begin to darken and pop.

Add the spices, along with the chicken and remaining ingredients, to the rice. Mix and chill.

SERVES 4—560 cal.; 11g (18% of cal.) total fat; 2.2g (4%) saturated fat; 93g (66%) carbohydrate; 48mg cholesterol; and 117mg sodium per serving

Rice and Fava Bean Salad

PARSLEY HAS A HIGH PROFILE IN THIS SALAD. USE THE FLAT-LEAFED VARIETY IF POSSIBLE.

2 cups long grain white, brown Texmati, or Arborio rice
3 tablespoons olive oil
1/2 pound scallops
1 15-ounce can fava beans, drained
1 cup chopped fresh parsley

8–10 cloves garlic, mashed
2/3–1 cup lemon juice
2 teaspoons grated lemon peel (optional)
2 teaspoons sweet Hungarian paprika
2 teaspoons ground cumin

Parboil the rice until it is barely tender. Drain and rinse with cold water. Put in a large bowl.

Heat 1 tablespoon of the oil in a heavy skillet over a moderate heat. Sauté the scallops in the oil until they turn white and are cooked through (about 2 to 5 minutes).

Add the scallops and all other ingredients to the rice. Mix briefly and chill for at least 2 hours before serving.

SERVES 4—612 cal.; 13g (19% of cal.) total fat; 1.8g (3%) saturated fat; 99g (65%) carbohydrate; 19mg cholesterol; and ±500mg sodium per serving

Variations. You can replace the scallops with other shellfish or a firm fish like monkfish. If fava beans aren't available, substitute cooked or canned garbanzo beans (chickpeas) or kidney beans.

Mail Order Sources

Well-stocked supermarkets carry most of the ingredients listed in this book. You'll find most of the remaining items in local natural food stores or ethnic markets. Check the Yellow Pages under the Grocery listings for likely sources. A few appear below. Those that fill mail-orders are marked with an asterisk. Write or call first for current catalogue and ordering information.

Dried Spices and Herbs

*Aphrodesia Products, 264 Bleeker Street, New York, NY 10014; (212) 989-6440

*Frontier Herbs, P.O. Box 188, Norway, IA 52318; (800) 786-1388

*Market Spice House, Pike Place Market, Seattle, WA (retail)
P.O. Box 2935, Redmond, WA 98073; (206) 883-1220 (mail order)

*Penzey's Spice House Ltd., P.O. Box 1448, Waukesha, WI 53187; (414) 574-0277

*Rafal Spice Co, 2421 Russell Street, Detroit, MI 48207; (800) 228-4276

*San Francisco Herb, 250 Fourteenth St., San Francisco, CA 94103; (800) 227-4530

Herb Plants and Seeds

*Companion Plants, 7247 N. Coolville Ridge Rd., Athens, OH 45701; (614) 592-4643. Catalogue: $2.00

*It's About Thyme, 11726 Manchaca Road, Austin, TX 78748; (512) 280-1192. Catalogue: $1.00, refundable with first order.

*Nichols Garden Nursery, 1190 North Pacific Hwy N.E., Albany, OR 97321; (503) 928-9280.

*Well-Sweep Herb Farm, 205 Mt. Bethel Rd., Port Murray, NJ 07865; (908) 852-5390. Catalogue: $2.00; cannot ship to CA, AZ, OR, or WA.

Ethnic Foods and Spices

Antone's Import Co., 807 Taft, Houston, TX 77109; (713) 526-1046
Mexican and Latin American ingredients

*Bangkok Market, Inc., 4757 Melrose Ave., Los Angeles, CA 90029; (213) 662-9705
Thai foods and spices

*Bazaar of India, 1810 University Ave., Berkeley, CA 94703; (800) 261-7662
Indian spices and foods

Bezjian's Grocery, Inc., 4725 Santa Monica Blvd., Los Angeles, CA 90029; (213) 663-1503
Indian and Middle Eastern foods and spices

*Bob's Red Mill, 5209 S.E. International Way, Milwaukee, OR 97222; (503) 654-3215
Whole grains and beans

Casa Peña, 1636 Seventeenth St., NW, Washington, DC 20009; (202) 462-2222
Mexican and Latin American ingredients

*Dean and DeLuca, 560 Broadway, New York, NY 10012; (800) 221-7714
Gourmet and ethnic ingredients and spices; Catalogue: $3.00.

G and L Import/Export, 4828 Twenty-second St., Tucson, AZ 85711; (602) 790-9016
Oriental and Indian ingredients

*Holland American, PO Box 1671, Bellflower, CA 90707; (310) 867-7589
Dutch and Indonesian foods

*Kalustyan, 123 Lexington Avenue, New York, NY 10016;
(212) 685-3416

Kam Man Food Products, 200 Canal St., New York, NY 10013;
(212) 571-0330
Chinese foods

*Katagari and Co., Inc., 224 East Fifty-ninth Street, New York, NY 10022; (212) 755-3566
Japanese ingredients

La Preferida Inc., 3400 West Thirty-fifth Street, Chicago, IL 60632;
(312) 254-7200
Latin American ingredients

Mi Rancho Market, 3365 Twentieth Street, San Francisco, CA 94110;
(415) 647-0580
Mexican ingredients

New England Food, 225 Harrison Avenue, Boston, MA 02111;
(617) 426-8592
Asian ingredients

*Paprikas Weiss, 1572 Second Ave., New York, NY 10028;
(212) 288-6117
European and Middle Eastern spices, grains, flours, and beans

*Pendery's, 304 East Belknap St., Fort Worth, TX 76102;
(800) 533-1870
Chilies and Mexican ingredients

Ratto's, 821 Washington Street, Oakland, CA 94607;
(510) 832-6503
International spices, condiments, grains and beans

*Sultan's Delight, PO Box 090302, Brooklyn, NY 11209;
(718) 745-6844 or (800) 852-5046
Mediterranean and Middle Eastern foods; please send stamped, self-addressed envelope for catalogue

Southeastern Food Supply, 11077 N.W. Thirty-sixth Street, Miami, FL 33167;
(305) 688-2228
Asian Food

*Star Market, 3349 N. Clark Street, Chicago, IL 60657;
(312) 472-0599
Asian (mostly Japanese) foods

Selected Bibliography

General References

Brown, Sarah, ed. *Microwave Cooking*. Pleasantville, N.Y.: Reader's Digest Home Handbooks, 1990.

Bumgarner, Marlene. *The Book of Whole Grains*. New York: St. Martin's Press, 1976.

Chang, K. C., ed. *Food in Chinese Culture*. New Haven: Yale University Press, 1977.

Cole, Candia. *Gourmet Grains: Maindishes Made of Nature*. Santa Barbara: Woodbridge, 1991.

Cole, John. *Amaranth from the Past for the Future*. Emmaus, PA: Rodale, 1979.

Ellis, Merle. *Cutting up in the Kitchen*. San Francisco: Chronicle Books, 1975.

Gelles, Carol. *The Complete Whole Grain Cookbook*. New York: Donald Fine, 1989.

Greene, Bert. *The Grains Cookbook*. New York: Workman, 1988.

Hinman, Bobbie. *Oat Cuisine*. Rocklin, CA: Prima, 1989.

Kafka, Barbara. *Microwave Gourmet*. New York: William Morrow, 1987.

Kawamura, Yojiro, and M. R. Kane, eds. *Umami: A Basic Taste*. New York: Marcel Dekker, 1987.

McGee, Harold. *The Curious Cook*. New York: Macmillan, 1990.

———. *On Food and Cooking*. New York: Macmillan, 1984.

Pitzer, Sara. *Whole Grains: Grow, Harvest, and Cook Your Own*. Charlotte, VT: Garden Way, 1981.

Reiser, Sheldon. "Health Implications of Food Carbohydrates: Heart Disease and Diabetes." In *Food Carbohydrates*. Edited by D. R. Lineback and G. E. Inglett. Westport, Conn.: Avi, 1982.

Saltzman, Joanne. *Amazing Grains*. Tiburon, CA: H. J. Kramer, 1990.

Sass, Lorna. *Cooking under Pressure*. New York: William Morrow, 1989.

Spiller, Gene, and Ronald Amen. *Fiber in Human Nutrition*. New York: Plenum Press, 1976.

Stoskopf, Neal. *Cereal Grain Crops*. Reston, VA: Reston Press, 1985.

Sweetman, Marion, and Ingeborg MacKellar. *Food Selection and Preparation*. 4th ed. New York: John Wiley & Sons, 1954.

Vahoury, George, and David Kritchevsky, eds. *Dietary Fiber and Clinical Aspects*. New York: Plenum Press, 1986.

Wood, Rebecca. *Quinoa: The Supergrain*. New York: Japan Publications, 1988.

Woodier, Olwen. *Corn Meals and More*. Pownal, VT: Storey Communications, 1987.

Zapsalis, Charles, and R. Anderle Beck. *Food Chemistry and Nutritional Biochemistry*. New York: John Wiley & Sons, 1985.

Nutritional Contents

Fletcher, Anne, *Eat Fish, Live Better*. New York: Harper and Row, 1989.

Margen, Sheldon, ed. *The Wellness Encyclopedia of Food and Nutrition*. New York: Rebus, 1992.

Nutritional Data. 6th ed. Pittsburgh, PA.: H. J. Heinz Co., 1962.

Pennington, Jean. *Food Values of Portions Commonly Used*. New York: Harper and Row, 1989.

Shils, Maurice, and Vernon Young. *Modern Nutrition in Health and Disease*. 7th ed. Philadelphia: Lea & Febiger, 1988.

USDA Handbook of the Nutritional Contents of Foods. New York: Dover, 1975.

Index

acidic flavorings, 4
adapted low-fat recipes
   asapao, 37, 38
   beef and broccoli with rice, 103, 110
   Chinese fried rice, 164, 166, 168
   macaroni salad, 197, 200, 201
   paella, 142, 145, 146
   pizza, 182
   spagetti with ragu sauce, 73, 76, 77
agrodulce sauce, 89
ajwain, 29
amaranth, 31
American Heart Association guidelines, 2
anchovies
   artichoke pizza, 185
   pasta puttanesca, 81
   pizza, 182
   sardine pissaladière, 188
   Sardinian couscous, 140
anticancer phytochemicals, 2
antiflatulent properties, 29
antioxidants, 2
apples, curried chicken salad, 226
arborio rice, 32
arborio rice and tuna salad, 216
arroz con pollo, 147

artichokes
   couscous with cardoons and lamb, 134-35
   heart-wise pasta salad, 211
   orzo pilaf, 152-53
   pasta with artichoke hearts, 98
   pizza, 185
asafetida, 29
asapao, 2, 35
   adapted, 37, 38
   traditional, 36
asparagus
   asparagus beef, 119
   rice salad with two tomatoes, 224
   risotto with asparagus, 70-71
   speckled rice salad, 222
avocado
   rye and melon salad, 215
   tea-scented salad, 223
bacteria, 18
bamboo shoots and pork, 120
bamie goreng, 174
bananas, West African rice and fish stew, 43
barley, 33
barley pilaf with lamb kabobs, 154-55
basic risotto, 65

basic stocks, 20-24
basic tomato sauce, 78-79
basil-flavored gnocchi, 59
basmati rice, 31, 32, 105
beans
    chili Colorado, 49
    cider soup, 55
    drunken beans and hominy, 44
    hopping John, 45
    pasta fagioli, 48
    pork and bean burrito, 196
    red beans and rice, 131
    rice and fava bean salad, 227
beef
    adapted ragu sauce, 76, 77
    asparagus beef, 119
    beef and broccoli with rice, 101-3,
        110
    beef empanada, 192-93
    beef kew, 123
    borscht, 42
    buckwheat noodles and glazed
        onions, 82
    buckwheat noodles with red-cooked
        beef, 100
    caraway noodles, 93
    Chinese broccoli beef, 110
    concentrated flavoring, 22
    cuts of, 10-11
    fried rice with a Korean flavor, 171
    hardy stir-fried vegetables, 126
    heart-wise pasta salad, 211
    Jollof rice, 158-59
    mushroom piroshki, 194-95
    spicy beef shreds, 112
    stock, 21
    stout noodles, 97
    tamale pie, 61
    temperature for cooking, 19
    traditional ragu sauce, 75

beef and broccoli with rice
    adapted, 103, 110
    traditional, 101-2
beer, stout noodles, 97
beets, borscht, 42
black olives, pasta with, 88
black pepper, 7
black and white pizza, 187
blood pressure, 3
bonito flakes, 27
borscht, 42
Boston butt, 13
brains, 11
braising, 11, 19
    ham, 24
breast (lamb), 13
British foods, mulligatawny, 51
broccoli
    beef and broccoli with rice, 101-3,
        110
    broccoli with hoisin sauce and lamb,
        128
    Chinese broccoli beef, 110
broccoli rabe, pasta with pine nuts, 91
brussels sprouts with pork, 124
buckwheat, 32
buckwheat noodles, 32
    and glazed onions, 82
    with red-cooked beef, 100
    Tibetan, 99
    yaki soba, 170
bulgur, 32
    fragrant pear and bulgur salad, 220
    pilafs with rose water, 26
    salad, 213
burrito, pork and bean, 196
butcher's terminology, 10

Cajun foods, red beans and rice, 131
calzone, sardine, 190-91

canola oil, 27
cantaloupe, rye and melon salad, 215
capered salad, 225
caraway noodles, 93
carbohydrates, complex, 1, 2, 4
cardiovascular diseases, 10
cardoons, couscous with cardoons and
    lamb, 134-35
Caribbean foods, hopping John, 45
carminative (antiflatulent) properties, 29
casseroles, 34-35
catfish, 17
  asapao, 38
  fidellini soup, 56
  West African rice and fish stew, 43
  whole wheat pasta salad, 208
cauliflower curry, 130
cayenne pepper, 29
chicken, 14-16
  arroz con pollo, 147
  asapao, 36
  bamie goreng, 174
  breast, 6
  chicken lo mein, 173
  curried chicken salad, 226
  dirty rice, 151
  fragrant pear and bulgur salad, 220
  General Tso's chicken, 118
  harira, 41
  Mexican lime soup, 57
  moo goo gai pan, 121
  mulligatawny, 51
  nasi goreng, 169-70
  orange-flavored chicken, 114
  pasta and chicken salad, 212
  pozole, 40
  quinoa pilaf with baked chicken legs,
    160-61
  rice salad with two tomatoes, 224
  risotto with grapes, 68

speckled rice salad, 222
stew with a Chinese taste, 53
stock, 22
thighs, 6
Turkish pilaf, 150
wild rice pilaf, 163
chickpeas, spicy, 132
chili Colorado, 49
chili paste with garlic, 25
chili peppers, 7, 29
chili soups
  chili Colorado, 49
  drunken beans and hominy, 44
Chinese foods
  adapted fried rice, 164, 166, 168
  asparagus beef, 119
  bamboo shoots and pork, 120
  beef and broccoli with rice, 101-3,
    110
  beef kew, 123
  broccoli beef, 110
  broccoli with hoisin sauce and lamb,
    128
  brussels sprouts with pork, 124
  buckwheat noodles with red-cooked
    beef, 100
  chicken stew, 53
  eggplant and pork, 125
  five-spice powder, 30
  fried rice, 168
  General Tso's chicken, 118
  hardy stir-fried vegetables, 126
  hoisin sauce, 25
  hot and sour fish, 115
  lamb-scented greens, 127
  lily buds, 27
  moo goo gai pan, 121
  orange-flavored chicken, 114
  oyster-sauced greens, 113
  pastas, 72

Chinese foods, (*Cont'd.*)
   snow peas with scallops, 111
   spicy beef shreds, 112
   spicy tofu and pork, 122
   star anise, 30
   sweet and sour pork, 117
   Szechuan peppercorn, 31
   traditional fried rice, 164, 165
   yu xiang pork, 116
cholesterol, 3
chuck (beef), 10-11
cider soup, 55
clams
   paella, 146
   spaghetti with red clam sauce, 95
   spaghetti with white clam sauce, 96
complex carbohydrates, 1, 2, 4
cooking meats, 19-20
cornmeal, 33
   peppered polenta, 60
   tamale pie, 61
country ribs (pork), 14
couscous, 32, 134-40
   with cardoons and lamb, 134-35
   cooking techniques, 104, 106-8
   and harissa, 26
   lamb couscous, 138-39
   orange flower water, 26
   Sardinian couscous, 140
   tuna-flavored couscous salad, 218
   Tunisian duck couscous, 137
crab
   gumbo, 46
   rye and melon salad, 215
   West African rice and crab, 133
curried chicken salad, 226
curry leaves, 29
curry powder, mulligatawny, 51
curry powder blends, 29
cutting boards, 18

dashi, 27
dirty rice, 151
diseases, cardiovascular, 1, 10
dressings for salads, 197
dried mushrooms, 7, 26-27
drunken beans and hominy chili, 44
dry flavorings, 26-27
dry soups; *see* sopa secas
duck, 16
   pasta salad with grapes and duck,
     206
   pungent pasta salad, 205
   Tunisian duck couscous, 137
   wild rice, papaya, and duck salad,
     217

eggplant and pork, 125
eggs, fettuccini carbonara, 87
electric rice cookers, 104, 106
empanadas, beef, 192-93
epasote, 29
Ethiopian foods
   ajwain, 29
   spicy chickpeas, 132
extracts, 25-26
   fish, 7
   meat, 7
extra-virgin olive oil, 27, 197
farfel, 72
fats
   flavor in, 7
   in meat, 1
   reduction of, 2
   in soups, 34-35
fava beans, rice and fava bean salad, 227
fennel, pasta and fennel salad, 209
fenugreek, 30
fettuccini carbonara, 87
fidellini soup, 56

fish, 6, 17; *see also* specific kinds
  cooking tips, 19
  extracts of, 7
  freezing of, 18
  fumet, 17, 23
  scalloped casserole, 64
  soup, 39
  storage of, 18
  West African rice and fish stew, 43
fish sauces, 26
five-spice powder, 30
flank (beef), 11
flavorings, dry, 26-27
Food Pyramid, 5
fragrant pear and bulgur salad, 220
French foods, pastas, 72
fried grains, 164-76
fruit, 2; *see also* specific kinds
  mancha manteles, 52
fumet, fish, 23
fusilli with tuna, 94

galuska, 72
garam masala, 31
garlic, 7
gizzard (poultry), 15
glanagal, 30
gnocchi, 33
  basil-flavored, 59
  spinach, 58
golden needles, 27
golden pilaf, 161
grains, 8, 31-33, 101-40
  cooking liquid and time, 109
  fried, 164-76
  grain-wrapped foods, 177-96
  pretoasted, 141-63
  salads, 197-227
  steamed, 101-40

granza rice, 32
grapes
  pasta salad with grapes and duck, 206
  risotto with grapes, 68
Greek foods
  orzo pilaf, 152-53
  pastas, 72
green beans, bamboo shoots and pork,
  120
greens
  lamb-scented greens, 127
  oyster-sauced greens, 113
ground meats, 10
  bacteria in, 18
  turkey, 16
gumbo, 46-47

ham, 13-14, 16
  braised, 24
  dry soup with mushrooms, 54
  fettuccini carbonara, 87
  gumbo, 46
  ham and rye salad, 214
  hopping John, 45
  jambalaya, 156-57
  juniper-scented pasta, 92
  lasagna with two fillings, 62
  microwave risotto, 67
  pasta with artichoke hearts, 98
  pasta with peppers and ham, 80
  pasta with pine nuts, 91
  pasta salad with kumquats and ham,
  204
  peppered polenta, 60
  spinach gnocchi, 58
  swiss chard pizza, 184
hantaka pepper, 29
hardy stir-fried vegetables, 126
harira, 41

harissa, 26
heart (beef), 11
heart (poultry), 15
heart-wise pasta salad, 211
herbs, 4, 7, 28-31
hoisin sauce, 25
   broccoli with hoisin sauce and lamb,
     128
hominy
   drunken beans and hominy, 44
   Mexican lime soup, 57
   pozole, 40
   tamale pie, 61
hopping John, 45
horseradish, 31
hot and sour sauces
   bamboo shoots and pork, 120
   hot and sour fish, 115

Indian foods
   ajwain, 29
   asafetida, 29
   basmati rice, 32
   cauliflower curry, 130
   curry leaves, 29
   fenugreek, 30
   garam masala, 31
   mogul pilaf, 148
   mulligatawny, 51
   nigella, 30
   pastas, 72
   tamarind concentrate, 26
Indonesian foods
   bamie goreng, 174
   black rice, 32
   Indonesian curry, 129
   ketjap asem, 25
   ketjap manis, 25
   laos, 30
   nasi goreng, 169-70

insects, 27
Iranian foods, mogul pilaf, 148
Italian foods; see also pastas; pizzas
   arborio rice, 32
   basil-flavored gnocchi, 59
   gnocchi, 33
   lasagna with two fillings, 62
   pasta fagioli, 48
   peppered polenta, 60
   risotto, 65-71
   sardine calzone, 190-91
   spinach gnocchi, 58

jambalaya, 156-57
Japanese foods
   dashi, 27
   miso pastes, 26
   ocha-zuki, 223
   oshi mugi, 33
   pastas, 72
   sansho pepper, 50
   sushi and sashimi, 31
   tea-scented salad, 223
   wasabi, 31
   yaki soba, 170
Jewish foods, pastas, 72
Jollof rice, 158-59
juniper berries, 30
   juniper-scented pasta, 92

kalonji, 30
kasha, 32
ketjap manis, 25
kha, 30
Korean foods, fried rice with a Korean
   flavor, 171
kumquats, pasta salad with kumquats
   and ham, 204

lamah, 189
lamb, 12-13
    barley pilaf with lamb kabobs, 154-55
    broccoli with hoisin sauce and lamb,
      128
    chili Colorado, 49
    couscous with cardoons and lamb,
      134-35
    lamah, 189
    lamb couscous, 138-39
    lamb-scented greens, 127
    leg of, 12-13
    mogul pilaf, 148
    orzo pilaf, 152-53
    pasta with black olives, 88
    Scotch broth, 50
    spicy chickpeas, 132
    temperature for cooking, 19
    Tibetan buckwheat noodles, 99
laos, 30
lasagna with two fillings, 62
Latin American foods; *see also* Mexican
    foods
    arroz acon pollo, 147
    beef empanada, 192
leg of lamb, 12-13
lemon juice, 4, 26
lentils
    harira, 41
    mulligatawny, 51
    rice and lentil pilaf, 162
lily buds, 27
lime soup, 54
lite products, 4
liver (beef), 11
liver (poultry), 15
lo mein, 173
loin (lamb), 13
loin (pork), 13
London broil, 11

macaroni salad
    adapted, 197, 200, 201
    traditional, 197, 199
magrebi couscous, 32
mail order sources, 228-30
mancha manteles, 52
meats; *see also* specific kinds
    cooking tips, 19-20
    extracts of, 7
    and fat, 1
    as flavorings, 2-3, 6-24
    freezing of, 18-19
    ground, 10
    pleasures of, 6-8
    quantity of, 8
    selecting cuts, 8-17
    storage of, 17-18
    trimmed meat yields, 9
mee krob, 72
megedarra, rice and lentil pilaf, 162
Mexican foods; *see also* Latin American
    foods
    cider soup, 55
    dry soup with mushrooms, 54
    epasote, 29
    fidellini soup, 57
    fried rice with a Mexican flair, 175
    lime soup, 57
    mancha manteles, 52
    pastas, 72
    pork and bean burrito, 196
    pozole, 40
    tamale pie, 61
microwave risotto, 67
microwaves, 104, 105, 108
Middle Eastern foods
    ajwain, 29
    basmati rice, 32
    bulgur salad, 213
    fenugreek, 30

Middle Eastern foods (*Cont'd.*)
garam masala, 31
harira, 41
harissa, 26
lamah, 189
nigella, 30
orange flower water, 26
pasta and chicken salad, 212
pastas, 72
rice and lentil pilaf, 162
rose water, 26
sumac, 30-31
tahini, 26
millet, 32
sunny millet salad, 221
minerals, 2, 4
miso pastes, 26
mogul pilaf, 148
monkfish, pasta, 85
monosodium glutamate (MSG), 26, 27
moo goo gai pan, 121
Moroccan foods
harissa, 26
pastas, 72
MSG (monosodium glutamate), 26, 27
mulligatawny, 51
mushrooms
dried, 7, 26-27
dry soup with mushrooms, 54
mushroom and mussel pizza, 186
mushroom piroshki, 194-95
porcini, 26-27
shiitake, 26-27
mussels, mushroom and mussel pizza,
186

nam pla, 26
nasi goreng, 169-70
nigella, 30

North African foods
couscous, 32
couscous with cardoons and lamb,
134-35
fenugreek, 30
lamb couscous, 138-39
scallop couscous, 136
nuoc mam, 26
nutritional standards, 1

ocha-zuki, 223
oils, 3, 19-20, 27
olive oil, extra-virgin, 27, 197
onions, 7
buckwheat noodles and glazed
onions, 82
orange flower water, 26
oranges
orange-flavored chicken, 114
pasta and monkfish, 85
pasta and prawns, 84
spicy pasta wheels, 86
organ meats, 11
Oriental foods; *see also* specific countries
chili paste with garlic, 25
glanagal, 30
golden needles, 27
oyster sauce, 26
sesame paste, 26
soba, 32
wood ear fungus, 27
orzo, 72
orzo pilaf, 152-53
oshi mugi, 33
oyster sauce, 26
oyster-sauced greens, 113

paella
adapted, 142, 145, 146
traditional, 142, 144

pancit guisado, 172
papayas, wild rice, papaya, and duck
    salad, 217
pastas, 33, 72-100; *see also* sauces;
    specific kinds of pastas
  bamie goreng, 174
  buckwheat noodles and glazed
    onions, 82
  buckwheat noodles with red-cooked
    beef, 100
  caraway noodles, 93
  chicken lo mein, 173
  cooking techniques, 73-74
  fettuccini carbonara, 87
  fidellini soup, 56
  fried rice stick noodles, 176
  fusilli with tuna, 94
  heart-wise pasta salad, 211
  juniper-scented pasta, 92
  lasagna with two fillings, 62
  macaroni salad, 201
  nonwheat, 74
  orzo pilaf, 152-53
  pancit guisado, 172
  pasta with agrodulce sauce, 89
  pasta with artichoke hearts, 98
  pasta basilico, 83
  pasta with black olives, 88
  pasta and chicken salad, 212
  pasta fagioli, 48
  pasta and fennel salad, 209
  pasta from two worlds, 90
  pasta and monkfish, 84
  pasta with peppers and ham, 80
  pasta with pine nuts, 91
  pasta and prawns, 84
  pasta puttanesca, 81
  pasta salad with grapes and duck,
    206
  pasta salad with kumquats and ham,
    204
  pasta salad with a taste of turkey,
    207
  pasta and shrimp salad, 210
  pasta and smoked turkey salad, 202
  peppered pasta salad, 203
  pungent pasta salad, 205
  spaghetti with homemade ragu sauce,
    77
  spaghetti with red clam sauce, 95
  spaghetti with white clam sauce, 96
  spicy pasta wheels, 84
  stout noodles, 97
  Tibetan buckwheat noodles, 99
  whole wheat pasta salad, 208
  yaki soba, 170
pastes, 25-26
pears, fragrant pear and bulgur salad,
    220
peas, risotto with, 69
pepper
  black, 7
  sansho, 30
peppercorn, szechuan, 31
peppers, chili, 29
peppers (sweet)
  pasta with peppers and ham, 80
  pasta and prawns, 84
  peppered pasta salad, 203
  peppered polenta, 60
perloo, 149
Philippine foods, pancit guisado, 172
pig's feet, 14
pilafs, 141-63
  arroz con pollo, 147
  barley pilaf with lamb kabobs, 154-
    55
  cooking techniques, 142-43
  dirty rice, 151

pilafs (*Cont'd.*)
  golden pilaf, 161
  jambalaya, 156-57
  Jollof rice, 158-59
  mogul pilaf, 148
  paella, 146
  perloo, 149
  quinoa pilaf with baked chicken legs, 160-61
  rice and lentil pilaf, 162
  Turkish pilaf, 150
  wild rice pilaf, 163
pine nuts, pasta with, 91
pineapple, sunny millet salad, 221
piroshki, mushroom, 194-95
pizzas, 177-89
  adapted, 182
  anchovy, 182
  artichoke pizza, 185
  black and white pizza, 187
  dough for, 180-81
  lamah, 189
  mushroom and mussel pizza, 186
  sardine pissaladière, 188
  sunny pizza, 183
  swiss chard pizza, 184
  traditional pepperoni and cheese, 179
polenta, 33
  peppered, 60
  tamale pie, 61
pork, 13-14
  bamboo shoots and pork, 120
  brussels sprouts with pork, 124
  cider soup, 55
  drunken beans and hominy, 44
  eggplant and pork, 125
  mancha manteles, 52
  pancit guisado, 172
  pasta with agrodulce sauce, 89

pasta fagioli, 48
pork and bean burrito, 196
pozole, 40
spicy tofu and pork, 122
sweet and sour pork, 117
temperature for cooking, 19
traditional ragu sauce, 75
yaki soba, 170
yu xiang pork, 116
poultry, storage of, 17; *see also* specific kinds
pozole, 40
prawns
  fried rice stick noodles, 176
  gumbo, 46
  Indonesian curry, 129
  pasta and prawns, 84
  perloo, 149
  risotto with asparagus, 70-71
pregnant women, 30
pressure cookers, 104, 106
proteins, 1, 2
quinoa, 33
  pilaf with baked chicken legs, 160-61
  salad with scallops, 219

rabbit, 16
ragu sauces, 73, 75-77
ribs (lamb), 13
rice, 101-33; *see also* pilafs; risotto; wild rice
  arborio, 32
  arborio rice and tuna salad, 216
  asapao, 36, 37, 38
  asparagus beef, 119
  bamboo shoots and pork, 120
  basmati, 32, 33, 105
  beef kew, 123
  black, 32

rice (*Cont'd.*)
broccoli with hoisin sauce and lamb, 128
brussels sprouts with pork, 124
capered salad, 225
cauliflower curry, 130
Chinese broccoli beef, 110
Chinese fried rice, 168
cider soup, 55
cooking techniques, 104-06
curried chicken salad, 226
dry soup with mushrooms, 54
eggplant and pork, 125
fried rice with a Korean flavor, 171
fried rice with a Mexican flair, 175
fried rice stick noodles, 176
General Tso's chicken, 118
granza, 32
gumbo, 46
hardy stir-fried vegetables, 126
hopping John, 45
hot and sour fish, 115
Indonesian black 222
Indonesian curry, 129
lamb-scented greens, 127
moo goo gai pan, 121
mulligatawny, 51
nasi goreng, 169-70
orange-flavored chicken, 114
oyster-sauced greens, 113
paella, 146
red beans and rice, 131
rice and fava bean salad, 227
rice salad with two tomatoes, 224
scalloped casserole, 64
snow peas with scallops, 111
speckled rice salad, 222
spicy beef shreds, 112
spicy chickpeas, 132
spicy tofu and pork, 122

sweet and sour pork, 117
tea-scented salad, 223
West African rice and crab, 133
West African rice and fish stew, 43
yu xiang pork, 116
rishta, 72
risotto
arborio rice for, 31, 65
with asparagus, 70
basic, 65
granza rice for, 65
with grapes, 68
microwave, 67
with peas, 69
rose water, 26
round (beef), 11
rump (beef), 11
Russian foods
borscht, 42
mushroom piroshki, 194-95
rye, 33
rye berries
ham and rye salad, 214
rye and melon salad, 215

salads, 197-227
arborio rice and tuna salad, 216
bulgur salad, 213
capered salad, 225
curried chicken salad, 226
dressings for, 197
fragrant pear and bulgur salad, 220
ham and rye salad, 214
heart-wise pasta salad, 211
macaroni salad, 201
pasta and chicken salad, 212
pasta and fennel salad, 209
pasta salad with grapes and duck, 206

salads (*Cont'd.*)
    pasta salad with kumquats and ham,
      204
    pasta salad with a taste of turkey, 207
    pasta and shrimp salad, 210
    pasta and smoked turkey salad, 202
    peppered pasta salad, 203
    pungent pasta salad, 205
    quinoa salad with scallops, 219
    rice salad with two tomatoes, 224
    rye and melon salad, 215
    speckled rice salad, 222
    sunny millet salad, 221
    tea-scented salad, 223
    whole wheat pasta salad, 208
    wild rice, papaya, and duck salad,
      217
salmon, 6, 17
    pasta and fennel salad, 209
salmonella, 19
salt, 4, 14, 16, 20, 81
sandwiches, 177
sansho pepper, 50
saponins, 33
sardines
    sardine calzone, 190-91
    sardine pissaladière, 188
Sardinian couscous, 140
sashimi, 31
sauces, 7, 25-26; *see also* pastas
    agrodulce, 89
    basic tomato, 78-79
    for pastas, 72-100
    spaghetti with ragu sauce, 73, 75-77
    spaghetti with red clam sauce, 95
    spaghetti with white clam sauce, 96
    sweet-sour, 89
sausage
    gumbo, 46
    microwave risotto, 67

    red beans and rice, 131
    risotto with peas, 69
    spicy pasta wheels, 86
    swiss chard pizza, 184
sautèing, 3, 7, 19-20
scallops
    black and white pizza, 187
    capered salad, 225
    pasta basilico, 83
    quinoa salad with scallops, 219
    rice and fava bean salad, 227
    scallop couscous, 136
    scalloped casserole, 64
    snow peas with scallops, 111
    sunny millet salad, 221
Scotch broth, 50
sea bass, 6, 17
    basic risotto, 65-66
    bulgur salad, 213
    fish soup, 39
    macaroni salad, 201
    peppered pasta salad, 203
    scalloped casserole, 64
    sunny pizza, 183
seaweed, 7, 27
semiyan, 72
semolina, 33; *see also* couscous
    basil-flavored gnocchi, 58
    spinach gnocchi, 58
sesame oil, 27
sesame paste, 26
sesame seeds, 26
shanks (lamb), 13
shark, 6, 17
    pasta from two worlds, 90
shellfish, 6, 17; *see also* specific kinds
    golden pilaf, 161
    jambalaya, 156-57
    mushroom and mussel pizza, 186
    paella, 146

sheriya, 72
shoulder (lamb), 12
shoulder (pork), 13
shrimp
   basil-flavored gnocchi, 59
   Chinese fried 168
   fried rice with a Mexican flair, 175
   gumbo, 46
   pasta and shrimp salad, 210
   tea-scented salad, 223
   wild rice casserole, 63
Smithfield hams, 14
snow peas with scallops, 111
soba, 32
sole, 17
sopa secas
   cider soup, 55
   dry soup with mushrooms, 54
   fidellini soup, 56
   Mexican lime soup, 57
soups, 34-35
   borscht, 42
   chicken, 53
   chili Colorado, 49
   cider soup, 55
   drunken beans and hominy, 44
   dry soup with mushrooms, 54
   fidellini soup, 56
   fish, 39
   gumbo, 46-47
   harira, 41
   hopping John, 45
   mancha manteles, 52
   Mexican lime soup, 57
   mulligatawny, 51
   pasta fagioli, 48
   pozole, 40
   rice and fish, 43
   Scotch broth, 50
soy sauces, 25

spaghetti with ragu sauce
   adapted, 73, 76, 77
   traditional, 73, 75
Spanish foods
   granza rice, 32
   paella, 146
spareribs (pork), 14
speckled rice salad, 222
spices, 2, 4, 7, 28-31
spicy pasta wheels, 86
spicy tofu and pork, 122
spinach
   fried rice with a Korean flavor, 171
   ham and rye salad, 214
   lasagna with two fillings, 62
   microwave risotto, 67
   quinoa pilaf with baked chicken legs,
     160-61
   scalloped casserole, 64
   spinach gnocchi, 58
   Tibetan buckwheat noodles, 99
   wild rice, papaya, and duck salad,
     217
squid, black and white pizza, 187
star anise, 30
stews; see soups
   stir-frying, 11, 101, 167-76
   bamie goreng, 174
   broccoli with hoisin sauce and lamb,
     128
   chicken lo mein, 173
   Chinese fried rice, 168
   fried rice with a Korean flavor, 171
   fried rice with a Mexican flair, 175
   hardy stir-fried vegetables, 126
   lamb-scented greens, 127
   lily buds, 27
   nasi goreng, 169
   pancit guisado, 172
   yaki soba, 170

stocks, 6
  basic, 20-24
  beef, 21
  bones for, 14, 15, 16, 17, 20, 21
  chicken, 22
  concentrated beef flavoring, 22
  dashi, 27
  ham, 24
  for soup, 34
stout noodles, 97
sugar, 4
sumac, 30-31
sun-dried tomatoes, 27
  pasta from two worlds, 90
  rice salad with two tomatoes, 224
  sunny pizza, 183
sunny millet salad, 221
sushi, 31
sweetbreads, 11
sweet-sour sauces
  pasta with agrodulce sauce, 89
  sweet and sour pork, 117
swiss chard pizza, 184
swordfish, 17
  cauliflower curry, 130
  hot and sour fish, 115
Szechuan peppercorn, 31

tabouli; see bulgur
tahini, 26
tamale pie, 61
tamarind concentrate, 26
tea-scented salad, 223
temperatures for cooking meats, 19
Texmati rice, 33
Thai foods
  fried rice stick noodles, 176
  kha, 30
  nam pla, 26

pastas, 72
thymus, 11
Tibetan buckwheat noodles, 99
toasting, 7, 141-63
tofu, spicy tofu and pork, 122
tomatoes, basic sauce, 78-79; see also
        sun-dried tomatoes
traditional high-fat recipes
  asapao, 36
  beef and broccoli with rice, 101-02
  Chinese fried rice, 164, 165
  macaroni salad, 197, 199
  paella, 142, 144
  pizza, 179
  spaghetti with ragu sauce, 73, 75
trichinosis, 19
triticale, 33
tuna, 6
  arborio rice and tuna salad, 216
  fusilli with tuna, 94
  tuna-flavored couscous salad, 218
turkey, 14-16
  pasta salad with a taste of turkey, 207
  pasta and smoked turkey salad, 202
turkey sausage, 14, 16
  red beans and rice, 131
Turkish pilaf, 150

umami, 7
USDA guidelines, 2, 5
uterine contractions, 30

veal, 12
vegetables, 2, 4, 8; see also specific kinds
  hardy stir-fried vegetables, 126
Vietamese foods, nuoc mam, 26
vinegars, 4, 197
vitamins, 2, 4

wasabi, 31
weight loss, 3
West African foods
    Jollof rice, 158-59
    rice and crab, 133
    rice and fish stew, 43
wild rice, 32, 33
    casserole, 63
    pilaf, 163
    wild rice, papaya, and duck salad,
      217

wine, 4
woks, 167
wood ear fungus, 27

yaki soba, 170
yu xiang pork, 116

zucchini, black and white pizza, 187